D1007466

"It has been almost forty years since Ronald Reagan famously declared, 'government is the problem,' and thus began the great experiment in glorifying private excess over public need. The results are in. We now live in the most extreme period of income inequality in our history, with millions earning a barely livable wage, while the richest just get richer. It wasn't just predictable, it was conclusively *predicted* by Barlett and Steele thirty years ago. This updated volume not only shows what has happened, it simply and clearly explains why. Let's hope today more are ready to listen." —MARK BOWDEN, author, *Black Hawk Down*

"The 1992 edition of *America: What Went Wrong?* was one of the most important works of journalism in the 20th century. This updated edition is even more compelling, as it lays bare our nation's shameful drift over the past three decades to an even more inequitable, unfair and unjust society. Barlett and Steele tell us not only what went wrong, but what's still going wrong and how only we, the citizenry, can fix it. Let's hope that this time around, the public and our elected representatives do a better job of listening and responding." —DAVID BOARDMAN, Dean of the Klein College of Media and Communication, Temple University

"*America: What Went Wrong?* is even more significant and relevant today than it was in 1992 when it was first published. The brilliant, two-time Pulitzer Prize winners have released a terrific, 'that was then, this is now' updated throughout edition of their muckraking classic about inequality in America. And it is an absolute MUST read!" —CHARLES LEWIS, Founder, The Center for Public Integrity

"This brilliant book is essential reading for anyone seeking the true story of how America works—or doesn't. Barlett and Steele lay out in meticulous detail how special interests continue to loot the American middle class, with disastrous results. They use up-to-the-minute data and compelling human stories to show how the average American has ended up far worse off than even the authors could have predicted three decades ago, when they first began their exploration of how special interests with deep pockets and friends in Washington fueled inequality in America. The book unfolds as a gripping economic detective story, an engrossing tale of real people beat by the system that will leave you angry and yearning for change." —JOE STEPHENS, Founding Director of the Program in Journalism, Princeton University

"The achievement of Barlett and Steele can hardly be overstated. I know of no other investigative report that displays a comparable ambition—nothing less than to document the drivers and effects of class warfare (to call it out by name) in the United States. The breadth and depth of the research and the potent clarity of the writing, moving from individual stories to crystalline exposition of arcane tax laws, raise the benchmarks for journalism. In this update, Barlett and Steele demonstrate that the trends they mapped in the early '90s have deepened, ruining the lives and futures of the American middle class. The book can be read as an indictment of financiers who looted the country and politicians who paved their path, but its ultimate target is a system, and systems can be changed, as the authors set out in their new epilogue. This book is not only unique, it's a masterpiece." —MARK LEE HUNTER, author, *Story-Based Inquiry: A Manual for Investigative Journalists*

"This important and timely update of a classic investigative work once again details the terrible—and increasing—inequities of the U.S. economic and legal system that bestows numerous favors on the rich while trampling the wages, benefits and hopes of middle-class citizens. *America: What Went Wrong? The Crisis Deepens* also serves as an exemplary textbook for young journalists who wish to expose the corrupt and abusive systems contributing to this ongoing crisis." —BRANT HOUSTON, Professor and Knight Chair of Investigative Reporting, University of Illinois Urbana-Champaign

"Reading this brilliant book on the long slow death of the American dream will give you strength to fight for its resurrection."
—TIM WEINER, Pulitzer Prize-winner author of *Legacy of Ashes* and *The Folly and the Glory*

"*America: What Went Wrong?* ... is Old News at its very best—meticulously researched, masterfully reported, and brimming with statistics and facts. It's a mural of American life that allows everyday people to tell stories about their jobs, their neighborhoods, and their families." —*Utne Reader*

"You'll find the book to be an eloquent and carefully researched picture of what many people have come to see as the dismantling of the American middle class. The authors interviewed people from all walks of life and sifted through thousands of documents to show how the lives of all of us have been touched by public acts—or inaction—and private greed." —*Amarillo (Texas) News-Globe*

"*America: What Went Wrong?* is the most powerful description of the nation's domestic problems I have read since Michael Harrington published *The Other America*." —*Charleston (West Virginia) Gazette-Mail*

"For those who want to understand why this country is in the economic mess it's in, (this) book will provide some straight answers. *America: What Went Wrong?*... is a must read for anyone concerned about the sorry state of our country." —*Greensboro (North Carolina) News and Record*

"The authors are craftsmen of perspective ... the portrait they paint of our economy (is) the picture of Dorian Gray, kept youthful looking by Tax-Code driven frenzies that mask a withering productive soul. ... their central theme becomes unassailable. As folks at the top acquire income tax breaks that the middle class hasn't the means to enjoy, the middle class shoulder more than their share of the national debt and thereby transfer their wealth to the top. So much for the trickle-down theory." —*Legal Times*

"We hardly notice the dreams are gone until books like *America: What Went Wrong?* come along. It mercilessly indicts the economic system we dreamed was an infinitely widening highway carrying us to ever-increasing prosperity." —*Fort Worth (Texas) Star-Telegram*

Also by DONALD L. BARLETT AND JAMES B. STEELE

The Betrayal of the American Dream

*Critical Condition: How Health Care
Became Big Business—and Bad Medicine*

The Great American Tax Dodge

America: Who Stole the Dream?

America: Who Really Pays the Taxes?

America: What Went Wrong?

Forevermore: Nuclear Waste in America

Howard Hughes: His Life and Madness

AMERICA: WHAT WENT WRONG?

THE CRISIS DEEPENS

DONALD L. BARLETT and JAMES B. STEELE

MISSION POINT PRESS

Mission Point Press
2554 Chandler Road
Traverse City, Michigan 49696
www.MissionPointPress.com

Cover design by Barrie Maguire

ISBN: 978-1-950659-50-0
Library of Congress Control Number: 2020906748

First published as *America: What Went Wrong,*
copyright 1992, by Donald L. Barlett and James B. Steele.

Printed in the United States of America

AMERICA: WHAT WENT WRONG?

THE CRISIS DEEPENS

CONTENTS

FOREWORD

America's middle class is in crisis, and it is a crisis that has been building for 50 years. This dispiriting American trajectory toward severe inequality—economically ravaging half the U.S. population, middle class and working class alike—requires a fresh and profound understanding if we are to change a devastating course.

Fortunately, this new edition of *America: What Went Wrong?*—the seminal work on the origins of inequality in America—is coming just at the time that our country seems to be waking up to the slow-motion disaster that gross income and wealth disparities have wrought. With this new, expanded book, subtitled *The Crisis Deepens*, and a growing American understanding of the issue, it is possible that we can fashion a whole new series of approaches to make sure resources and opportunity are available to all in America.

Beginning in the 1970s, we have seen the needs and interests of the American working and middle classes relentlessly savaged for the past half-century. This has involved politicians of all stripes and businesses at every level of the U.S. economy. Many of us who are doing OK have lamented the unfairness of our system, but we have done little politically to force change. Now we have a society in which opioid addiction, death by drug overdose and suicide have become epidemic.

Inequality of wealth and income is more severe than at any time in the 20th century, matching even the famously unfair system of the Gilded Age 120 years ago. Some 58 percent of American families have no savings, no cushion and are at the whim and mercy of any fateful mishap—a health crisis, a fire, a car accident, the loss of a job. Working-class and middle-class despair is rampant.

Three decades ago, the great American investigative reporters Donald L. Barlett and James B. Steele chronicled the systematic unraveling of the economic security of most of working America in their famous book, *America: What Went Wrong?* It stayed at No. 1 on The New York Times Bestseller List for weeks and had a profound impact on the political campaigns of the 1990s.

That account was originally published as a series of articles in The *Philadelphia Inquirer* when I was serving as editor of the paper. It engendered the most astonishing public response I have ever seen to a series of articles: Thousands of readers lined up on Broad Street, snaking down toward City Hall from the Inquirer Building, all anxious to get a reprint. We received more than 20,000 letters and phone calls from grateful readers telling us how glad they were that we had told their story. It was this outpouring that led Barlett, Steele and me to fashion a strategy to expand the series into the book.

It was later recognized by New York University as one of the 100 most important works of journalism of the 20th century, and it remained in print and in circulation for years. But the great shock for us at the time was that because the book was so far ahead of the rest of the country, it didn't change things. Some people dismissed it as extreme, and others doubted things were as bad as the articles had depicted.

But, today, citizens at every level of American society and every political persuasion recognize the brutal impact of inequality. No one doubts the serious social situation we have allowed our democracy to devolve to: over half the country disaffected, unwilling to believe in the fairness or justice of our system; millions so angered by what they rightly feel is a system artfully stacked against the interest of the many and in the interest of the few that they indulge in populist rage that threatens the stability of society.

This is so clearly a time that can benefit from the message of—and the spectacular factual weight of—*America: What Went Wrong? The Crisis Deepens.* No other work has so clearly, so powerfully documented how we got into this mess—and what we need to do about it. Fortunately for all of us, Barlett and Steele are bringing forth an edition that has been carefully updated, with fresh reporting and writing on the current American predicament.

This book will certainly stand the test of time. But it is not an historical account from a short period of time long ago. It is as relevant today—perhaps more relevant—than at any time in our history. It is essential that Americans understand that the fix for our problem is not just an election. It isn't just Donald Trump. The trouble with so many of us is that we seem to believe that if we can just get Trump out of the White House that everything will be fine. It won't. Certainly, electing a competent leader is the necessary first step. The elections matter, of course; but still we will have massive obstacles to overcome. And only if the public has a strong understanding of where we are and how it went wrong can we hope to take the meaningful actions that can repair our system.

This new edition offers that understanding. We must heed its message now.

—Maxwell King
    Former editor of The *Philadelphia Inquirer*
    and President of the Pittsburgh Foundation

PROLOGUE

We can have concentrated wealth in the hands of a few
or we can have democracy. But we cannot have both.
—Justice Louis Brandeis

Listen to the people in charge of the U.S. economy tell you how well everything was going in 2019.

On June 11, 2019, Larry Kudlow, director of the White House's National Economic Council, told television viewers: "The U.S. economy is very strong. I think we're in very good shape…"

On Sept. 18, Jerome Powell, chairman of the Federal Reserve, told Congress: "The U.S. economy has continued to perform well. We are into the 11th year of this economic expansion … The job market remains strong."

On Nov. 29, Steven Mnuchin, secretary of the U.S. Treasury, told reporters: "We have the stock market at an all-time high, unemployment at an all-time low, wages growing. The president has delivered a great economy to the American people just as he promised."

And President Trump himself tweeted on Aug. 29: "The economy is doing great, with tremendous upside potential."

Tremendous upside potential?

You might have a different view – one you held even before the coronavirus struck. Especially if you were one of the 4,500 auto workers who lost your job at the General Motors assembly plant in Lordstown, Ohio, that closed in 2019.

Or one of the 44,000 Verizon Wireless employees who lost a job that year as the company downsized.

Or one of the 3,000 Celadon Co. truck drivers who were stranded in their rigs on America's highways when their company abruptly shut down in 2019.

Or one of the 30,000 employees of Toys R Us who lost a job after a Wall Street-inspired takeover went bust.

You also might have a different view if you are a member of

America's disappearing middle class—whether blue-collar worker, white-collar worker, mid-level manager or professional.

And you especially might have a different view if you are one of the millions of Americans seeking to attain a middle-class status that's beyond your reach.

But that's because you see things differently from those in Washington.

You are on the bottom looking up.

Those in charge, on the other hand, are on the top looking down: Call it the view from Washington and Wall Street.

Those peering down from those lofty perches in 2019 pointed to low unemployment numbers as proof of how well the economy was doing. But those numbers disguised an all-too-familiar fact of life for too many Americans: After losing a good-paying job, many workers do find work, but at jobs that pay far less and offer limited benefits, if any. So, yes, they're employed. But they're in a much worse situation—sometimes working two or even three jobs trying to make ends meet.

This is how the destruction of the middle class relentlessly grinds up more and more people and families, their fates obscured by official statistics as defined by those at the top.

The rosy view of those above can be easily explained by looking at their paychecks.

Let's start in 1959, a time of growing middle-class prosperity. The top 4 percent earned as much as the bottom 35 percent. By 1970, the top 4 percent of the workforce earned as much as the bottom 38 percent—not such a big increase.

But by 2017, the latest year for which data from federal income tax returns is available, it was a different story. The top 4 percent earned as much as the bottom 57 percent. In stark dollars, those at the top reported an average salary of $334,000. For those at the bottom, the average was only $22,000—painful evidence that the middle class was in sharp decline.

And these numbers deal only with wages and salaries. They do not include interest and dividends; gains from the sale of stocks, bonds and other capital assets, or income from other investments. That income, too, flows overwhelmingly to the wealthiest.

When we first wrote about the "one percenters"—a term that was later popularized to describe the wealthiest of the wealthy—their average annual income was $464,800 in 1992. It rose to $1.57 million in 2017, an increase of 238 percent. And that was just the average for those at the top. That year, a record number of individuals and families—20,223—reported income of $10 million or more on their tax returns.

For a growing number of individuals and families, the exploding difference in income among the people at the top and everyone else means the end of the American dream and the destruction of the middle class.

Everyone has their own definition of the middle class, but however you define it, Washington perennially pays lip service to its needs. When passing tax legislation, presidents and congresses alike always claim that the bill aims to help average Americans when the opposite is usually true.

One of America's deepest and most enduring beliefs is that the U.S. is the land of opportunity. Over and over you hear it voiced in Congress in a way that helps Congress paper over the depth of the middle-class crisis. There's still opportunity in America but not for everyone. For the vast majority, opportunities are shrinking. Most Americans are just hanging on, hoping to retain what they have, with little prospect of improvement.

How dire is it? The New York Federal Reserve concluded in 2019 that four in 10 Americans, if confronted with an unexpected expense of $400, would not have the cash to cover it, adding that "over one-fifth of adults are not able to pay all of their current month's bills in full."

None of this is surprising to many young people who are saddled by debt in jobs that don't pay enough to meet their obligations and who can't afford to start a business, buy a house or begin a family. The American dream, so long a beacon that lighted the way for each new generation, has gone dark.

The America of today, so at odds with the image that Washington boosters like to project, has been a long time coming.

When this book was first published in 1992, in the midst of the presidential race, it caused a sensation. It documented how the good-paying jobs, health care and pensions for millions of Americans were imperiled and how the middle class, the backbone of America, was shrinking as a direct result of actions taken by Washington and Wall Street.

"For the first time in this century," the book warned, "members of a generation entering adulthood will find it impossible to achieve a better lifestyle than their parents."

Controversial at the time, that statement has become widely accepted, not only by the public but also by academics whose statistical studies have reconfirmed its validity.

A bestseller for eight months, the book was cited widely by candidates running for office. Bill Clinton, who was photographed holding up the book while campaigning for president, said he was "profoundly influenced" by its conclusions of what had happened to the middle class. Twenty-six years later, Clinton was still citing the book as one of the formative influences of his presidency, telling the *New York Times* that it "strengthened my determination to try to reverse trickle-down economics and achieve a fairer and more prosperous economy."

The book hit a nerve with middle-class people who despite their hard work couldn't understand why they were falling behind economically. The book showed them that it wasn't their fault, that they were victims of public and private actions that were undermining their way of life.

We have updated and expanded this book because it is as relevant as ever. Many of the currents we identified that were dragging down the middle class in 1992 are surging to an alarming degree.

In this book we tell the story of how we got here—the laws and the decisions made in Washington and Wall Street that set in motion these changes – and we point in the direction our country is headed.

Many of the people whose stories were first told in this book will seem familiar: workers who have lost their jobs, parents who cannot afford health care for their children, seniors who must decide every month between filling a prescription or buying groceries. The prices paid for essentials in 1992 seem quaint, but for millions of Americans today the struggle is the same—a losing battle to maintain a middle-class lifestyle.

Each chapter contains a new introduction and has been updated to show why the nation's middle class is in even more difficult financial straits than in 1992.

Most of the original charts have been allowed to stand with updates on current developments. These provide a view of deeply troubling trends in showing the size of the gap between the haves and have-nots then, how the gap has widened, and the ever-greater distance we must go to bridge that gap.

One set of numbers shows just how wide the gap has become since publication of the first edition. In 1992, the top 5 percent of taxpayers earned 30 percent of the total income. By 2017, America's wealthiest 5 percent had upped their share to 37 percent.

As the rich become ever richer, working Americans continue to lose ground, with an impoverished old age looming for millions who don't have pensions or sufficient retirement savings. More than half of working-age Americans have no retirement plan of any kind.

To this bleak picture has been added an additional crisis for the middle class: student debt. As middle-class incomes stagnated and the states—long the main support of public higher education—cut funding, students from middle-income families have been forced to borrow to pay for college.

Student debt now stands at $1.5 trillion—second only to mortgages—and is rising at a rate of nearly a billion dollars a year, saddling current and future generations with a burden that families before them never had to endure.

Why do we allow this to go on?

Why does America, year in and year out, allow policies that are destroying the middle class and heap new burdens on average Americans that make things even worse?

The answer lies in the nature of the American experiment.

From our beginning, Americans were ambivalent about the role of government in society. With the memory of an overbearing King George and Parliament fresh in mind, the young nation came into being with a profound distrust of a strong central government.

WHAT'S STILL GOING WRONG

The wage and salary structure of American business, encouraged by federal tax policies, continues to push the nation toward a two-class society. Data from 2017 shows an ever-larger gap.

In 1959 (each symbol = 2 million workers):

◀ **The top 4%**
(2.1 million individuals and families) earned $31 billion in wages and salaries – the same as

the bottom 35% ▶
(18.3 million individuals and families).

In 1989 (each symbol = 2 million workers):

◀ **The top 4%**
(3.8 million individuals and families) earned $452 billion in wages and salaries – the same as

the bottom 51% ▶
(49.2 million individuals and families).

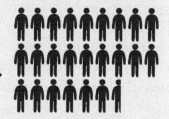

In 2017 (each symbol = 2 million workers):

◀ **The top 4%**
(5 million individuals and families) earned 1.7 trillion in wages and salaries – the same as

the bottom 57% ▶
(72.5 million individuals and families).

Source: Internal Revenue Service

To keep government at bay, the founders enshrined the principle of personal liberty in the Declaration of Independence and the Constitution, and wrote into the Bill of Rights many freedoms that they felt would be a bulwark against a strong central government like the one they had just toppled in the colonies. This is why the Constitution guarantees freedom of worship, freedom of speech, freedom of assembly and many other freedoms.

Nowhere does the Constitution explicitly grant freedom to make money, but it's one of those rights that's understood to be part of the pursuit of happiness.

Yet the freedom to make money periodically leads to all sorts of economic mayhem in America when the excesses of the private market cause deep economic pain for millions. These financial catastrophes are then followed, sometimes, by pushback from government as an attempt to restore some balance to the system.

The robber baron era of empire building of the late 19th century led to anti-trust laws and consumer protections such as the Pure Food and Drug Act. The unregulated financial market of the 1920s crashed with the Great Depression, which spawned financial regulation and Social Security. The business-friendly 1950s led to the activist 1960s, when government adopted Medicare. The Great Recession of 2008 that caused millions of Americans to lose their houses and their health care led to stronger financial oversight as well as Obamacare—a modest benefit compared with Social Security and Medicare, but a recognition that government had to step in because the private market had failed.

As a rule, the wealthy believe in as little government as possible. This gives them free rein to go about their business of making money with few if any constraints on their freedom to do so.

As a rule, average Americans believe in a more active role for government to provide programs from infrastructure to health care that benefit the greater good.

Over the past half-century, with a couple of modest exceptions, the pendulum has swung disastrously onto the side of the wealthy and those who oppose government action in the economy. The result has kept the poor in poverty, clamped a death grip on the middle class and made the rich richer.

In program after program you see the effects of this trend. The first federal student loan program was staffed by civil servants. Under Ronald Reagan it was turned over to private companies, whose executives used the program to enrich themselves—one of whom had so much cash in his pocket that he built his own private 18-hole golf course. In the meantime, millions of former students are weighed down with loans they'll never be able to repay.

America is out of balance with the money flowing to ever more powerful corporations and to a small percentage of the population, the inevitable result of a decades-long propaganda campaign by conservative think tanks, television pundits, right-wing demagogues, and their lackeys in Congress to persuade the American people that government is their enemy.

No one disputes that the free market is a powerful force that stimulates innovation and a multitude of new enterprises that create vast individual fortunes. But it hasn't lifted all boats. Too many Americans are mired in place or losing ground. Relegating government to the sideline has created an increasingly unequal society, and restoring that balance would not affect the lifestyle of a single wealthy family in America.

The consequences of U. S. policies hostile to government were brutally exposed by the onset of the coronavirus. The federal government had no national plan to deal with it – no plan to make sure that vital equipment to save lives got to the health care community, no plan to warn all citizens of the danger the virus posed, no plan to institute containment measures to slow its spread. The response to a national calamity was left to the woefully unprepared private market and to divergent state and local governments. But the disaster was of a magnitude that required coordinated public action from coast to coast, not private initiative.

The problem went beyond the bumbling Trump administration, which refused to face the danger until the virus reached America's shores. Years of touting the benefits of a market-driven health care system by opponents of government left the nation with fewer hospital beds per capita than any other major developed nation. The number of hospital beds shrank 16 percent from 1975 to 2018 during a period when the U.S. population increased by 50 percent. The U. S.

figure, 2.8 beds for every 1,000 persons, was dramatically lower than that of France (5.9 beds per 1,000); Germany (8 beds per 1,000), and Japan (13 beds per 1,000). Even China, with 4.34 beds per 1,000, could take care of a greater share of its people than the U.S.

When the pandemic and its economic impact have passed and the familiar rhythms of American life have returned, the problems the virus exposed will still be with us and crying for action. For all the pain the pandemic has caused, it signals to the nation an opportunity to restructure government to meet the needs of all its citizens, not just on health care but on taxes and economic security so that we can finally start to reduce income inequality and make good on the promise of the American dream for all America.

More than ever, the time has come to reverse this half-century-long march to plutocracy, to acknowledge that after decades of corporate excesses and private greed, the time has come for government to reassert itself on behalf of all the people, to create a tax system that rewards all Americans, not just the rich, to fashion a regulatory environment that balances the interests of workers and companies, to create a framework that assures all Americans of basic health care and a decent retirement, and to invest in America, thereby creating good-paying jobs so that all hard-working men and women will have a ticket to the middle class.

The structural problems in our system that are dismantling the middle class are not new. But they are intensifying. What is new is an urgent need to confront them and to rebuild the middle class. Unless these trends are reversed, the American dream is over, with an elite class of Americans at the top and the vast majority of Americans at the bottom. The U.S. will then look more like a banana republic than the world's first modern democracy.

But there are some hopeful signs: We see in many young people, especially those who have become active in the 2020 presidential race, a desire to adopt a better health-care system, a more equitable tax code, a higher minimum wage and to curtail the virtually unrestrained power of large corporations to mistreat their workers and despoil the environment.

They are our hope. They are America's hope. They know the time has come to take back the country.

AMERICA: WHAT WENT WRONG?
THE CRISIS DEEPENS

Chapter One

DISMANTLING THE MIDDLE CLASS

INTRODUCTION

We are brought up in America to believe that everyone should play by the same rules, but those who run the country these days play by their own rules.

And their rules are destroying the American middle class.

Their policies on taxes, jobs, health care and retirement are always presented as ways to help the middle class, but those policies usually turn out to benefit them, not most Americans.

Their latest major attack on the middle class came in the misleadingly named Tax Cuts and Jobs Act of 2017, the much-ballyhooed Trump tax bill. As a result of this act, tax cuts for the wealthy will pour at least half a trillion additional dollars into the pockets of the top 1 percent over the next decade. Roughly 1.5 million people out of a population of 330 million Americans will get a staggering windfall.

For the remaining 150 million Americans who file a tax return, the bill is mostly a wash. When rising costs in essentials such as housing and health care are counted, even those who might have derived a small benefit will see it vaporize.

What's most shocking about this policy is that it isn't new. Washington has been doing this relentlessly for years—passing laws and implementing regulations that harm most Americans, as we'll see below. And this toxic trend keeps gathering steam.

Rigging the Game

Worried that you're falling behind, not living as well as you once did? Or expected to?

That you're going to have to work extra hours, or take a second job, just to stay even with your bills?

That the company you've worked for all these years may dump you for a younger person?

Or that the pension you've been promised may not be there when you retire?

Worried, if you're on the bottom rung of the economic ladder, that you'll never see a middle-class lifestyle?

Or, if you're a single parent or part of a young working family, that you'll never be able to save enough to buy a home?

That you're paying more than your fair share of taxes?

Worried that the people who represent you in Congress are taking care of themselves and their friends at your expense?

You're right.

Keep worrying.

Those people in Washington who write the complex tangle of rules by which the economy operates have rigged the game—by design and default—to favor the privileged, the powerful and the influential. At the expense of everyone else.

Seizing on that opportunity, an army of business buccaneers began buying, selling and trading companies the way most Americans buy, sell and trade knickknacks at a yard sale. They borrowed money to destroy, not to build. They constructed financial houses of cards, then vanished before they collapsed.

Caught between the lawmakers in Washington and the dealmakers on Wall Street have been millions of American workers forced to move from jobs that once paid $15 an hour into jobs that pay $7. If, that is, they aren't already the victims of mass layoffs, production halts, shuttered factories and owners who enrich themselves by doing that damage and then walking away.

As a result, the already-rich are richer than ever; there has been an explosion in overnight new rich; life for the working class is deteriorating, and those at the bottom are trapped.

Members of the generation entering adulthood in the 21st century will find it impossible to achieve a better lifestyle than their parents. Most will be unable to even match their grandparents' middle-class status.

Indeed, the growth of the middle class—one of the underpinnings of democracy in this country—has been reversed. By government action.

Taken as a whole, the rules that govern the game have:

» Created a tax system that is firmly weighted against the middle class.

» Enabled companies to trim or cancel health-care and pension benefits for employees.

» Granted subsidies to businesses that create low-wage jobs that are eroding living standards.

» Undermined longtime stable businesses and communities.

» Rewarded companies that transfer jobs abroad and eliminate jobs in this country.

» Placed home ownership out of reach of a growing number of Americans and made the financing of a college education impossible without incurring a hefty debt.

Look upon it as the dismantling of the middle class. And understand that, barring some unexpected intervention by the federal government, the worst is yet to come. For we are in the midst of the largest transfer of wealth in the nation's history. It is a transfer from the middle class to the rich—courtesy of the people in Washington who rewrote the rules.

Those who have taken advantage of the changed rules are beneficiaries of the transfer. People like Andrew G. Galef, an art collector, millionaire investor and resident of one of the nation's wealthiest enclaves, Bel Air, Calif. Meanwhile, those who have played by the old rules are victims of the transfer. People like Mollie James, a factory worker, mother of four, and grandmother of six, living in a working-class neighborhood in Paterson, N. J.

Andrew Galef never met Mollie James, but a decision he made

in 1989 had a profound effect on her life. Galef eliminated Mollie James' job.

For more than three decades, James worked at the Universal Manufacturing Co. in Paterson, rising from assembly-line worker to become the only female operator of a large metal-stamping machine. In the process, she prospered to a wage of $7.91 an hour, or more than $16,000 a year.

In June 1989, MagneTek Inc., a Galef company that had bought Universal, halted manufacturing in New Jersey—terminating James' job, along with the jobs of 500 others. The manufacturing operation was transferred to Blytheville, Ark., where wages were lower, and part of the existing manufacturing operation in Blytheville was moved to Mexico, where the wages were even lower—less than $1.50 an hour.

For her 33 years of service, Mollie James received a severance check that, after deductions, came to $3,171.66—or a little less than $100 for each year she had worked. At the age of 65, that would qualify her for a monthly pension of $101.76. That is about half the $2,400 that Andrew Galef spent in a single year to feed, groom and care for the family dog, according to his second of three wives.

The extreme differences between the lifestyles of the rich and those of ordinary working people have existed always. But there is a notable difference today: The ranks of the Andrew Galefs are growing by the thousands. The ranks of the Mollie Jameses are swelling by the millions. And the ranks of those in between are shrinking.

Once upon a time, membership in the middle class was open to everyone. Now it is severely restricted. And existing memberships are being revoked. A few statistics, drawn from an analysis of a half-century of tax and economic data, tell part of the story.

THE SHRINKING MIDDLE CLASS. Nearly 34 million individuals and families who earned salaries filed federal tax returns for 1989 reporting adjusted gross incomes between $20,000 and $50,000. They represented the heart of America's working middle class. Median family income that year amounted to $34,213—meaning that half of all families earned more, half earned less.

TWO-CLASS SOCIETY

Increase in total salaries of people
earning more than $1 million:

2,184%

WHAT WENT WRONG

The total amount of dollars in
salaries funneled to the rich soared
in the 1980s — as did the number
of rich themselves. Meanwhile, the
total dollars in wages that went to
the middle class increased an
average of just 4 percent a year,
or 44 percent over the decade.

It was a phenomenon
unlike any America had
seen in this century.

Increase in total
salaries of people
earning $20,000
to $50,000:

44%

Increase in
total salaries of
people earning
$200,000 to $1
million:

697%

SOURCE: Internal Revenue Service

In the chart on your left we highlighted the startling separation between the middle and upper classes that was occurring in the 1980s. Since the '80s, though, the rich have continued to receive ever-higher pay raises: In the decade beginning in 2010, taxpayers who earned more than $1 million saw a pay increase of 71 percent; middle-class workers, just 12 percent.

In 2017, the 410,000 individuals and families who earned $1 million or more took home in combined pay more than all the 10.5 million taxpayers earning from $40,000 to $50,000.

Source: Internal Revenue Service

But the middle is shrinking when measured against comparable income groups of earlier years. The middle-income group accounted for 35 percent of all tax returns showing income from a job in 1989. That was down from 39 percent in 1980.

UPDATE

The steady decline in the number of middle-class American families continues: When the data we used to define the middle class is adjusted for inflation, middle-class earnings would range from $40,000 to $100,000. In 2017, the latest year for which data is available, the total number of tax returns in that income group was 40 million—just 31 percent of the total who filed tax returns, a decrease of 4 percent in the middle class since 1989.

Even those who have kept a foothold in the middle class have seen their income shrink. Median family income was $34,213 in 1989. If income for those families had kept up with inflation from 1989 to 2017, it would have risen to $68,607. Instead, it was only $61,372—10 percent less.

THE GREAT SALARY GAP. Between 1980 and 1989, the combined salaries of people in the $20,000-to-$50,000 income group increased

44 percent. During the same period, the combined salaries of people earning $1 million or more a year increased 2,184 percent.

Viewed more broadly, the total wages of all people who earned less than $50,000 a year—85 percent of all Americans—increased an average of just 2 percent a year over those 10 years. At the same time, the total wages of all millionaires shot up 243 percent a year. Those figures are not adjusted for inflation, which cuts across all income groups but hits the lower and middle classes hardest.

THE BULGING RANKS OF THE RICH. Between 1980 and 1989, the number of people reporting incomes of more than a half-million dollars rocketed from 16,881 to 183,240—an increase of 985 percent. That represented the largest percentage increase in the 20th century. It even exceeded America's other era of excess, the 1920s.

During that decade, the number of people reporting incomes of more than a half-million dollars rose from 156 in 1920 to 1,489 in 1929—a jump of 854 percent. The 1920s, like the 1980s, were marked by an uncontrolled financial frenzy on Wall Street and a government responsive to special interests.

More significant for most people is a comparison with the 1950s, the decade that saw the largest expansion of the country's middle class. It was a time when ever more Americans climbed the economic ladder and substantially improved their living standard. It was also a time when the number of people reporting more than a half-million dollars in income barely rose, from 842 in 1950 to 1,002 in 1959, a gain of 19 percent.

The decade began and ended with fewer people reporting such incomes than had during the 1920s, even though the population had increased by more than 50 percent and a 1950s dollar did not have as much buying power as a 1920s dollar. One reason for the slow growth: In the 1950s, taxable income above $400,000 was taxed at a rate of 91 percent. In 1991, the maximum tax rate for individuals was 31 percent. That's a tax-rate reduction of 66 percent. In both the 1920s and the 1980s, Congress enacted large tax cuts for the wealthy.

Because of the dramatic increase in their numbers, the over-$500,000 group is accounting for a larger share of overall income tax collections at the same time their individual payments have fallen off sharply. In 1980, they paid $8.1 billion in taxes, or 3 percent of total individual income taxes. In 1989, they paid $59.4 billion, or 14 percent of the total.

 UPDATE

Our earlier findings about the bulging ranks of the rich riled up those who thought the American middle class was doing just fine.

They contended that by spotlighting the growing number of rich Americans that we were decrying success and, worse, fomenting class warfare.

As dramatic as the 1992 numbers were, the ranks of the rich had only begun to bulge. In 1992, the top 1 percent accounted for 14.8 percent of total income reported to the IRS. By 2017, the top 1 percent were receiving 20.9 percent of total income, and that was before the Trump tax bill of 2017 put even more money in their pockets.

In the 25 years from 1992 to 2017, the total income of the top 1 percent as a group went from $538 billion to $2.4 trillion—an increase of 350 percent. During that same quarter-century, median family income did not even keep pace with inflation, rising from $52,615 to $61,372—an increase of 17 percent, or less than one percent a year.

RISING TAXES OF THE MIDDLE CLASS. In 1970, a family with income of $9,000 to $10,000—median family income that year was $9,867—paid a total of $1,689 in combined local, state and federal income and Social Security taxes.

In 1989, a family with income of $30,000 to $40,000—median family income that year was $34,213—paid $8,491 in combined local, state and federal income and Social Security taxes. Thus, while these taxes consumed 17.8 percent of a middle-class family's earnings in 1970, by 1989 they took 24.3 percent of the family's income. When real estate taxes, sales taxes, gasoline taxes and other excise taxes and local levies that have gone up are added in, the middle-class family's overall tax burden rises to about one-third of family income.

UPDATE

The heaviest tax burden for low-income and moderate-income families is the payroll tax.

This is the tax automatically deducted from every paycheck for Social Security and Medicare. Many lower-income people pay no income taxes because they earn so little. But whatever they earn, they must pay the payroll tax if they collect a paycheck. The tax is calculated on gross pay with no deductions.

Unlike the income tax, which theoretically requires those who earn more to pay more, the payroll tax hits low-income workers the hardest. Workers earning $40,000 pay 7.65 percent of their gross earnings. Self-employed workers must pay 12.4 percent. But for millionaires the effective rate can be 2 percent or lower because they no longer have to pay Social Security taxes after their incomes reach $137,700.

ILLUSORY TAX ON THE WEALTHY. When Congress enacted the Tax Reform Act of 1986, lawmakers hailed its alternative minimum tax provision as the most stringent ever, guaranteeing that nobody would escape paying at least some tax. Financial publications sounded warnings to their readers. The *Wall Street Journal* said the new law "would toughen the alternative minimum tax" and *Fortune* magazine predicted that "a lot more taxpayers are likely to be hit."

Congress's Joint Committee on Taxation, declaring that the alternative minimum tax was necessary "to ensure that no taxpayer with substantial economic income can avoid significant tax liability," estimated that the amended provision would generate an additional $8.2 billion in revenue from 1987 to 1991.

Rep. Marty Russo, the Illinois Democrat who was a member of the tax-writing House Ways and Means Committee and an architect of the alternative minimum tax, said during debate on the bill: "I take particular pride when I hear my colleagues ... say that this bill has the toughest minimum tax they have ever seen. It makes sure everybody pays a fair share."

It did not. Under the existing law that year, 198,688 individuals and families with incomes over $100,000 paid alternative minimum taxes totaling $4.6 billion. Three years later, in 1989, under the new law praised by Russo and his colleagues, 49,844 individuals and families paid alternative minimum taxes totaling $476 million.

Passage of "the toughest minimum tax ever" resulted in a 75 percent drop in the number of people who paid the tax, and a 90 percent drop in the amount they paid. On average, a millionaire in 1986 paid an alternative minimum tax of $116,395. Three years later, a millionaire paid $54,758. That amounted to a 53 percent tax cut.

At first glance, the drop-off in alternative minimum tax collections might seem to suggest that the system was working as planned. After all, the 1986 law eliminated many tax shelter schemes that had triggered the alternative minimum tax in the past. Thus, it would appear that those at the top were paying more in taxes at the regular rate and were not subject to the more-strict alternative minimum tax.

This was certainly true in some individual cases. But for millionaires and other upper-income people as a group, it was not. From 1986 to 1989, the average tax bill of millionaires—exclusive of the alternative minimum tax—fell 27 percent, dropping from $864,068 to $634,196. At the regular tax rates, that represented a tax savings of $229,873.

A comparison with individuals and families who reported incomes of more than $1 million in 1980 is even more stark. From 1980 to 1989, their average tax bill—again exclusive of the alternative minimum tax—plunged from $980,869 to $634,196. That amounted to a 35 percent tax cut, giving those people an extra $346,673 in spending money.

During that same period, the alternative minimum tax payments of the same income group fell from $144,474 to $54,758. That amounted to a 62 percent tax cut, giving those people another $89,716 in spending money.

TRAPPED AT THE BOTTOM. Almost half of all Americans who had jobs and filed income tax returns in 1989 earned less than $20,000.

Tax 'reform': Small break for you, big breaks for the rich

The Tax Reform Act of 1986 cut everyone's taxes.
But three years later, some fared much better than others:

INCOME BRACKET	SIZE OF TAX CUT	AVERAGE 1989 TAX SAVINGS PER RETURN
UP TO $10,000	11%	$37
$10,000 – $20,000	6%	$69
$20,000 – $30,000	11%	$300
$30,000 – $40,000	11%	$467
$40,000 – $50,000	16%	$1,000
$50,000 – $75,000	16%	$1,523
$75,000 – $100,000	18%	$3,034
$100,000 – $200,000	22%	$7,203
$200,000 – $500,000	26%	$24,603
$500,000 – $1,000,000	34%	$86,084
$1,000,000 OR MORE	31%	$281,033

The chart we published in 1992 showed the huge tax cut the rich received from the Tax Reform Act of 1986. Congress continues to shower the wealthy with gifts. The Tax Cuts and Jobs Act of 2017 gave those earning $1 million or more a year an average tax cut of $64,428. Taxpayers earning from $50,000 to $75,000 received $840. Those making from $40,000 to $50,000 got $525.

Source: U.S. Congress, Joint Committee on Taxation

Of the 95.9 million tax returns filed that year by people reporting income from a job, 47.2 million came from people in that income group. They represented 49 percent of all such tax filers.

Between 1980 and 1989, the average wage earned by those in the under-$20,000 income category rose $123—from $8,528 to $8,651. That was an increase of 1.4 percent. Over the decade, the average salaries of people with incomes of more than $1 million rose $255,088—from $515,499 to $770,587—an increase of 49.5 percent. That, it should be stressed, was their increase in wages and salaries alone.

The figure does not include other types of income, such as dividends and interest, or profits from the sale of stocks, bonds, real estate or other capital assets.

For those at the top, such income far exceeds salaries. In 1989, salaries, on average, amounted to just 29 percent of the total income received by people earning more than $1 million. In the case of individuals and families in the $500,000 to $1 million bracket, salaries amounted to 50 percent of their overall income.

The story is different for members of the middle class and lower-income groups. They are dependent on their paychecks to meet daily living expenses. Take individuals and families who earned between $30,000 and $40,000 in 1989. Of their total income, 88 percent came from wages and salaries. It was 86 percent for those in the $50,000 to $75,000 income class, as well as the $10,000 to $20,000 income group.

More working Americans than ever find themselves at the bottom of the income ladder.

Despite low unemployment leading up to 2020, which in the past usually raised wages and salaries, the financial squeeze has intensified.

Of the 126.2 million returns filed in 2017 by people reporting income from a job, 62.1 million earned less than $40,000 —49.2 percent of all taxpayers. That was slightly higher than we reported in 1992.

Millions of Americans are living on the edge. In its 2019 report on the economic well-being of Americans, the New York Federal Reserve found that more than 25 percent of Americans "skipped necessary medical care in 2017 due to being unable to afford the cost." In this same survey which found that four in ten Americans don't have enough cash to meet a $400 emergency, the Fed concluded that in order to meet such an expense "27 percent would borrow or sell something to pay for the expense, and 12 percent would not be able to cover the expense at all."

THE GOOD LIFE—TAX FREE. During 1989, some 37,000 million-aires supplemented their other income with a weekly tax-free check for $2,607. That was $135,548 for the year. No tax owed.

The money came from the return on their investment in bonds issued by local and state governments. The interest on those bonds is exempt from federal income taxes. Altogether, some 800,000 people with income over $100,000 picked up $20.1 billion from their exempt-bond holdings, thereby escaping payment of $5.6 billion in federal income taxes.

That lost revenue, as you might guess, was made up by other taxpayers, among them the 26.5 million people with income under $20,000 a year who paid taxes on the interest earned from their savings accounts. All together, these people paid about $7.1 billion in federal income taxes on savings account interest that averaged $1,782 for the year.

Many of the same millionaires escaped payment of billions of dollars in state income taxes as a result of their investment in U.S. government securities, which are exempt from state and local taxes.

SUBSIDIZING THE AFFLUENT. If you earned $20,000 in 1990, you paid $1,530 in Social Security taxes. Of that figure, $1,240 was earmarked for Old Age and Survivors' Insurance; the remaining $290 for Medicare.

So where, exactly, did your $1,240 go?

Most people think it goes into a special fund that is set aside for their own future retirement. It does not. Instead, it goes to current retirees, including wealthy Americans, who are already receiving their Social Security. In 1989, the top four-tenths of 1 percent of all people filing tax returns with reported incomes of more than $100,000 received $4.9 billion in Social Security payments.

That sum exceeded the Social Security tax withheld from the paychecks of about 2 million workers in Massachusetts earning less than $30,000 a year. Plus more than 1 million workers in South Carolina in the same income category. Plus more than 3 million workers in Illinois. And about 1 million workers in Oregon.

Think of it as a simple transfer of money.

Of course, the wealthy pay into Social Security, too. But the $4.9 billion they receive is more than the Social Security taxes paid by about 7 million workers who earn less than $30,000 a year. And it is turned over to 400,000 people who earned more than $100,000 a year. Only 14 percent of the over-$100,000 set collects Social Security. But in coming years that number will grow. That means ever more workers in the under-$30,000 set will be tapped to pay the bill.

For all this, you can thank a succession of Congresses and presidents who set the rules for the American economy. Congress does so when it enacts new laws and amends or rescinds outdated ones and then provides the resources that determine whether the laws will be enforced. The president does so through the various departments and regulatory agencies that implement new regulations and amend or rescind outdated ones—and then either enforce or ignore the regulations.

Both the Congress and the president do so when they succumb to pressure from special interests and fail to enact laws or implement regulations that would make the economic playing field level for everyone. Taken together, the myriad laws and regulations—from antitrust to taxes, from regulatory oversight to bankruptcy, from foreign trade to pensions, from health-care to investment practices—form a rule book that governs the way business operates, that determines your place in the overall economy.

Think of it as the U.S. government rule book.

It is a system of rewards and penalties that influences business behavior, which in turn has a wide-ranging impact on your daily life. From the price you pay for a gallon of gasoline or a quart of milk to the closing of a manufacturing plant and the elimination of your job. From the number of peanuts in your favorite brand of peanut butter to the amount of money you will collect in unemployment benefits if you are laid off. From whether the shirt or dress you are wearing is made in Fleetwood, Penn., or Seoul, South Korea, to whether the company you work for expands its production facilities in the United States, thereby creating jobs, or opens a new plant in Puerto Rico or Mexico instead.

From whether the grapes you eat are grown in California or Chile to the amount of money you will receive in your pension check when you retire—or whether you will even receive a pension check. From the amount of interest you earn on your passbook savings account to whether your weekly paycheck may be cut when your employer sells out to a competitor.

It should be noted that conditions beyond the government rule book also are at work in the economy. They, too, play a part in determining one's fortunes. There is a preoccupation with resorting to litigation to settle most any type of conflict or slight, real or imagined. There is a systemic failure in schools to provide the basic technological education required for the business world of the 21st century. Also, there is a declining work ethic that raises costs and contributes to the production of defective merchandise. There is an unthinking adherence to arcane work rules that breed inefficiency.

Nonetheless, if all these problems were erased overnight, the plight of the middle class would remain essentially unchanged.

For it is the rule book that determines who, among the principal players in the economy, is most favored, who is simply ignored and who is penalized. Those players include management, employees, customers, stockholders and the community where a business is located.

The players often have conflicting interests.

Arthur Liman, a prominent New York defense lawyer who represented convicted junk-bond creator Michael R. Milken, once put it this way: "I don't see how a board, elected by shareholders, can be expected to protect, for example, the interests of the community or the interests and diversity in the economy. That, perhaps, has to come from the rules of the game that are established by government, by democratic processes. I think boards have to represent the shareholders."

Indeed so. But those who establish the rules of the game long ago ceased to represent the middle-class players. As a result, the middle-class casualties of the government rule book already can be counted in the millions. In the years ahead, they will be many times that number.

Here is a summary of what seems likely to come, barring a sweeping reversal in federal policy:

» Workers will continue to be forced to move from jobs that once paid well into minimum wage jobs that pay less. Some will be consigned to part-time employment. Some will lose all or part of their fringe benefits long taken for granted.

» Women and African Americans will continue to move into the workforce, but they will receive substandard wages, substandard pensions and substandard fringe benefits. For the first time, they will be joined by a new minority—white males in both manufacturing and service jobs.

» Workers will be compelled to forego wage increases to shoulder a growing percentage of the cost of their own health-care insurance. Some will find their coverage sharply limited. Some will lose their health-care coverage entirely.

» The elimination of jobs that once paid middle-class wages will continue uninterrupted, due in part to an ongoing wave of corporate restructurings and bankruptcies, the continuing disappearance of some industries and the transfer of others to foreign countries.

» Local, state and federal taxes will continue to consume a disproportionate share of the income of ordinary workers. At the same time, the income of wealthy Americans that goes untaxed will continue to grow.

» Massive debt loads incurred by corporations and the federal government will require ever growing sums of money for interest payments, meaning less money for new plants and equipment, less money to create jobs, less money to rebuild a collapsing infrastructure—highways, bridges, water and sewer lines.

» Men and women, banking on pensions they believe the federal government has insured, will discover at retirement that their pensions are not guaranteed. Some will receive only a fraction of the promised benefits. Some will receive nothing.

» For the first time since the Great Depression, a growing number of workers will receive no pension at all. At the other extreme, about 20 percent of the workforce will receive hefty pensions—in many cases more in retirement than they earned while at work.

None of this, it should be underscored, is related to a recession. Because these conditions are structural, built into the economy by the rule book's authors, they will be largely unaffected by any upturn in business.

Casualties of the New Economic Order

Larry Weikel and Belinda Schell know all about the future. For them, it arrived in 1990 when they paid the price for Wall Street's excesses—and Congress's failure to curb those excesses.

Weikel lived with his wife in Boyertown, Penn. Their children were grown. Schell lived with her husband and three children, two teenagers and a 7-year-old, in Royersford, Penn.

Both worked at the old Diamond Glass Co. plant that had long been a fixture in downtown Royersford. Until, that is, the takeover craze of the 1980s led to its closing, the elimination of their jobs and the jobs of 500 coworkers—and profits of tens of millions of dollars for those behind it all.

Their stories are the stories of middle-class jobholders everywhere. In interviews across America, we heard a constant refrain. It was a litany sounded in city after city, from Hagerstown, Md., to South Bend, Ind., from Hermann, Mo. to Martell, Calif. Over and over, blue-collar and white-collar workers, mid-level managers—middle class all—talked of businesses that once were but are no more. Sometimes the business was glassmaking. Sometimes it was printing. Or timber. Or shoemaking. Or meatpacking. But always the words were the same.

They talked about owners and managers who had known the employees by name, who had known their families, who had known the equipment on the floor, who had walked through the plants and offices and stopped to chat. They talked about working with—and for—people who were members of an extended corporate family. And, finally, they talked—some with a sense of bewilderment, some with sadness, some with bitterness—of the takeovers, of the new owners and of the new managers who replaced the old.

Sometimes those managers knew the workers' names, but never the people behind the names. The managers had only a nodding acquaintance with the equipment. And they were obsessed with meeting ever-rising production quotas.

Listen to Larry Weikel, who grew up in Spring City, Penn., went to Springford High School, joined the Air Force, spent four years in the service, returned home and, in 1966, went to work at the Diamond Glass Co., a family-owned business that dated to 1874: "Everybody knew everybody. Everybody was friendly. The supervisors were all nice. The owner would come in and talk to you. It was just a nice place to work. It was a nice family, you know ... I loved to go to work."

Belinda Schell, born in Keyser, W.V., the daughter of a glassmaker, remembers how difficult it was to get a job at Diamond. Everyone, it seemed, wanted to work there. "It took me about two years to get into the plant," she said. That was 1984.

But already the plant was operating under the new economic rules. The company embarked on a course that thousands of other businesses had embarked on and would follow—because the rules by which the American economy operates actually encourage it.

That course went something like this: Take the company public, borrow a lot of money to expand by acquiring other glass companies, run up the price of the stock and sell it off at a nice profit.

At first, the process moved slowly. The company, which had changed its name to Diamond-Bathurst Inc. after a management buyout, picked up a second glassmaking plant in Vienna, W.V., from a bankrupt producer in 1981. Two years later, in 1983, it went public. Then, in April 1985, Diamond-Bathurst purchased Container General Corp., a Chattanooga, Tenn., glass manufacturer with 12 plants. And in July 1985, the company purchased most of the assets of Thatcher Glass Co. of Greenwich, Conn., a manufacturer with six plants that was operating under the protection of bankruptcy court.

Thatcher, like so many companies in the 1980s, went through a leveraged buyout in which managers and investors purchased the company with mostly borrowed money. So much borrowed money that the company eventually was forced into bankruptcy court. That same month, Diamond-Bathurst moved from the drab second-floor offices above the aging Royersford plant into a modern office complex built into a hillside in the wooded and rolling countryside in Malvern, Penn. As Frank B. Foster III, the company's president and chief executive officer, put it at the time: "We became in three short months one of the largest glass container manufacturers in the United States, with projected annualized sales of $550 million." To finance it all, Diamond-Bathurst borrowed big. Its debt rocketed 700 percent, going from $13 million in 1984 to $104 million in 1985.

Wall Street loved it. The stock shot up from a low of $6 a share to a high of $29. Later, it split. Sales climbed from $62 million to $408 million. Profits went from $2 million to $11 million.

The *Philadelphia Inquirer* in July 1985 quoted a First Boston Corp. securities analyst, Cornelius W. Thornton, as saying: "There's a whole lot of synergism in this deal. I don't think the question is can Diamond pull it off. I think they've done it." They hadn't. But Wall Street has a short attention span and many investors already had made a killing.

It soon became clear that Diamond-Bathurst would be unable to make the interest payments on its mountain of debt. That debt was made possible by a Congress which, at the time, was working on a tax bill that would eliminate the deductibility of most forms of consumer interest but retain the interest deduction for corporations.

Without that deduction, much of the corporate restructuring that took place in the 1980s, and the job loss that followed, might never have occurred, since the deals depended on the tax advantage. The use of debt to buy and dismantle companies—instead of to build them—was exploding. Congress, in hammering out the Tax Reform Act of 1986, chose to ignore that phenomenon.

In any event, Diamond-Bathurst posted a $6.2 million loss for 1986 rather than the profit that earlier had been forecast by stockbrokers and company management.

In June 1987, Moody's lowered the credit rating on Diamond-Bathurst's bonds.

Company executives already had closed one manufacturing plant after another—in Indianapolis; Wharton, N.J.; Mount Vernon, Ohio; Vienna, W.V., and Knox, Penn., abolishing the jobs of several thousand workers.

It was not enough. In August 1987, a heavily indebted Diamond-Bathurst was acquired by a competitor, the new corporate headquarters in Malvern was closed and more than 250 salaried workers were dismissed. The buyer was Anchor Glass Container Corp. of Tampa, Fla., a descendant of a leveraged buyout.

When the new owners arrived, Larry Weikel, by then a shift foreman; Belinda Schell, a clerk, and other workers noticed an immediate change. "It just became so competitive," Weikel said, "and things just started getting nasty and out of hand. It just seemed like they didn't care what you did to get the numbers ... They'd expect you to get on somebody about a problem that wasn't their fault to start with."

Schell said Anchor Glass sent in managers from its plants in other parts of the country, and they issued conflicting orders. Jobs were eliminated and the remaining employees were pressured to increase output. But there was no investment in more modern equipment or new technology. The final day of production came in August 1990. Weikel, Schell and the remaining 275 or so employees were out of work.

Once again, their stories were much like the stories that we heard in scores of interviews across the country. With few exceptions, the former Anchor Glass workers have moved into jobs that paid lower wages and reduced health-care benefits. Weikel worked part time at a marine-supply store run by his brother-in-law. His wife worked in a sewing factory, earning about $6 an hour. When he lost his job, he refinanced the mortgage on the family home and began draining their savings. Jobs that paid the $15 an hour he earned at Anchor Glass did not exist.

Said Weikel: "That's all I ever did in my life, work in a glass plant. I went to work there when I came out of the service and, you know, I really never learned anything because all I did was make bottles, and there's not much call for that. I could re-educate myself, I guess, but I don't want to get into another mess like that. I could get a job any-where, I mean making $5, $6 an hour. But that's not worth my time ... I would do it if I was starving. But I'm not. My kids are grown and I'm not worrying about it that much anymore. I spent 23 years worrying about it ... All I really have to do is make enough money to feed my wife and myself."

Belinda Schell, with a growing family, had no choice but to go back to work. At Anchor Glass, she earned more than $10 an hour. At her new job, as a nursing home aide, she earned considerably less. It is an occupation that the federal government touts as a growth industry that will provide many jobs—mostly low-paying—as the aged population continues to grow.

Belinda Schell's husband, who like Weikel earned $15 an hour at Anchor Glass, found a job in another manufacturing plant in King of Prussia. He, too, earned less than before.

Schell said her brother-in-law encountered another obstacle when he sought a job at lower pay than he had made: "They would tell him he made too much money and he wouldn't be satisfied.

He was making $16 at Anchor Glass and they said he wouldn't be satisfied making $8. But people like that don't know what it's like to go through a plant closing when you have a mortgage and children to feed. He has two children. He had just bought a new home the year before." Schell said he finally found other work, but at lower pay than he made at the glass plant. As for other coworkers, she said, "some of them that are working are only making $5 to $7 an hour, which doesn't compare with what we were making at Anchor … I don't know anybody that is making what they made at Anchor Glass."

For Larry Weikel, the experience was disheartening: "You know what hurts me, that I was liked there at that plant one time. And then for this to happen Twenty-three years in there, you know, and everything was great. And then an outfit comes in like this and destroys you.

"It seems like I prostituted my whole young life to that company and then they turn me out to pasture …I spent Saturdays and Sundays down there. I didn't do anything with the kids. I didn't go to ballgames. I didn't do that. I was always working. And then they turn around and do something like that to you."

Weikel, Schell and the other Diamond Glass employees were working under America's old economic rules that, for many, provided a job and good salary and health care and pension for life in exchange for a commitment to the company.

The new rules were quite different, and the owners of the Anchor Glass company that bought Diamond Glass knew them intimately. In fact, you might even say that one of Anchor Glass' original owners helped write those rules. He was former U.S. Treasury Secretary William E. Simon, who was catapulted onto the *Forbes* magazine directory of the 400 richest Americans by taking advantage of the tax deduction for corporate debt.

Anchor Glass Container Corp. was itself the product of a leveraged buyout. It was formed in 1983 by Wesray Corp. and executives of the glass container division of the Anchor Hocking Corp., one of the country's glassmaking institutions. Wesray was an investment banking firm founded by Simon along with Raymond G. Chambers, an accountant. It was one of the first of what would be many leveraged buyout firms that acquired companies with mostly borrowed money.

After making cosmetic changes that often included job cutbacks and other short-term cost-reduction measures, the companies would be sold, in whole or in part, at a substantial profit—or taken public, another form of sale.

Newspapers and financial publications regaled readers with Simon successes during the 1980s—among them Anchor Glass.

In an article published in October 1988, the *Los Angeles Times* reported that after Simon helped engineer the Anchor Glass buyout, "managers cut the workforce, slashed expenses and made a successful acquisition."" Simon, the Times said, "made more than 100 times his money."

When Anchor Glass purchased the old glass container division of Anchor Hocking, the transaction was financed with the patented Simon debt formula: $76 million in borrowed money and $1 million investment by Wesray and others. You might think of that kind of arrangement this way: Let's say you want to buy a house for $100,000. You visit your friendly neighborhood bank and offer to put about $1,500 down. That's not the kind of deal you can get.

But Simon and his associates got a much better one when they organized Anchor Glass. After Anchor Glass borrowed the $76 million, according to documents filed with the U.S. Securities and Exchange Commission (SEC), $48.5 million of that sum was reloaned to Simon and friends. They, in turn, used $24 million of that money to buy the land and buildings of the various glass plants. Then they leased the land and buildings back to their new company, Anchor Glass, for 20 years.

In other words, the new owner of the glass plants, Anchor Glass Container Corp., would pay rent on the land and buildings to Simon and the other investors.

There was still more. Simon and his associates bought the furnaces and other glassmaking equipment in the various plants in exchange for a note promising to pay $43.6 million. Then they leased the glassmaking equipment back to Anchor Glass.

Several years later, Anchor Glass, in a report filed with the SEC, said the transactions were too generous to Simon and the other investors: "These arrangements were entered into when the company was privately owned, were not the result of arm's-length bargaining and on the whole were not as favorable to the company as could have been obtained from unrelated third parties."

There were other deals. Wesray picked up investment banking fees for handling the purchase of the glass-container properties and the acquisition of Midland Glass Co. Anchor Glass purchased its casualty and liability insurance and its employee health and benefit insurance from two brokerage firms in which Simon and his colleagues also held an interest. That was worth more millions of dollars in fees. And finally, there was the Anchor Glass corporate headquarters in Tampa. It, too, was owned by Simon and associates, who leased the building to the company.

In 1986, Anchor Glass, which had been a private company, offered stock for sale to the public. By 1988, according to an SEC report, Simon had sold his holdings. His total profits from the many and varied deals are unknown. But they run into the tens of millions of dollars.

One more note: In 1989, Anchor Glass was sold. The buyer was Vitro S.A., a Mexican glass company that ships products into the United States, competing with American-owned companies. Vitro is part of the corporate empire of Mexico's Sada family, ranked among the world's billionaire families by *Forbes*. The Mexican company's first moves included a decision to close the glass plant in Royersford. And another plant in Vernon, Calif. And another plant in Gulfport, Miss. and another plant in San Leandro, Calif.

Downward Mobility

What happened to Weikel and Schell and other glass plant workers is not at all unusual. Nor is what happened to the company they worked for. Nor the money being made by investors and corporate executives. Their story is the story of millions of middle-class Americans who are being forced out of higher-paying jobs into lower-paying jobs, or who have lost their benefits, or both.

VANISHING FACTORY WORKERS. In a letter to Congress in January 1989, President Reagan spoke enthusiastically of the many jobs his administration had created since 1980: "Nearly 19 million non-agricultural jobs have been created during this period ... The jobs created are good ones. Over 90 percent of the new jobs are full-time, and over 85 percent of these full-time jobs are in occupations in which average annual salaries exceed $20,000."

In fact, the job growth was centered in the retail trade and service sectors, which pay the lowest wages. Higher-paying jobs in manufacturing disappeared at a rate unmatched since the Great Depression. In the 1950s, businesses added 1.6 million manufacturing jobs. They added 1.5 million such jobs in the 1960s, and 1.5 million in the 1970s. But in the 1980s, corporations eliminated 300,000 manufacturing jobs.

While the number of manufacturing jobs fell 1.3 percent from the 1970s to the 1980s, dropping from an average of 19.6 million to 19.3 million, the number of retail trade jobs climbed 32.5 percent, rising from 12.8 million to 17 million. The retail trade workers, whose numbers are growing, earn on average $204 a week. The manufacturing workers, whose numbers are dwindling, earn $458 a week.

Those numbers understate the problem. For the percentage of the overall workforce employed in manufacturing, people who make things with their hands—cars, radios, refrigerators, clothing—is plummeting. During the 1950s, 33 percent of all workers were employed in manufacturing. The figure edged down to 30 percent in the 1960s and plunged to 20 percent in the 1980s. By 1992, it was 17 percent—and falling.

 UPDATE

Employment in manufacturing is down to just 8 percent of the total U.S. workforce.

The decline in this vital sector of the economy has been especially acute since 2000, falling from 17.3 million to 12.8 million jobs in 2019. Technological change and offshoring have eroded this former bastion of middle-class security and no new categories of good-paying jobs have appeared to offset the losses.

A typical manufacturing worker earns on average $1,128 a week. Retail trade jobs pay just about half that, an average of $603 weekly. Jobs in personal care, the fastest-growing job sector of the economy, pay even less: an average of $460 a week.

The loss of jobs in manufacturing has rippled through the economy, affecting many more middle-class workers in addition to those who lost their jobs in manufacturing. The Economic Policy Institute has calculated that for every 100 jobs lost in manufacturing, 744 jobs are lost indirectly—more than from any other category of employment.

ORGY OF DEBT AND INTEREST. One major reason for the declining fortunes of workers: American companies went on a borrowing binge through the 1980s, issuing corporate IOUs at the rate of $1 million every four minutes, 24 hours a day, year after year. By decade's end, companies had piled up $1.3 trillion in new debt—much of it to buy and merge companies, leading to the closing of factories and elimination of jobs.

That debt required companies to divert massive sums of cash into interest payments, which in turn meant that less money was available for new plants and equipment, less money for research and development. During the 1950s, when manufacturing jobs were created at a record pace, companies invested $3 billion in new manufacturing plants and equipment for every $1 billion paid out in interest. By the 1980s, that pattern had been reversed: Corporations paid out $1.6 billion in interest for every $1 billion invested in manufacturing plants and equipment.

Similarly, during the 1950s, for every $1 billion that corporations paid out in interest on borrowed money, they allocated $710 million for research and development. By the 1980s, corporations spent only $220 million on research and development for every $1 billion in interest payments.

Through the 1980s, corporations paid out $2.2 trillion in interest, more than double their interest payments through the 1940s, 1950s, 1960s and 1970s—combined. It was enough money to create seven million manufacturing jobs, each paying $25,000 a year.

UPDATE

Corporate America is on a runaway borrowing binge in the 21st century that makes the "orgy of debt" era seem quaint.

Corporate debt in 2019 neared $10 trillion—nearly 10 times what it was in the 1980s, when it shattered all previous records.

Where is all that borrowed money going? If it's used to build plants, modernize equipment or expand the business—as was the case decades ago—then it creates jobs and improves the nation's overall well-being. But in the 21st century, much of the borrowed money is going into lining the pockets of the wealthy.

A report by the Federal Reserve Bank of New York concluded in 2019 that a "large share of the borrowing that companies are currently doing is not being used to invest in growing their own productive capacity." That's Fed-speak for not investing in the business. So where did the companies invest? In their shareholders and executives. The Fed concluded that the borrowed money was going for "acquisitions, stock buybacks and dividends..." and labeled it an "inefficient" use of debt—in other words, inefficient for the nation, although quite efficient for those who own or run a company.

This huge indebtedness also poses a potential threat to workers in yet another way: During economic downturns, jobs and employee benefits are always the first to be cut by heavily indebted corporations so they can pay interest on their debt. And then, if the debt burden is still too heavy, companies close their doors.

BLOATED PAY FOR EXECUTIVES. While companies are cutting jobs that pay middle-income wages and adding large numbers of lower-paying jobs, they are paying ever-larger salaries and bonuses to people at the top. To put this in perspective, if the pay of manufacturing workers had gone up at the same pace as executive pay, a factory worker would earn $81,000 a year.

While the news media have written at length on corporate salaries, publications have suggested that highly paid executives are the exception. They are not. An analysis of tax return data shows that in 1953, executive compensation was the equivalent of 22 percent of corporate profits. By 1987, executive compensation was the equivalent of 78 percent of corporate profits.

Measured from a different perspective, in 1953 corporations paid their executives $8.8 billion in salaries, stock bonuses and other compensation. That year, those corporations paid $19.9 billion in federal income taxes. By contrast, in 1987, corporations paid their officers $200 billion in compensation, while they paid $83.9 billion in federal income taxes. That means businesses paid $2.3 billion in taxes for every $1 billion paid in executive salaries in 1953. By 1987, that pattern was reversed: Businesses paid $2.4 billion in executive salaries for every $1 billion in taxes.

 UPDATE

Business guru Peter Drucker, a friend of corporations and the people who ran them, once devised a formula that he felt fairly measured the appropriate gap between a CEO's pay and that of a company's workers.

In Drucker's view, formed in the 1960s, the ratio should be 20 to 1. For every dollar an employee earned the CEO should earn no more than $20. Drucker explained his reasoning: "That ratio is the limit beyond which (executives) cannot go if they don't want resentment and falling morale to hit their companies."

By 1992, after a decade of runaway corporate excess, the ratio had ballooned to 58 to 1. CEO pay has continued to skyrocket, and by some accounts the ratio is 312 to 1.

A factory worker who earned $8 an hour in the 1960s worked for a top boss whose pay was $150 an hour. By 2019, the boss of an employee earning $15 an hour was pocketing upward of $45,000 an hour.

Examples of excessive annual executive compensation abound: Elon Musk of Tesla, $512 million; Brendan Kennedy of Tilray, $256 million; Tim Cook of Apple, $141.6 million; Stephen Schwarzman of Blackstone, $69 million.

Even executives who perform poorly are richly rewarded. The most stunning case might be Jeffrey Immelt of General Electric. In the 16 years Immelt was CEO, General Electric's stock fell 33 percent—a $150-billion loss in value. As shareholders lost billions and workers lost jobs, Immelt pulled in millions. In his last three years on the job, 2014-16, Immelt was paid in excess of $50 million, and he walked out the door with a payout of $211 million.

THE DOWNWARDLY MOBILE. Measured in terms of buying power, the wages of manufacturing, retail trade and other service industry employees during the 1980s fell far short of their parents' and grandparents' earnings.

To understand why, let's go back to 1952 and the opening of Levittown, Penn., the world's largest planned community, a symbol of a flourishing middle class.

It took a factory worker one day to earn enough money to pay the closing costs on a new Levittown house, then selling for $10,000. More important, that was an era when the overwhelming majority of families buying homes relied on the income of one wage-earner. In 1991, it took a factory worker 18 weeks to earn enough money to pay the closing costs on that same Levittown home, selling for $100,000 or more.

Unfortunately, even if the factory worker of the 1990s had the minimum down payment, his income would be insufficient for him to qualify for a mortgage. That's because it now requires two incomes for most families to come up with a larger down payment and to meet higher monthly mortgage and tax payments. Workers in the retail and service industry are even worse off, which helps explain why so many Americans can't afford to own a house.

This is especially true for young families, who in decades past were the traditional homebuyers.

On a more mundane level, a store clerk in 1952 had to work two hours to pay for 100 postage stamps. In 1991, a store clerk had to work six hours to buy 100 stamps.

All these things—shrinking paychecks, disappearing factory jobs, fat salaries for corporate executives, uncontrolled business debt, a deteriorating standard of living—are the visible consequences of the distorted government rule book.

Other consequences are harder to see. But look closely and you will find them. They range from mounting racial tensions between whites and African Americans competing for a shrinking number of middle-class jobs to an increase in employee theft and shoplifting. From fraudulent workers compensation claims to a growing refusal on the part of citizens to pay taxes that they owe. From a shifting of the responsibility for social welfare programs from the federal government to the state governments, from the state governments to local governments. From an increase in domestic violence to a declining quality of care for residents of nursing homes.

What does the government rule book have to do with care in a nursing home?

Meet Mengabelle Quatre, a former resident of a California nursing home operated by Beverly Enterprises Inc.

Actually, let's begin with Beverly Enterprises, the product of a new economic order—one envisioned by Michael R. Milken and his Wall Street associates and made possible by rules set down by Congress. Like so many other businesses of the 1980s, its rapid expansion was fueled by easy debt. The company grew by acquiring small, independent nursing homes and building new ones, financed with junk bonds, bank loans and, in part, taxpayer dollars through industrial revenue bonds.

The number of beds in its facilities increased from 51,300 in 1981 to 121,800 in 1986. Revenue rose from $486 million to $2 billion. Profits went from $16 million to $51 million. And its stock shot up from $2.50 a share to $22.50, generating millions of dollars in profits for investors.

Along the way, Beverly Enterprises emerged as the nation's larg-

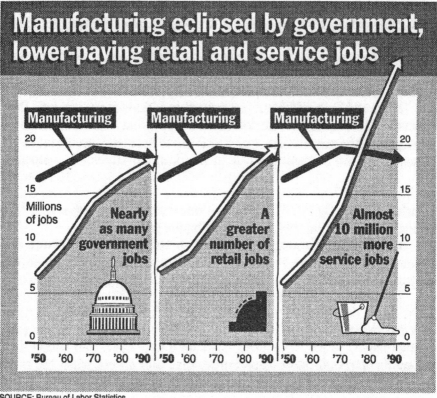

Manufacturing eclipsed by government, lower-paying retail and service jobs

Manufacturing | Manufacturing | Manufacturing

20

15

Millions of jobs

Nearly as many government jobs

A greater number of retail jobs

Almost 10 million more service jobs

10

5

0

'50 '60 '70 '80 '90 | '50 '60 '70 '80 '90 | '50 '60 '70 '80 '90

SOURCE: Bureau of Labor Statistics

... WHAT WE'VE FOUND NOW

It was clear in 1990 that manufacturing jobs were on the decline. That trend has continued, with such jobs falling to 12.8 million in 2019 from 18.4 million in 1991. Retail jobs also dropped from 20 million in 1990 to 15.6 million. Only service-providing jobs, exclusive of retail, increased – to 115.3 million.

Source: U.S. Bureau of Labor Statistics

est nursing home operator. Its investment adviser, Drexel Burnham, which had managed a $100-million securities offering for the company in 1983, was bullish on the prospects of making ever more money on the elderly. In a 1985 report to its clients, Drexel Burnham recommended the purchase of Beverly Enterprises stock, saying there were many opportunities for expansion.

"There is still a formidable pool of small independents," the investment firm said, adding that "management's goal is a steady stream of small acquisitions..."

In a report a year later, Drexel Burnham predicted that the company's profits would reach $86 million in 1987 and said "there is no shortage of growth prospects for Beverly." And in May 1987, The *Wall Street Journal* reported that a Beverly executive had confirmed that estimates by securities analysts of profits for the year between $54 million and $71 million were "in the ball park."

It turned out to be a different ballpark. For Beverly's earnings—like the earnings of so many businesses built on debt—evaporated. Instead of the $86-million profit forecast by Drexel Burnham, the company lost $33 million in 1987. It lost $24 million in 1988. And another $104 million in 1989.

As the company sought to cut costs, it developed a reputation for paying low wages and having a high turnover rate among employees. Those two conditions often led to substandard care. The wages were so low, the staffing so minimal at some Beverly-operated nursing homes, that regulatory authorities in one state after another cited the company time and again for patient neglect.

Beverly also lost a civil lawsuit in which damages were awarded to residents of its nursing homes in Mississippi who complained about a reduced quality of life due to general neglect and abuse. And the National Labor Relations Board joined the critics when an administrative law judge in 1990 cited Beverly for unfair labor practices at 33 nursing homes in 12 states.

In a December 1988 article recounting Beverly's declining fortunes, The *New York Times* reported: "Perhaps the most damaging blow to Beverly's reputation occurred in California two years ago. The state alleged that poor care at a handful of Beverly's 90 homes caused nine deaths, and inspections turned up 50 life-threatening citations over a 15-month period."

All of which brings us to Mengabelle Quatre. Suffering from seizures and cancer of the bronchial tubes, unable to walk without assistance and otherwise confined to a wheelchair, she was admitted to a Beverly nursing facility on Oct. 13, 1989. Seven weeks later, on a quiet Saturday afternoon on Dec. 2, 1989, Mengabelle Quatre died at the age of 69 at the Beverly Manor Convalescent Hospital in Burbank, Calif., not far from the make-believe world of Hollywood film studios.

A few lines from her death certificate sum up what happened:

"Death was caused by: Thermal injuries."

"Manner of death: Accident."

"Describe how injury occurred: Clothing caught on fire while smoking."

Confined to a wheelchair in a facility operated by Beverly Enterprises—the banner draped over the entrance proclaims "Love Is Ageless; Visit Us"—Mengabelle Quatre, a printer in a movie lab for 35 years, burned to death, in the middle of a hospital, while she was smoking a cigarette.

State investigators later described the incident: "(An employee) stated in an interview that at approximately 3:10 p.m. on Dec. 2, 1989, he heard someone screaming, ran to the patio adjacent to the TV room where he observed (the patient) on fire. He extinguished the fire and yelled for someone to call the paramedics." Quatre was taken to an acute-care hospital where she died five hours later. According to the state investigation, "the county coroner reported that the resident had died of thermal burns ... of yellow-brown to black discoloration over 50 percent of her body. The burns ranged between her front mid-thighs to the top of her head."

A California Department of Health Services investigation concluded that Beverly Enterprises "failed to ensure that (Quatre) smoked only in a designated area under supervision" and failed to implement a "plan which required the patient's smoking materials to be kept at the nurses station and the patient to smoke in a designated place supervised by the staff."

Drexel Burnham Lambert, which helped bankroll Beverly Enterprises, collapsed in 1990, entered bankruptcy and was dissolved in what was the largest Wall Street failure since the Great Depression.

The longtime investment bank, with roots in the 19th century, had been the principal purveyor of so-called junk bonds—non-investment grade bonds that earned a higher rate of interest than traditional corporate bonds because the investments they financed were considered riskier.

The bonds were promoted by Michael Milken, Drexel's bond trading chief, and became a favorite of corporate raiders and other aggressive financiers in leveraged buyouts, mergers, acquisitions, hostile takeovers and corporate restructurings. By the late 1980s, Drexel was one of the most powerful and feared presences on Wall Street.

Drexel's downfall began when a client implicated the bank and Milken in an illegal insider-trading scheme, and both were charged with securities fraud. Drexel paid a $650-million fine before the company was dissolved, and Milken pleaded guilty to securities fraud, was fined $600 million and sentenced to 10 years in prison. He served 22 months and was released in 1993.

President Donald Trump pardoned Milken in 2020, citing the "incredible job" he had done supporting cancer research.

Life on the Expense Account

The government rule book that helped create the environment in which Mengabelle Quatre died also makes possible quite a different lifestyle.

Meet Thomas Spiegel. He is the former chairman and chief executive officer of Columbia Savings & Loan Association, a Beverly Hills-based thrift that The *New York Times* described in February

1989 as an institution that "has been extremely successful investing in junk bonds and other ventures." Spiegel was a major fund-
raiser and financial supporter of political candidates, Democrats and
Republicans alike. He and his family lived in a six-bedroom Beverly
Hills home complete with swimming pool, tennis court and entertainment pavilion.

Spiegel thrived at Columbia during the 1980s, a time when the
executive branch of the federal government loosened regulatory
oversight of the savings and loan industry. Working with his friend
and business associate Michael Milken, whose Drexel Burnham
Lambert Inc. office was just down the street in Beverly Hills, Spiegel
used depositors' federally insured savings to buy a portfolio of junk
bonds, the high-risk debt instruments that promised to pay big dividends.

Columbia's profits soared. Earnings jumped from $44.1 million in
1984 to $122.3 million in 1985 and $193.5 million in 1986 before trail-
ing off to $119.3 million in 1987 and $85 million in 1988.

Spiegel's compensation for those years averaged slightly under
$100,000 a week.

He spent $2,000 for a French wine-tasting course, $3,000 a night
for hotel suites on the French Riviera, $19,775 for cashmere throws
and comforters, $8,600 for towels, and $91,000 for a collection of
guns—Uzis, Magnums, Sakos, Berettas, Sig Sauers.

Not unusual outlays, you might think, for someone who collected
a multimillion-dollar yearly salary. Only in this case, according to
a much-belated federal audit, it was Columbia—the savings and
loan—not Spiegel, that picked up the tab.

There is nothing new about lavish corporate expense accounts.
The practice of converting personal living expenses to a deduction
on a company or business tax return has been around as long as the
income tax. It is a practice that Congress has been unable to come up
with rules to effectively curb. But in the 1980s, corporate tax write-
offs for personal executive expenses as well as overall corporate
excesses—from gold-plated plumbing fixtures in the private office to
family wedding receptions in Paris and London—reached epidemic
proportions.

The reasons varied. Among them:

» The pace of corporate restructuring brought on by Wall Street created a climate in which once-unacceptable practices became acceptable, indeed, were even chronicled on radio and television, in newspapers and magazines.

» In a monumental change in the rules, Congress deregulated the savings and loan industry, in effect opening the doors to the vaults of the nation's savings institutions, while at the same time discouraging meaningful audits or crackdowns when irregularities were detected.

» The Internal Revenue Service lacks the staffing and time to conduct the intense audits of companies that would uncover such abuses. And even if the resources were available, an impenetrable tax code places too many other demands on the agency.

All this made possible a Tom Spiegel—and an army of other corporate executives who lived high on their expense accounts. Federal auditors eventually found that Spiegel used Columbia funds to pay for trips to Europe, to buy luxury condominiums in Columbia's name in the United States and to purchase expensive aircraft. From 1987 to 1989, for example, Spiegel made at least four trips to Europe at Columbia's expense, the auditors reported, staying at the best hotels and running up large bills:

They included, the report said: "...$7,446 for a hotel and room service bill for three nights in the Berkeley Hotel in London ... for Spiegel and his wife ... in November 1988 ... $6,066 for a hotel and room service bill for three nights in the Hotel Plaza Athénée in Paris ... in July 1989."

The Spiegels' most expensive stay was in July 1989 at the Hotel du Cap on the French Riviera, where the family ran up a $16,519 bill in five days. When they weren't flying to Europe, the Spiegels spent time at luxury condominiums, acquired at a cost of $1.9 million, at Jackson Hole, Wyo., Indian Wells, Calif., and Park City, Utah.

To make all this travel easier, Spiegel arranged for Columbia, a savings and loan that had no offices outside California, to buy corporate aircraft, including a Gulfstream IV equipped with a kitchen and lounge.

Federal auditors say that Columbia paid $2.4 million "for use of corporate aircraft in commercial flights for the personal travel for Spiegel, his immediate family and other persons accompanying Spiegel." Columbia wrote off those expenses on its tax returns, thereby transferring the cost of the Spiegel lifestyle to you, the taxpayer.

The Federal Office of Thrift Supervision filed a complaint against Spiegel, seeking to recover at least $19 million in Columbia funds that it claimed he misspent. Spiegel's lawyer, Dennis Perluss, said Spiegel would contest the charges.

"All of the uses that are at issue in terms of the planes and the condominiums were for legitimate business purposes," Perluss said.

But you are paying for more than Spiegel's lifestyle. You're also going to be picking up the tab for his management of Columbia. After heady earnings in the mid-1980s, Columbia lost twice as much money in 1989 and 1990—a total of $1.4 billion—as it had made in the previous 20 years added together. Federal regulators seized Columbia in January 1991. Taxpayers paid for a bailout estimated to be as high as $1.1 billion.

That final figure depended, in part, on how much the government collected for the sale of the corporate headquarters on Wilshire Boulevard in Beverly Hills. When construction started, it was expected to cost $17 million. By the time work was finished, after Spiegel had made the last of his design changes—"the highest possible grade of limestone and marble, stainless steel floors and ceiling tiles, leather wall coverings"—the cost had soared to $55 million.

It could have been even higher, except that one of Spiegel's ambitious plans never was translated into bricks and mortar. According to federal auditors, he had wanted to include in the building "a large multi-level gymnasium and 'survival chamber' bathrooms with bulletproof glass and an independent air and food supply."

Just whom Spiegel thought might attack the bathrooms of a Beverly Hills savings and loan is unclear.

Spiegel later settled the federal case against him by agreeing to pay a fine of $275,000, neither admitting nor denying the charges that had been brought against him.

An Indifferent Congress

Congress has done little to curb the abuses of the 1980s. Consider, for a moment, Congress's response to the leveraged buyout and corporate restructuring craze of the 1980s that led to the loss of millions of jobs. As mergers, acquisitions, hostile takeovers and buyouts swept corporate America in the 1980s, defenders of the restructuring process contended it was merely another stage of the free-market economy at work.

During an appearance before a congressional committee in 1985, Joseph R. Wright Jr., then deputy director of President Reagan's Office of Management and Budget, summed up the prevailing attitude: "There is substantial evidence that corporate takeovers, as well as mergers, acquisitions and divestitures are, in the aggregate, beneficial for stockholders and for the economy as a whole."

It is true that the restructuring of business is as old as business itself. So, too, the demise of corporations that are mismanaged or that manufacture products for which there is no longer any demand. The Baldwin Locomotive Works once sprawled over 20 acres in Philadelphia and more than 600 acres in Eddystone, Penn. At the company's peak, it employed 20,000 people. When the market for steam locomotives disappeared, so, too, did Baldwin.

In those days, when factories and technologies died out—and workers lost their jobs—new factories and new technologies replaced the old. Always at higher wages. But what sets the current era apart from the past is this: There are no new manufacturing plants to replace today's Baldwins. And the remaining jobs pay less. While the government rule book encourages deal-making over creating jobs, rewards those who engineer new pieces of paper to be traded on

Wall Street rather than those who engineer new products that can be manufactured and sold, Congress has displayed little interest in making changes.

From the mid-1980s on, lawmakers distributed news releases decrying corporate excesses. They made speeches deploring the loss of jobs. They conducted hearings exploring the possibility of enacting legislation to curb abuses. They issued reports reciting their findings.

At one point, the flurry of activity stirred concern on Wall Street. An article in a January 1989 issue of The *Wall Street Journal*, under the headline, "Wall Street Fears That Congress Will Put Brake on LBOs," began: "Fears are mounting on Wall Street that Congress may actually do something to slow down the gravy train of takeovers and leveraged buyouts."

The fears were misplaced. Lawmakers were content with giving the appearance of action: News releases. Speeches. Hearings. Reports. But nothing else. Especially no legislation.

As one congressional staff member put it when he explained why committee hearings trailed off:

"There simply is no interest among lawmakers in this."

Indeed not. But Congress was merely following the lead of the White House and Presidents Reagan and Bush.

President Bush summed up his attitudes on corporate takeovers in a question-and-answer interview with *Business Week* magazine: "To the degree that there are egregious offenses in these short-term takeovers that result in increased debt, I think we ought to take a look. But I have no agenda on that. I'm always a little wary about the government trying to solve problems when, historically, the marketplace has been able to solve them."

Members of Congress, for their part, seemed satisfied with the arguments mounted by the experts who insisted that all was working well and that new laws were unnecessary. To Capitol Hill they came to testify, from the Harvard Business School, from Wall Street investment houses, from law firms specializing in mergers and acquisitions, from the offices of corporate raiders. People like Carl C. Icahn, who spoke on the virtues of corporate takeovers during an appearance before a House Energy and Commerce subcommittee in March 1984.

Icahn already had made hundreds of millions of dollars in raids on such companies as Texaco Inc., Hammermill Paper Co., Uniroyal Inc. and Marshall Field & Co.

It was the year before he would take over Trans World Airlines Inc., a company from which he personally would extract millions of dollars, fire thousands of employees and pilot to the edge of bankruptcy.

Downplaying concerns about layoffs that follow mergers and acquisitions, Icahn told lawmakers: "Generally, if the company is doing pretty well ... there are not an awful lot of layoffs, and the layoffs that do occur are really getting rid of some of the fat that is not productive for society."

Similar views were expressed by Icahn's fellow raiders and others who profited from the restructuring of business—Wall Street investment advisers, bankers, lawyers, accountants, brokers, pension fund managers, arbitrageurs, speculators and a close circle of hangers-on.

This army of dealmakers turned the government rule book to its own advantage, seizing on provisions that place a higher value on ever-larger profits at the expense of long-term growth and more and better-paying middle-class jobs. In doing so, they made billions of dollars.

Popular wisdom has it that the worst has passed, that it was all an aberration called the 1980s. The age of takeovers and leveraged buyouts. The decade of greed. And greed has been officially declared dead by trend-trackers. A higher economic morality is supposedly operating. Popular wisdom is wrong. The declining fortunes of the middle class that began with the restructuring craze will continue.

There are, an analysis suggests, two reasons: First, there is the global economy—the current buzz-phrase of politicians and corporate executives. As will be described in a later chapter, the global economy will be to decades ahead what corporate restructuring was to the 1980s. Decisions that produced short-term profits at the expense of jobs and future profits were justified because they increased "shareholder value." Today, the same decisions are being made with the same consequences—only this time the justification is "global competition."

Second, the fallout from the 1980s continues as more companies file for protection in bankruptcy court, more companies lay off workers to meet their debt obligations, more companies reorganize to correct the excesses of the past.

Wall Street's Greatest Achievements

Meet Edwin Bohl of Hermann, Mo. He, like Larry Weikel and Belinda Schell, knows all about the future.

The place to begin Bohl's story is with a company called Interco Inc., a once-successful Fortune 500 conglomerate whose products included some of the best-known names in American retailing—Converse sneakers, London Fog raincoats, Ethan Allen furniture, Florsheim shoes. That was in 1988, the year the investment banking firm, Wasserstein Perella & Co., set out to reorganize Interco, a St. Louis-based company with scores of plants operating in the United States and abroad.

Interco could trace its origins back more than 150 years. It was one of the country's largest industrial employers, with 54,000 workers. It had annual sales of $3.3 billion. It had paid dividends continuously since 1913.

In the summer of 1988, a pair of corporate raiders out of Washington, D.C., brothers Steven M. and Mitchell P. Rales, targeted Interco for takeover, offering to buy the company for $64 a share, or $2.4 billion. To fend off the Raleses, Interco's management turned to Wasserstein Perella, which came up with a plan valued at $76 a share. Interco, obviously, did not have that kind of cash lying around. So the plan called for the company to borrow $2.9 billion.

The financial plan was the sort that Wall Street embraced with great enthusiasm. Supporters of corporate restructurings insisted that debt was a positive force, imposing discipline on corporate managers and forcing them to keep a tight rein on costs. Michael C. Jensen, a professor at the Harvard Business School, was one of the academic community's most vocal supporters of corporate restructurings: "…The benefits of debt in motivating managers and their organizations to be efficient have largely been ignored."

As it turned out, Interco failed to be a textbook model for the wonders of corporate debt. Instead of encouraging efficiency, it compelled management to make short-term decisions that harmed the long-run interests of the corporation and its employees. Within two weeks of taking on the debt, Interco closed two Florsheim shoe plants—and sold the real estate. Interco announced that the shutdowns would save more than $2 million. That was just enough to pay the interest on the company's new mountain of debt for five days.

At the Florsheim plant in Paducah, Ky., 375 employees lost their jobs. At the Florsheim plant in Hermann, Mo., 265 employees were thrown out of work. None was offered a job at another plant.

Hermann is a picturesque town of 2,700 on the Missouri River, about 70 miles west of St. Louis. Settled by Germans from Philadelphia in the 1830s, it remains heavily German. The town's streets are named after noted Germans. The local telephone book reads more like a directory from a town on the Rhine than one on the Missouri. As might be expected from such a heritage, the deeply engrained work ethic served the town's largest employer well. Beginning in 1902, that employer was known down through the years simply as "the shoe factory."

It was a model of stability for the town and one of the manufacturing jewels of the International Shoe Co., later Interco, its owner. Because of the factory's efficient workforce, whenever Florsheim wanted to experiment with new technology or develop a new shoe, it did so at Hermann. The plant had a long history of good labor relations. And it operated at a profit. So why, then, did Interco choose to close the factory?

Listen to Perry D. Lovett, who was city administrator of Hermann when the plant shut down and who discussed the closing with Interco officials: "We talked to the senior vice president who was selling the property and he told me this was a profitable plant and they were pleased with it. The only thing was, this plant and the one in Kentucky they actually owned. The other plants they had, they had leased. The only place they could generate cash was from the plant in Hermann and the one in Kentucky.

"He said it was just a matter that this was one piece of property in which they could generate revenue to pay off the debt. And that was it. That brought it down."

In short, a profitable and efficient plant was closed because Interco actually owned—rather than leased—the building and real estate. And the company needed the cash from the sale of the property to help pay down the debt incurred in the restructuring that was supposed to make the company more efficient.

Hardest hit by the closing, Lovett said, were the older people: "Here were folks who had never worked anywhere else ... They had gotten out of high school and they went to work in the shoe factory..."

So it was with Edwin Bohl.

Bohl began as a laborer in 1952. "I think I started for 70 cents an hour," he recalled. Except for two years out to serve in Korea, he worked at the plant, rising to a supervisory position until its closing 37 years later.

The announcement of the shutdown came without warning a few weeks before Christmas of 1988. There was a meeting that morning, Bohl remembered, in which there was talk about increased benefits and changes in the way shoes were made. "They had given me a bunch of new chemicals," he said, "that I was to use in the finishing department. They had told us that everything was looking good." A company executive was supposed to fly in from Chicago that same morning. No one said exactly why, but his plane was delayed.

"The minute we came back from lunch," Bohl said, "they called us supervisors together ...The man read us the papers and said there were no jobs held for anybody ... They told us they had to close the plant because of the restructuring ... They had to raise money ... They told (us) it was not because of the quality. We were rated the top in quality and cost ... We had no idea this would happen."

Unexpectedly, Edwin Bohl found himself on the unemployment rolls at age 58. He was given a choice: He could wait until he reached retirement age and collect his full pension. If he did so, he would have to pay for his own costly health insurance. Or he could take early retirement, with a sharply reduced pension, and the company would continue to pay his health insurance.

"I sacrificed 29 percent of my pension to get it (the health insurance)," he said, adding, "if I hadn't taken early retirement, my insurance would have been sky high. You really didn't have much choice." Bohl, who was earning $19,000 a year at the shoe factory, found part-time work in the local Western Auto store. The job paid $4 an hour.

Lamented Bohl's wife, Geraldine: "We thought this would be the best time of our life. Now he doesn't know when he's going to get a day off. You either take a poor retirement and have your insurance or have your retirement and pay for high insurance."

As for Bruce Wasserstein and Joseph Perella, whose firm collected $9 million in fees for arranging the restructuring that left Interco with $2.9 billion in debt—which ultimately forced the company into bankruptcy court—they have a somewhat different perspective of their efforts at reshaping corporate America. In February 1989, Perella modestly assessed his firm's contributions for The *Wall Street Journal*: "No group of people—not just me and Bruce—ever accomplished so much in such a short period of time in Wall Street's history."

Chapter Two

LOSING OUT TO MEXICO

INTRODUCTION

No one can say with absolute certainty how many U.S. manufacturing jobs have been exported to Mexico over the years. It's at least one million, and no doubt many more, especially if you count the jobs that would have been created in American plants had all those facilities remained in the U.S.

Although NAFTA, the North American Free Trade Agreement, is commonly blamed for these losses, U.S. corporations were moving to Mexico and exporting jobs to other developing countries long before NAFTA was signed in 1993. Attracted by low wages and virtually no oversight of labor conditions or environmental standards, U.S. companies could freely cut costs abroad and reward stockholders back home. It's no surprise that corporations have taken advantage of opportunities to lower their costs—that's their mission. The outrage is that a false promise allowed these companies to export American jobs in the first place.

"Free trade" agreements were sold over and over by politicians and so-called experts in both parties who claimed that they would create more jobs than they would kill. One former U.S. Treasury Department official, Gary Hufbauer, predicted on the eve of NAFTA's passage that it would "generate a $7 to $9 billion (trade) surplus that would ensure the net creation of 170,000 jobs in the U.S. economy the first year." Instead, NAFTA created an immediate trade deficit with Mexico and a net loss in jobs after it wiped out hundreds of thousands of U.S. manufacturing jobs.

This has been the story for decades: No trade deal has ever created more jobs than it eliminated. Average working people understand this, and it's a big reason why so many of them, angered by so many false promises, turned to Donald Trump in 2016.

"What Are We Going to Do Now?"

Rosa Vasquez and Mollie James shared a common interest. Vasquez worked for the company that once employed Mollie James. That's where similarities end. James earned $7.91 an hour. Vasquez earned $1.45 an hour.

James lived in a six-room, two-story house on a paved street in a working-class neighborhood of Paterson, N.J. Vasquez lived in a one-room shack in a Mexican shantytown reachable only by foot along a dirt path. James' house had electricity and indoor plumbing. Vasquez's house had neither. When Mollie James watched television, she turned on the set in her living room. When Rosa Vasquez watched television, she connected a car battery to a 13-inch black-and-white set.

For 33 years, Mollie James worked for a company that manufactured electrical components for fluorescent lights in New Jersey. Rosa Vasquez went to work for the same company, making the same kinds of products at a new plant in Mexico.

Mollie James' story is that of many Americans: After decades of working for one employer, they suddenly found themselves out of work—unable to secure another job and deprived of benefits they had counted on for their later years.

Universal Manufacturing Co., the company that employed James, was founded in 1947 as a recent invention—fluorescent lights—grew in popularity. Universal manufactured a mechanism called a ballast that regulated the flow of electricity to the light.

Mollie James went to work at Universal's Paterson plant in 1955 for 95 cents an hour. She worked as a laminator, a tester, a machine operator and finally a press operator. "I could do any job in the plant," she said proudly. Although there was usually abundant overtime, James held a second full-time job for 18 years to bring in more money to raise and educate her four children.

Universal's original owners knew the workers and routinely walked through the plant talking to them, James recalled. "We were more or less like a family," she said. "The owner would come out and talk to us and would help us in any way that he could. He saw that many of us got homes through their help, by speaking to a bank or even making you a personal loan. They were concerned about the welfare of the workers." If something didn't work, James said, the owners wanted to know so they could make adjustments and produce a better product. "We were number one," she said.

In 1986, Universal was acquired by MagneTek Inc. of Los Angeles. MagneTek had been formed in 1984 by a Los Angeles investment company, the Spectrum Group, headed by Andrew G. Galef, a business consultant who specialized in advising troubled businesses. The company was an early beneficiary of Michael R. Milken's junk bond machine. Drexel Burnham Lambert Inc. served as MagneTek's investment adviser underwriting millions of dollars in high-yield bonds that enabled the company to acquire Universal and other businesses.

MagneTek went public in 1989 with investment analysts predicting a bright future. "We think this stock has above average intermediate term prospects," Merrill Lynch said in 1989, "(and) looks even more reasonably priced on prospects in the period beyond, which accounts for our buy, long term rating."

Andrew Galef became MagneTek's chairman and received generous bonuses. More important, the Spectrum Group—of which Galef was the sole stockholder—collected annual fees for providing "management services" to MagneTek, according to SEC reports. Spectrum also made similar arrangements with other companies that Galef reorganized, including the Warnaco Group Inc., a textile manufacturer, and Exide Corp., a maker of automotive and industrial batteries. In the five-year period from 1986 to 1991, Spectrum received $3.6 million in fees from MagneTek alone.

Galef and his third wife lived in the fashionable Bel Air section of Los Angeles, popular with entertainers and movie executives. The flavor of Galef's lifestyle emerged in court papers filed in 1987 during a divorce action initiated by his second wife, Billie: "At Christmas we always had a large dinner party with at least 200 guests ... Travel was also extensive. Last July, we went to Australia, Hong Kong, China and Japan for approximately three weeks. We stayed, as we always do, in first-class hotels, ate at the best restaurants and generally traveled by limousine.

"In September, we took the Concorde to Paris and London, where we spent a week, again staying at the best hotels and eating in the best restaurants."

While Galef and his wife were jetting about the world, his managers at the Paterson plant where Mollie James worked were assuring employees that nothing would change under MagneTek, the new owner. "They came through the plant and talked to each worker and told us we wouldn't have anything to worry about because they would always have operations in Paterson," James said. "They gave us the impression that we had great prospects here. They told us they were going to get us new equipment, new machinery."

All the promises notwithstanding, the new equipment failed to materialize. Instead, the existing equipment began to disappear. When Mollie James and her coworkers would leave the factory one day, the equipment, such as a large stamping machine, was in place, bolted to the floor. And then, she remembered: "You'd come in the next morning and it would be gone. There'd be a bare space on the floor."

Employees discovered later that the equipment had been shipped to other MagneTek plants. The company subsequently sent Paterson workers to those plants to train other people to use the machines that had once provided work in Paterson. Incidents such as that made employees wonder if the plant's days were numbered. Nonetheless, MagneTek continued to say it would never close Paterson. "They told us we were doing a great job," James remembered.

But one day a notice went up on the plant bulletin board. Effective June 30, 1989, Universal's 38-year-old Paterson plant would be shut. "It was very devastating," James said. "People asked, 'What are we going to do now?' We just always thought we would have a job." In July 1989, the plant that had once employed 500 people became a distribution center, receiving products made at other MagneTek facilities. James was offered a job in the shipping department. But at 58, she was unable to lift the heavy boxes. She was out of work.

Rush to the Border

As MagneTek stopped manufacturing in Paterson, the company reached full production at a 150,000-square-foot plant in Matamoros, Mexico, a burgeoning border town across the Rio Grande from Brownsville, Texas.

While Galef declined to discuss MagneTek's move to Mexico—"Mr. Galef usually doesn't do interviews," a secretary said—another company official explained the transfer. Robert W. Murray, vice president of communications and public relations, said that production operations at Paterson were transferred to a plant in Blytheville, Ark., and that part of the Blytheville operations were, in turn, moved to Matamoros.

Commenting on the shutdown of production in Paterson, Murray said that "on a local basis, it can be a tragedy. That, we regret. But to keep our 16,000 people employed, we need to stay in business ... But the market—the labor market that was once called the United States—is now North America, and I include in that Central America ... Regions rather than countries are now competing on a world scale. We've got to cooperate with both our neighbors to the north, Canada, and with Mexico to the south to put together the kind of competitive package that can really compete on a world scale."

The MagneTek plant is part of Mexico's maquiladora program, a venture started to attract U.S. companies to establish assembly plants there. The government encouraged such plants by setting a low tariff on finished goods shipped back to the United States. Originally, maquiladoras assembled components shipped in from the states by American corporations. Many of these so-called assembly plants became full-scale manufacturing facilities performing the same type of work that was once done by American workers, but at much lower wages.

With the backing of government rule makers, maquiladora plants blossomed along the border. The strip of land that runs for 1,500 miles from California to Texas has become a highway of Fortune 500 companies. All along the Mexican side of the border are names long associated with the other side—General Motors, Fisher-Price, Trico, Parker-Hannifin, Xerox, Ford, Kimberly-Clark, IBM, Samsonite, General Electric and Rockwell. By 1990, more than 1,800 plants were operating in Mexico employing more than 500,000 workers.

When Donald Trump campaigned for president, he repeatedly called NAFTA, the 1993 North American Free Trade Agreement "the worst trade deal ever made." For many American corporations, NAFTA was an expansion of the trade policies they had pursued in the maquiladora program. After renegotiating NAFTA, Trump as president called the new agreement "the best and most important trade deal ever made by the U.S.A."

What a stretch. The new pact is essentially NAFTA with a new name, the United States-Mexico-Canada Agreement (USMCA). There are some minor changes to dress it up and create the illusion of real change, but they will do little to help U.S. manufacturing workers who lost so many jobs in the original NAFTA.

Supporters touted sections aimed at strengthening labor rights in Mexico with tougher enforcement provisions. We'll see how that goes; when it comes to a country's domestic laws, multinational agreements rarely result in significant enforcement of labor laws.

American corporations breathed a sigh of relief that the broad outlines of the original NAFTA had been preserved and they rushed to lobby for passage of the new pact.

There were some winners: America's dairy farmers. They won the right to export more milk to Canada, hardly a big job generator. Another provision buried in the 741-page treaty will let U.S. winemakers sell wine in the government-owned liquor stores of British Columbia, the Canadian province with a population about the same as Missouri.

Like virtually every other president before him who's negotiated a trade deal, Trump called USMCA a great victory, when in fact it will do little to create jobs in the U.S.

With few exceptions, the new plants replaced facilities that once provided jobs for U.S. workers in the states. Like the Zenith Electronics Corp. plant in Reynosa, across the Rio Grande from McAllen, Texas. In 1965, every color television set purchased in the United States was made by an American-owned company in a domestic plant. In that year, Americans purchased 2.6 million sets manufactured by companies like Sylvania, Motorola, Admiral, Philco, Sunbeam, RCA, Quasar, Magnavox and Wizard.

Twenty-six years later, in 1991, sales of television sets to U.S. consumers soared to 21 million. But only one company was still making the sets in the United States—Zenith Corp., at a lone domestic plant in Springfield, Mo.

By 1992, there were none. In 1991, Zenith announced that it was ending production in Springfield and shifting the jobs to a Zenith plant in Reynosa, Mexico.

For the American television industry, the end came with a swiftness that would have seemed inconceivable a generation ago, when more than two dozen American-owned plants were turning out all the television sets purchased in this country. That was before Japanese television manufacturers began dumping huge quantities of low-priced receivers on the American market.

When American manufacturers objected to what they called unfair trade practices, the Japanese claimed that they were able to undersell American makers because their products resulted from greater cost efficiencies. But American television makers said that there was no evidence to support that assertion. As proof, they pointed to the fact that the Japanese were selling television sets to Americans at much lower prices than they were selling them in Japan.

As Zenith asserted in a 1977 report: "The fact that the Japanese manufacturers, whose lowest priced 19-inch offerings in Japan are priced at about $500, are selling similar receivers to American private brand retailers at prices that permit resale in the United States at under $300, provides substantial support for the premise that those receivers are being dumped in the United States."

In 1971, the U.S. Tariff Commission had agreed, ruling that the "industry in the United States is being injured by reason of the importation of television receivers from Japan, which are being sold at less than fair value…" Fines and duties totaling several hundred million dollars were later assessed against the Japanese television makers. But years of legal wrangling and diplomatic maneuvering followed, with the Japanese companies ultimately paying only nominal amounts.

Zenith also filed a lawsuit against the major Japanese manufacturers, charging them with violating U.S. antitrust and antidumping laws. The case found its way to the U.S. Supreme Court, which ruled on behalf of the Japanese. By the time litigation and the regulatory proceedings were over, the American television industry was history.

Every American-owned company had either shut down its television production line or been sold to the Japanese. Except Zenith. The company known for innovation and quality—"The quality goes in before the name goes on"—continued to maintain one production plant. Zenith's sprawling Springfield plant—it covered an area the size of 29 football fields—was the town's largest private employer and a steady source of earnings for 1,750 local residents.

Until 1992. Having lost $500 million in revenue over the previous five years, the company announced that it had to cut costs. When labor contracts expired in 1992, a total of 1,350 employees were let go and the work shifted to Mexico. In a statement that has become all too familiar to middle-class Americans, Jerry K. Pearlman, Zenith's chairman and president, explained that the Springfield shutdown, while "painful," was necessary for Zenith to remain competitive: "This further consolidation of our operations is a necessary component of Zenith's programs to reduce costs and improve profitability." And the chief way to reduce costs, Zenith officials acknowledged, was to take advantage of Mexico's low wage rate.

 UPDATE

For American companies considering a move to Mexico, the overwhelming attraction remains Mexico's cheap labor. In 2019 the average wage paid to U.S. manufacturing workers was $20 an hour. In Mexico it was $2.

U.S. JOBS CROSS THE BORDER

WHAT WENT WRONG

American corporations are closing plants or slashing work forces in the U.S. and shifting the jobs to Mexico. Since 1965, more than 1,800 plants employing more than 500,000 workers have been built there, most by U.S. corporations.

2,800 (est.)

2,500

2,000

1,850

1,500

Hundreds of Mexican factories...

1,000

500

0

'65 '70 '75 '80 '85 **'90 '95**

800,000 (est.)

600,000

530,000

400,000

...with thousands of workers

200,000

0

'65 '70 '75 '80 '85 **'90 '95**

SOURCE: Secretariat of Programming and Budget, Secretariat of Commerce and Industrial Development, Mexico City

We estimated in 1990 that the flight of jobs from the United States to Mexico would only increase. Indeed, from 1993, when the North American Free Trade Agreement (NAFTA) was approved, until 2016, more than 80,000 U.S. manufacturing plants closed, dropping from 380,000 in 1993 to 291,543 in 2016. It's not known exactly how many plants relocated to Mexico after NAFTA, but the number is in the thousands. Thousands of other companies closed plants and then subcontracted work once performed in the States to Mexican suppliers.

Source: U.S.Bureau of Labor Statistics

Robert W. Mingus, president of local 1453 of the International Brotherhood of Electrical Workers, which represented the Zenith workers, did not blame the company for the shutdown. He blamed the last four presidents, the Commerce Department and members of Congress, both for not doing more to counter Japanese moves and for making it possible for U.S. industry to relocate to Mexico. "We're encouraging our industrial base right out of this country," he said.

UPDATE

Mexico has become an auto industry powerhouse, producing one million vehicles a year mostly at the expense of U.S. autoworkers. Due to overseas imports and production shifts to Mexico, the number of passenger cars manufactured in the U.S. since 1999 has been cut in half—from 5.6 million to 2.8 million in 2019.

The new Trump trade pact with Mexico and Canada of 2019 (USMCA) calls for a higher percentage of parts to come from North America and for higher wages for Mexican autoworkers, but the United Auto Workers is not impressed. It isn't a "fix" for the problems created by NAFTA, said UAW President Rory Gamble. "Hundreds of thousands of U.S. jobs that have gone to Mexico since NAFTA came into being 25 years ago will not return because of USMCA."

In Matamoros, where Mollie James' company relocated, maquiladora operations are like those found in Tijuana, Mexicali, Juarez, Nuevo Laredo and other border towns. Plants make everything from cosmetic brushes to auto flashers. Rosa Vasquez, one of 1,500 employees—mostly female—at the MagneTek facility in Matamoros, began working the 4:30 p.m. to 1:30 a.m. shift in July 1988, the year the plant opened. She earned 179,000 pesos, or about $59, a week.

MagneTek, in a report filed with the Securities and Exchange Commission, cited the benefits of this low-wage haven: "The company has consolidated manufacturing and relocated product lines to facilities having lower per-unit labor and overhead costs. For example, the company has established a full-scale manufacturing facility in Mexico, where it benefits from lower wage rates."

Mollie James didn't understand. "The company said we were hurt by foreign trade," she said. "But this company has plants in Mexico. Why isn't that foreign trade?" Rosa Vasquez did understand. She needed the money from the plant—even if it was only enough to buy essentials. Asked how she spent her earnings, she answered: "The children, food, clothing for the children, clothing for us."

To get to and from work, most MagneTek workers rode crowded, stuffy yellow vans called Maxi-Taxis that were designed for 12 passengers but that carried twice that many in cramped, often sweltering conditions for journeys that took up to an hour. In this sense Vasquez was fortunate. She walked to work.

Her home was one of about 200 primitive dwellings in a colony of poor people called "Vista Hermosa" bordering the MagneTek plant. Vista Hermosa ("beautiful view") was a collection of ramshackle dwellings made of wood or cement blocks, in varying stages of disrepair. Wooden outhouses served as toilets. People lighted their houses with kerosene lamps. Chickens and pigs wandered about.

Vasquez and her husband lived behind the plant, where the roar of MagneTek's air-conditioning system could be heard 24 hours a day.

She described her home as a "small wooden house." It is actually one room, 12 feet long and 10 feet wide, with a tin, peaked roof. It contains a double bed, two small dressers, a table, a cupboard, clothes hamper, two chairs and a propane stove.

Vasquez and her husband, Alberto, a carpenter, lived at the house during the week while their two children stayed nearby with her parents. Although she worked until 1:30 a.m., she rose early to take her small boys to pre-school each morning, riding 30 minutes by bus each way. She and her husband believe in education. The only object on the walls of their modest home is a poster showing a child bent intently over a desk with the slogan above, "Total Principio es Dificil." An ode to hard work, the expression translates roughly as "Starting all over is difficult."

For entertainment, the family watched television at the house of Rosa Vasquez's parents, using a car battery to power the set. Every two weeks a brother put the battery in an old car and drove around to charge it up.

Promoters of free trade with Mexico have long pointed to Mexico's large population as a potential market for American-made products. American workers, they assured, had nothing to fear from such an arrangement because it would open the door for U.S. products in Mexico's vast domestic market. That's the theory. Reality has been quite different.

 UPDATE

The big market for the sale of American goods in Mexico predicted by NAFTA promoters hasn't materialized, mainly because the wages of Mexican workers are so low that they can't afford most American consumer products. Instead, NAFTA paved the way for record-breaking trade deficits with Mexico.

The U.S. had a trade surplus with Mexico when NAFTA was approved in 1993. Now the U. S. has annual trade deficits of about $70 billion caused largely by the importation of goods manufactured in Mexico by American companies—companies that once produced those products in the States.

Even the wages earned by the Rosa Vasquezes—which are at the high end of the Mexican wage scale—do not translate into a standard of living comparable to that enjoyed by Rosa's counterpart, Mollie

James. As a result, the material goods that are common features of middle-class American households are beyond the reach of the Vasquezes.

Like refrigerators. Even if Vista Hermosa had electric power, and even if the Vasquezes could afford electricity, they still couldn't afford a refrigerator. In Matamoros, refrigerators sold for the equivalent of two months' wages. Even so, Rosa Vasquez felt fortunate. She had a job, which is more than Mollie James could say.

After the Paterson plant closed in 1989, Mollie James collected unemployment benefits for six months and then went back to school. She learned how to repair computers but did not find anyone to hire her.

"When you are ... going on 59, it is very hard to get a job," she said. "Any time you put your age down, they say nicely, 'We will contact you.'" For 18 months she paid for her own health benefits but it became too expensive at $114 a month. "I hope for the best," she said.

Mollie James liked her job at the Paterson plant and took pride in her work. Years earlier, she had to overcome management's reluctance to allow a woman to operate a large metal stamping machine. But she passed the 30-day tryout and ran the machine until the plant closed. "I've seen men lose fingers," she recalled, "but thank God I never lost anything."

Except, in the end, her job.

 UPDATE

Of all the hardworking Americans we met for this book, none impressed us more deeply than Mollie James. She wasn't happy about losing her job after more than 30 years, but she tried to move forward by retraining herself to work with computers.

As much as any one person, she symbolized the story of middle-class America: She worked hard, took on new work assignments, bought a house and raised her family. She did all the right things—then got tossed out of a job at an age when she couldn't find work.

After Bill Moyers read her story and those of other victims we chronicled in *America: What Went Wrong?*, he made two hour-long documentaries for his PBS program *Listening to America*. Among those who agreed to tell their story on television, Mollie James was pivotal. She was articulate, passionate and very angry over what had happened to her, though she did not voice her anger. She knew that the same thing was happening to middle-class people all over America, so she knew she was not alone. But she couldn't understand why government policies were allowing it to happen. Ultimately, she asked a question that still hasn't been answered: "Why can't something be done?"

Mollie James died in 2003.

Chapter Three

SHIFTING TAXES—FROM THEM TO YOU

INTRODUCTION

The single greatest driver of income inequality in America is the U.S. tax system.

Over the past 40 years, Washington has steadily cut the tax rate of the richest Americans. In 1980, the highest rate was 70 percent; today the top rate is 37 percent.

The estate tax, once considered America's insurance policy to ward off the growth of a financial aristocracy, has been eliminated for all but the megabillionaires.

And corporations enjoy the lowest tax rate in the past half century, giving them more money to reward stockholders with fatter dividend checks.

All this has put more money into the pockets of people who already had a lot of money.

This is why the gap between the wealthiest 1 percent and everyone else in America is greater than at any time in the past hundred years.

Once it was different. For the half century leading up to the 1970s, the incomes of those at the top and of most Americans grew at roughly the same rate. This shared prosperity created a robust middle class.

But starting in 1981 and continuing ever since with a couple of exceptions, Washington has upset the balance by lowering tax rates for the wealthy on most of their income while failing to fund public programs that would benefit all Americans.

Why do so many Americans go along with this?

One theory is that average Americans harbor a dream of one day becoming rich and want those low rates in place when that happens.

A more likely explanation is because they've been lied to repeatedly by the tax cutters who make false claims as to who will benefit from tax cuts. That tradition has flourished under President Donald Trump.

"The rich will not be gaining at all," Trump claimed on Sept. 12, 2017, while promoting what would be his signature legislative achievement, the Tax Cuts and Jobs Act of 2017.

From a president who has served up a record number of whoppers, this was one of the biggest.

Not only did the rich gain, but they gained more per capita than any other income group, according to Congress's nonpartisan Joint Committee on Taxation. Those earning $1 million or more received an average tax cut of $64,428 a year; middle-class taxpayers earning from $50,000 to $75,000 received $840.

The Magic Wand

Once upon a time, in a faraway land called Texas, two men owned a bank. They called it Guaranty Federal Savings & Loan. The two men paid themselves lots of money and loaned other people lots of money. But they wanted to make even more money, so they met with people from a distant kingdom with very tall buildings called Wall Street.

They liked the Wall Street people very much and decided to buy pieces of paper from them called bonds. They bought and sold the pieces of paper over and over again. When they made money doing this, they kept it for themselves. When they wanted even more money to build castles of sand in yet another kingdom, they just took it out of the bank.

This worked OK. Until one day the bank ran out of money. Then some government people came to Dallas to look into the way they ran the bank. These people called the two men crooks and put them in a building with bars on the windows.

The government people took the bank away from the two men and sold it to a big Texas company. Then the government people gave the big Texas company lots of money so the bank wouldn't run out again. Best of all, the government people also gave the company a very special magic wand that came with the bank.

The wand is called NOL, and it is wondrous. It makes taxes disappear. The government actually invented the wand. By waving the wand, the big Texas company that now owns the bank can make taxes vanish for years and years and years. The money it used to pay in taxes it can keep for itself. Isn't this a nice deal for the big Texas company?

Nicer than you think.

First of all, the wand invented by the government people is available to only a select few. You, for example, can't have one. What's more, you pay for the wands that do get passed around.

NOL stands for net operating loss deduction, a tax break that allows corporations to reduce this year's taxes—and next year's taxes, and so on—because of money lost last year. Through the 1980s, the NOL enabled corporations to escape payment of more than $100 billion in income taxes.

But it is not the largest of the many generous write-offs available to businesses. The deduction that corporations can take for interest paid on borrowed money costs the government nearly $100 billion in a single year, dwarfing the amount that NOLs diverted from the U.S. Treasury. The deduction for interest on corporate debt has long been part of the U.S. tax code. But in the 1980s' frenzy of unchecked corporate restructuring, as businesses raced to see which could borrow the most money, it ballooned out of control.

A catalogue of other deductions—ranging from the write-off for so-called intangibles, to special deals that exempt select businesses and investors from payment of taxes—runs to many more billions in lost tax revenue. All these are reasons that individual taxpayers are picking up an ever-larger share of the national tax burden while corporations pay a steadily decreasing share.

Corporations such as Temple-Inland Inc., the big Texas company that got the magic wand when it acquired Guaranty Federal Savings & Loan Association of Dallas. That's the savings and loan run by the two men from Dallas, Paul Sau-Ki Cheng and Simon Edward Heath. The Wall Street people were from Drexel Burnham Lambert

Inc. and E.F. Hutton & Co. Inc. By the time Cheng and Heath had finished working their financial wizardry, Guaranty Federal was insolvent. Federal regulators seized it in 1988 and turned it over to Temple-Inland.

As a result of what the government has charged was "fraudulent bond-trading" transactions, along with illegal dealings that led to the conviction of Cheng and Heath, the savings and loan ended up with a net operating loss of more than $300 million. So for many years to come, Temple-Inland could use those old losses incurred by the savings and loan's former owners to reduce its taxable income and avoid paying taxes.

What makes the Guaranty Federal story so remarkable is this: First, taxpayers are paying, and will continue to pay, to bail out the failed savings and loan—that is, to restore depositors' money. Then, taxpayers will pay yet again to make up for the taxes Temple-Inland won't be paying because its profits can be offset by the savings and loan losses incurred years earlier by two men who went to jail.

Direct cost of the bailout: An estimated $3.9 billion, which will go straight from you and other taxpayers to Guaranty Federal and its new owner, Temple-Inland. Indirect cost: an estimated $590 million in lost tax revenue. That missing revenue will be made up by you and other taxpayers—or be added to the federal debt, in which case you'll pay the interest charges on it.

The tax beneficiary, Temple-Inland, is a diversified corporation based in Diboll, Texas. The company's interests, which include forest products, building materials, mortgage banking and insurance, generate more than $2 billion in annual revenue. Its largest stockholder is Oppenheimer Group Inc., parent of Oppenheimer & Co. Inc., the Wall Street investment banking and securities firm.

In 1990, the first full year that Temple-Inland took advantage of the Guaranty Federal tax breaks, its federal income tax payments plummeted 66 percent. According to a report filed with the U.S. Securities and Exchange Commission (SEC), the company's profits rose from $207 million in 1989 to $232.5 million in 1990. But its taxes fell from $84 million to $29 million. If you were in the $30,000 to $40,000 income group and received a similar tax break, you'd have an extra $48 every week in your paycheck.

Guaranty is only one of hundreds of savings and loans that taxpayers are rescuing, Temple-Inland only one of scores of companies profiting from the bailout. The projected cost to taxpayers: a half-trillion dollars. If you make $20,000 to $30,000 a year, you might think of that sum this way: Every dollar that you and all others in your income group pay in federal income taxes for the next decade will, in effect, go to the savings and loan industry.

For this, you can thank the people in Washington—a succession of Congresses and presidents, administrators and regulators, Democrats and Republicans—who write the government rule book, the accumulation of laws and regulations that provide the framework for the country's economy.

A Tax Bill of Zero

As might be expected, some people profit handsomely from the rule book. Like Ted Arison of Miami Beach, Fla., and Tel Aviv. You may not recognize the name. But you may have seen the TV commercials for his company, starring Kathie Lee Gifford (cohost of the syndicated TV show "Live With Regis and Kathie Lee") who, in assorted costumes, dances across the decks of the "fun ships" of Carnival Cruise Lines Inc. singing "Ain't We Got Fun?"

From 1985 to 1988, Carnival Cruise Lines, which promises evenings of "dazzling entertainment, romantic dancing and fast-paced casino action" aboard a fleet of ships with names such as Fantasy and Ecstasy, produced total profits of $502.5 million.

The corporate income tax rate during those years ranged from 46 percent in 1985 to 34 percent in 1988, meaning that Carnival paid about $200 million in federal taxes.

Right?

Wrong. Carnival paid not a cent in U.S. corporate income taxes on that half-billion dollars in profits. Its corporate tax rate was zero. That's because Carnival benefits from a government rule book that exempts shipping companies incorporated in foreign countries from having to pay U.S. income taxes.

It is a special-interest provision, like so many others, that friendly members of Congress have preserved through repeated revisions in the Internal Revenue Code—revisions that they often call "tax reform." Although Carnival's offices are in Miami and its Caribbean-bound ships leave from Miami, the company is incorporated in Panama. Its subsidiaries are organized in Liberia, the Bahamas, the British Virgin Islands and the Netherlands Antilles.

Carnival's situation is not unique. Hundreds of corporations have eliminated or drastically reduced their federal tax bills through similar special-interest tax laws. But the immunity from federal corporate income taxes helps explain why Ted Arison, the Israeli-born founder of the company, was designated by *Forbes* magazine in 1991 as one of the 15 richest people in the United States, with wealth estimated at $2.3 billion.

How is it possible for any corporation to escape paying taxes after passage of the 1986 Tax Reform Act, the legislation that members of Congress hailed as restoring fairness to the American tax system? The legislation that Sen. Bob Packwood, the Oregon Republican who was one of the two chief architects of the tax law, said was so tough that "there will not be a profit-making corporation in the country that can escape taxation." The legislation that Sen. John F. Kerry, Democrat from Massachusetts, said "will make that kind of unfairness a thing of the past" and permit "the American people to move once again to trust their federal government."

They said it. The tax act did not do it. For the five years preceding passage of the tax act, Carnival recorded profits of $279 million, and paid no federal income taxes. In the two years following passage, it recorded profits of $349 million—on which it paid no federal income taxes.

The 1986 act did make one change that affected Arison personally. It required large shareholders like him to report a portion of their company's earnings on their individual income tax return. But the company had a solution for Arison's personal tax bill, as it disclosed in a report filed with the SEC in March 1990. As Carnival explained it, if the company's taxable income amounted to, say, $200 million, a stockholder who owned 80 percent of the company's stock (as

Arison, in fact, did at the time) would be required to report $160 million in income on his personal tax return. At an effective tax rate of 30 percent, he would owe taxes of $48 million.

Not to worry. Carnival would declare a dividend equal to the $48 million and give it to the stockholder (that is, to Arison) to pay his taxes. As Carnival put it in the SEC report: "The company anticipates that it will pay quarterly dividends aggregating with respect to each year an amount at least equal to the principal shareholder's tax rate..."

If there were a comparable deal for you, it might function something like this: Let's say you earn $30,000 to $35,000 a year working for the Kellogg Co., the Battle Creek, Mich., company that manufactures and markets Corn Flakes, Raisin Bran, Frosted Mini-Wheats and other ready-to-eat cereals and convenience foods. At the end of the year, your federal tax bill is $3,710. So the Kellogg Co. declares a special dividend and gives you a check for $3,710.

Sure. In the real tax world, you must pay your own income taxes, and the Kellogg Co. must—and does—pay corporate income taxes. For Carnival and companies like it, the rules are different.

But when Carnival acquired Holland America Line in January 1989, it was obliged to begin paying some income taxes. The reason: Holland America operates tours and hotels within the United States that do not enjoy the same tax immunity granted to the cruise business.

Thus, in 1989 and 1990, Carnival paid $11 million in federal income taxes on profits of $411 million. That's a tax rate of 2.7 percent, about half the rate paid by individuals and families with incomes of $7,000 to $9,000.

Carnival's tax-free status for its cruise operations has been one of its big selling points with Wall Street, driving up the stock price and helping make Arison a billionaire. Time and again, securities analysts have singled out Carnival's tax advantage and assured investors that there was little reason to fear that Congress would end the preferential treatment.

In 1987, the securities firm Bear Stearns & Co. issued an investment report advising its clients: "We are not aware of any initiatives now being considered by Congress to amend the 1986 tax changes in ways that will be detrimental for Carnival. In fact, when sponsors of the bills were working out final provisions last year, several interested parties were aiming to include language that would have further solidified exemptions…" Translation: Friendly members of Congress were prepared to write an amendment to the Internal Revenue Code guaranteeing the tax exemption of Carnival and similar companies.

One year later, a report by Provident National Bank reaffirmed the Bear Stearns view: "We believe that future taxation is not likely, and would point out that the company has taken a number of safeguards aimed at preserving its tax-free status for the foreseeable future." In December 1989, the Robinson-Humphrey Co. Inc., another securities firm, recommended that its clients buy Carnival stock in part because the company "does not pay U.S. federal income taxes."

This exemption is but one of the thousands of provisions that make up the government rule book, for which you pick up the tab.

UPDATE

Some things never change. The 2017 Trump tax bill showered scores of profitable corporations with billions of dollars in tax benefits that they didn't need and didn't deserve.

Take a look at this list of corporations. Do any names seem familiar? The dollar figure in parenthesis after each represents the amount of federal income taxes they paid in 2018:

Amazon ($0)	Netflix ($0)
Chevron ($0)	Prudential ($0)
Eli Lilly ($0)	
General Motors ($0)	
Halliburton ($0)	
IBM ($0)	

Middle-Class Tax Squeeze

To understand why you pay the taxes you do, think of your paycheck as part of two government pies. The first pie is made up of total income taxes collected from all individuals and all corporations. The amount that you, as an individual, pay is determined, in part, by the amount Congress says companies should pay. If Congress collects more from businesses, you pay less. If Congress says some businesses may pay reduced taxes, you pay more.

The second pie is made up of combined income taxes and Social Security taxes collected from individuals. The amount that you pay if you earn, say, between $25,000 and $35,000 is determined, in part, by the amount that Congress says people who earn more than $100,000 should pay. If Congress collects more from people at the top, you pay less. If Congress says people at the top should pay less, you pay more.

Now consider a few statistics drawn from an analysis of a half-century of government tax and economic data. They will explain why you are accounting for an ever-larger slice of the two government pies.

ITEM: During the 1950s, when more Americans than ever attained middle-class status, the federal government collected $478 billion in combined individual and corporate income taxes in the decade. Of that, corporations paid 39 percent; individuals 61 percent.

During the 1980s, individual and corporate income tax collections soared to $4 trillion. Of that $4 trillion, the corporate share dwindled to 17 percent; the individual share swelled to 83 percent.

UPDATE

The share of income taxes paid by corporations will amount to less than 10 percent of total income tax collections in 2019. The single largest drop followed passage of the Trump tax bill in 2017 that handed corporations their largest tax windfall ever.

Corporations will save $1 trillion—that's $1,000,000,000,000—over the next decade as a result of Congress cutting their tax rate from 35 percent to 21 percent. Proponents claimed that the tax cut would spur investment, but so far companies are mostly investing in their stockholders, not the nation, by handing out larger dividend checks or buying back stock, driving up its price.

Who will pay for this tax cut? You will. The gap in federal revenues created by the tax cuts to corporations will have to be filled. The federal government will borrow more money, adding to the national debt, and more of your income taxes will go to pay interest on the national debt, leaving less money for public programs that might benefit the nation as a whole.

ITEM: Corporations have succeeded in reducing their share of the tax burden, in part, through a long-standing provision in the government rule book that permits a virtually unlimited tax deduction for their interest on debt. During middle-class America's golden years, the 1950s, corporations paid $44 billion in interest on borrowed money and more than four times that amount, $185 billion, in federal income taxes.

By the 1980s, an era of frenetic corporate borrowing and unabashed congressional support of special interests, that pattern was reversed. During that decade, corporations paid $2.2 trillion in interest on borrowed money and $675 billion in income taxes.

Thus, in the 1950s, companies paid $4 billion in taxes for every $1 billion they paid in interest. In the 1980s, they paid $3 billion in interest for every $1 billion paid in taxes. That means if your income was less than $30,000 a year during the 1980s, every penny that you—and the other 70 million people who were in that income bracket—paid in federal income tax over the entire decade went just to offset the taxes lost because corporations could write off the interest they paid on their borrowings.

 UPDATE

The taxpayer-subsidized write-off for corporate debt has been a huge benefit to private equity funds. Their business model involves borrowing huge sums of money mostly from Wall Street banks, then buying existing companies, jettisoning workers, closing down divisions, and then selling—for a fee and profit—what's left of the remaining company to a third party.

From $700 billion in assets in 2000, private equity has grown to $5.8 trillion in 2018, according to Americans for Financial Reform. It is safe to say that without this taxpayer-provided benefit the private equity industry as we know it today would not exist.

Growing right along with private equity has been the size of the taxpayer-funded write-off that has made it all possible. Corporations wrote off $4.5 trillion in interest payments in the past decade and saved billions in taxes.

The Trump tax bill of 2017 slightly reduced the value of the interest deduction, but the loss to private equity and corporations will be more than offset by the reduction in the corporate tax rate the bill also provided.

ITEM: Congress has written the government rule book so that Social Security taxes consume an ever-larger share of the weekly paychecks of low- and middle-income Americans, while the affluent are exempted from similar increases. As a consequence, the average family or individual has less money to spend for housing, food, clothing and education.

Look at the plight of median-income families, those who fall in the middle of the American economy, with half of all workers earning more, half less. During the 1950s, median-income families paid a total of $744 in Social Security taxes for the entire decade—or 1.7 percent of their income. In the 1980s, they paid $19,114 in Social Security taxes—or 7 percent of their income.

For more affluent families—say, those with incomes of 10 times the median—the Social Security burden increased, but it was much lighter. During the 1950s, affluent families also paid $744 in Social Security taxes. That amounted to two-tenths of 1 percent of their income. In the decade of the 1980s, the more affluent families paid $26,683 in Social Security taxes—still less than 1 percent of their income.

A BILLION-DOLLAR BREAK FOR BIG BUSINESS

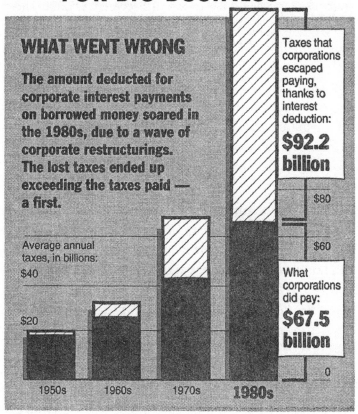

WHAT WENT WRONG

The amount deducted for corporate interest payments on borrowed money soared in the 1980s, due to a wave of corporate restructurings. The lost taxes ended up exceeding the taxes paid — a first.

Average annual taxes, in billions:

$40

$20

1950s   1960s   1970s   **1980s**

Taxes that corporations escaped paying, thanks to interest deduction:

$92.2 billion

$80

$60

What corporations did pay:

$67.5 billion

0

This chart shocked readers when we first published it. How could they not know, they asked, of a tax break of this magnitude that was enriching corporate America? The deduction for interest paid on corporate debt is still on the books. But there's a difference. Where it took a decade for corporations to avoid $92 billion in corporate taxes, we estimate that by 2019 it was lowering their tax bills by that much every few months.

Source: Internal Revenue Service

ITEM: The Social Security tax and federal income tax combined are weighted against middle- and lower-income workers, making it more difficult for both groups to maintain their standard of living or to improve their lot.

In 1970, people with incomes between $25,000 and $30,000 were solidly upper-middle class, earning about three times the median family income of $9,867. They paid, on average, $5,092 in combined income and Social Security taxes. By 1988, another generation in the same $25,000 to $30,000 income category had fallen several rungs down the economic ladder. Their earnings actually dropped below the median income of $32,191. To make matters worse, they paid $4,794 in combined income and Social Security taxes, or only $298 less than their more prosperous counterparts of 1970.

ITEM: While maintaining or increasing the tax burden on middle- and low-income workers, Congress has cut taxes for many of the nation's wealthiest people by one-third or more. In 1970, individuals and families with incomes between $500,000 and $1 million paid, on average, $304,408 in combined federal income and Social Security taxes. By 1989, individuals and families in that income group paid $168,714—or $135,694 less than 19 years earlier. That amounted to a tax cut of 45 percent.

By way of comparison, during the same period, the combined income and Social Security taxes of people in the $25,000 to $30,000 income group fell from $5,092 to $4,645—a decline of 9 percent. If the 7.6 million individuals and families in that middle-class group had benefited from the same tax-rate cut as the more affluent taxpayers, they each would have received a tax reduction of $2,291 instead of the $447 they got.

As you might expect, the people who write the tax laws have painted a different picture.

Dan Rostenkowski, the Democratic representative from Illinois who was chairman of the House Ways and Means Committee and one of the two principal authors of the 1986 Tax Reform Act, portrayed himself as the defender of the middle class during debate on the legislation. At one point, Rostenkowski posed these rhetorical questions for his colleagues:

"Today's vote is very straightforward. Do we want to give this country tax reform—or don't we? Do we want to give back to middle-income taxpayers the fairness they do not believe will ever come? Or do we want to stand for the status quo which goes hard on the poor—and easy on the rich?"

The answer—documented in tax data—is that Congress has stood for the rich. In 1985, the year before the tax overhaul bill was passed, those with incomes between $30,000 and $40,000 paid combined federal income and Social Security taxes of $6,663. That was 19 percent of their income. In 1989, three years after "tax reform," they paid $6,177, or 17.6 percent. That amounted to a 7 percent cut in tax rates.

By comparison, during that same period, those with incomes between $500,000 and $1 million saw their combined taxes fall from $243,506 to $168,714. That amounted to a 31 percent cut in tax rates—nearly five times the rate-cut for middle-class taxpayers.

If Rostenkowski and his colleagues were adamant about the good deeds they were doing for the middle class in 1986, they were equally insistent that the pending bill would transfer the tax burden from individuals to corporations. Rostenkowski said: "The bill will shift more than $120 billion in tax liability from individuals to corporations—restoring a balance that existed at the start of this decade."

Not really. In February 1986, months before passage of the 1986 tax act, Congress estimated that corporate tax collections under existing law would amount to $410 billion from 1987 through 1990. The new tax law, which Congress sold as transferring taxes from individuals to corporations, resulted in actual corporate collections of $375 billion during the four years. Instead of generating $120 billion in new corporate tax revenue, the law produced $35 billion less than had been projected under the old law.

As for Rostenkowski's claim that the act would restore the balance between corporate and individual tax payments that had existed in the early 1980s, consider this: In 1980, corporations accounted for 21 percent of total income taxes collected from individuals and corporations. In 1990, corporations accounted for 17 percent. That was down 4 percentage points. Not up.

It is such creative math that has led to an exploding federal deficit, which is a major factor in your falling standard of living.

Legalized Loansharking

Despite three laws passed by Congress mandating a phased elimination of the federal deficit by 1991—and then by 1993 and then by 1995—the red ink in 1992 topped $350 billion, a record, exceeding the deficits of the 1930s, the 1940s, the 1950s, the 1960s and part of the 1970s all combined.

To better appreciate the consequences of congressional arithmetic, you might consider that in 1960, $9 of every $100 that individuals paid in federal income taxes went not for education or health or social services, but for interest on the debt. In 1991, it was $30 of every $100. The interest payments represent the largest transfer of wealth in this century—with the money going from middle-class job holders to the investors who own the debt.

To put what is happening in more personal terms, think about the federal debt this way. Some years ago, your parents borrowed money from your rich uncle and now you must pay back the loan. Let's suppose that, as in most families, both you and your spouse work, and your combined paychecks total $600 a week, which makes you a certified member of the middle class. Now, give your rich uncle $180—or 30 percent of your income. Give him another $180 next week. And every week, for the rest of your life.

And presume that when you die, your children will keep paying it. Except they'll make the payments to the rich uncle's children.

It is the ultimate loansharking operation, one that organized crime leaders could only dream about. For all that money will go for interest on the debt. The debt itself will never be paid.

Oh, that uncle? He may be American. But chances are increasing that he is Japanese, Swiss, German or Arab, since foreign nationals own a growing share of the U.S. debt. As recently as 1969, foreign investors held just $10 billion of U.S. debt, or less than 5 percent of total federal debt held by the public. By 1990, the $10 billion had ballooned to $405 billion, or 17 percent of the debt.

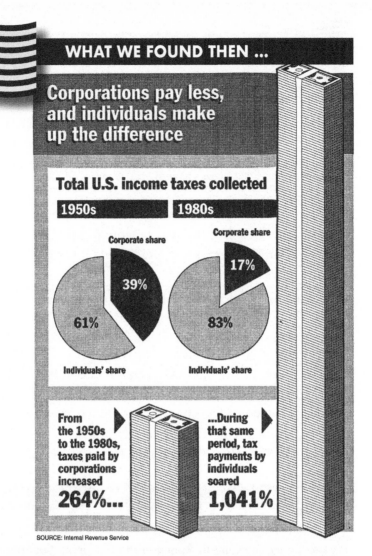

Corporations pay less, and individuals make up the difference

Total U.S. income taxes collected

1950s

Corporate share

39%

61%

Individuals' share

1980s

Corporate share

17%

83%

Individuals' share

From the 1950s to the 1980s, taxes paid by corporations increased **264%...**

...During that same period, tax payments by individuals soared **1,041%**

SOURCE: Internal Revenue Service

... WHAT WE'VE FOUND NOW

We noted how the corporate share of income taxes shrunk considerably by the '80s. That trend has continued – down to 10 percent in 2018, even before the full impact of the 2017 Trump tax cuts for corporations took effect. Tax experts predict that corporations will account for less than 10 percent of the total income taxes paid in 2020. In 2018 individuals paid $1.9 trillion; companies $262 billion.

Source: Internal Revenue Service

UPDATE

The percentage of U.S. debt owned by foreigners climbed to 29.3 percent in 2019.

The Japanese owned the largest amount: $1.13 trillion. China owned $1.11 trillion of U.S. debt, and the next largest were the United Kingdom, $334.7 billion, and Brazil, $310 billion.

It is a sure bet that a growing portion of the taxes withheld from your paycheck each week will be going to pay interest on the debt. That's because Congress and the presidents are on a roll. Make that 12 Congresses and five presidents.

At midnight on Monday, Sept. 30, 1992, the U.S. Government closed the books on its 23rd consecutive year of deficit spending. That's the longest-running streak of red ink in the nation's history. The previous record—16 consecutive years—ran from 1931 to 1946, the hard years of the Great Depression and World War II.

An entire generation came of age never knowing a federal government that spent less than it took in. The last time that Congress and the president chose to operate within the country's means, actually posting a surplus, albeit a modest one of $3.2 billion, was 1969.

UPDATE

As a result of a tax increases on wealthy taxpayers and a strong economy, the Clinton Administration reversed decades of red ink by posting budget surpluses in 1998, 1999, 2000, and 2001. But then President George W. Bush pushed through tax cuts that mostly benefited wealthy Americans. Ever since, the U.S. has been back in the red.

Lest you think the annual federal deficits have little relevance to your daily life, mull over these numbers: During the 1980s, the government paid out $1.13 trillion in interest on its debt, which consists of all the yearly deficits added together. That's $1.13 trillion in taxpayer dollars.

To put the number in perspective, consider what the federal government will spend in 1992 to reduce the infant mortality rate in the United States. Keep in mind that infant death rates in some U.S. cities rival the rates of developing nations. That $1.13 trillion would be enough money to double current spending on programs to reduce infant deaths—and to continue spending at that level, year after year, until the second half of the 21st century. Or you might want to think about $1.13 trillion this way: If your weekly paycheck was $700 or less during the 1980s, every penny you paid in federal income taxes went to the people who own that debt.

In many cases, they are people and corporations and institutions that pay no federal income taxes like you do. Or they pay taxes at a rate below what you pay. Which means a chunk of your weekly paycheck was transferred to wealthy investors. That chunk will grow substantially. During the 1980s, interest payments averaged $113 billion a year. In the early 1990s, interest payments averaged $195 billion a year.

How have a succession of Congresses and presidents fashioned a policy that has produced the civilized world's first permanent deficit? In part, by engaging in practices for which other people are sent to prison. In part, by playing a Washington game called Creative Math.

During his inauguration address in 1981, President Reagan railed against the deficits that the federal government had been accumulating. "For decades," he said, "we have piled deficit upon deficit, mortgaging our future and our children's future ... To continue this long trend is to guarantee tremendous social, cultural, political, and economic upheavals." The deficit that year, attributable to Congress and the administration of President Jimmy Carter, was $74 billion. The following year, the first under President Reagan, the deficit jumped to $120 billion—history's first $100-billion-plus deficit.

One year after that, in 1983—the year by which Reagan promised he would produce a balanced budget—the deficit spiraled to $208 billion. It had taken the federal government more than two centuries to pile up a $100-billion deficit in a single year. Reagan doubled that mark in one year.

Members of Congress, Democrats and Republicans alike, caught on to the Creative Math quickly. In 1985, Congress, with great fanfare, enacted the Balanced Budget and Emergency Deficit Control Act. More popularly known by the name of its authors, Gramm-Rudman-Hollings, it imposed automatic spending cuts if the government failed to meet fixed deficit-reduction goals. It provided for the deficit to be reduced to $172 billion in 1986, $144 billion in 1987, $108 billion in 1988, $72 billion in 1980, $36 billion in 1990 and zero in 1991.

Sen. Ernest F. Hollings, Democrat from South Carolina, told his colleagues the law assured that "we are going to have truth in budgeting. The lack of truth in budgeting is why we have gotten by with the charade of what a magnificent job we have done each year on the budget, how we have cut the budget and brought the deficit down— only to learn later that, on average, the deficit has increased about $20 billion each year."

Reagan was equally enthusiastic when he signed the legislation, foreseeing the end of government deficits in five years: "For years we've been warning that the growing deficit reflects a dangerous increase in the size of government ... Now Gramm-Rudman-Hollings locks in a long-term commitment to lowering and eventually eliminating deficits."

As it turned out, the first year, 1986, set the tone for the future. In 1981, President Carter had forecast a budget surplus of $138 billion for 1986. In 1984, President Reagan forecast a $177-million deficit for 1986. And in 1985, Gramm-Rudman-Hollings set the maximum deficit at $172 million for 1986. The deficit eventually hit $238 billion.

That was off $66 billion from the Gramm-Rudman-Hollings mandated maximum of $172 billion. Off $61 billion from President Reagan's predicted deficit of $177 billion. Off $376 billion from President Carter's predicted surplus of $138 billion. So much for the way lawmakers and presidents count.

Truth to tell, the numbers were worse. The real deficit was $283 billion. But the Social Security and other trust funds had surpluses. So Congress and the President took the $45-billion surplus in the trust funds—money that in part was to have been set aside for future Social Security payments—and spent it instead for other government programs, thereby masking the true size of the deficit. That is a practice for which other people go to prison.

By law, money in a trust fund may be spent only for the specific purpose for which the trust fund was created. Unless you happen to be Congress or the president. In which case you may remove $138 billion from Social Security and other trust funds—which Congress and two presidents did through the 1980s—and divert the money elsewhere.

In any event, the deficit numbers were going the wrong way. To deal with the errant figures, Congress passed another version of the Gramm-Rudman-Hollings law in 1987, setting revised deficit goals. The new deficit figures: $136 billion in 1989, $100 billion in 1990, $64 billion in 1991, $28 billion in 1992, and zero in 1993. Once again, though, the numbers did not seem to add up quite right. The 1989 deficit ended up at $153 billion, instead of the promised $136 billion.

Congress then did what only Congress can. It came up with a supplemental deficit-control law called the Omnibus Budget Reconciliation Act of 1990.

Lawmakers promised that it would soak up nearly $500 billion in red ink over the next five years.

The *New York Times*, in an article recounting passage of the measure in October 1990, called it "the most important legislation ever written to reduce the budget deficit." The *Wall Street Journal* labeled it the "most serious deficit-cutting package in modern times." And The *Philadelphia Inquirer* described it as "the largest deficit-reduction package in history" and "a first step toward reversing the fiscal legacy of the free-wheeling '80s."

It was unprecedented. Sen. Warren B. Rudman, the New Hampshire Republican who was coauthor of the ongoing Gramm-Rudman laws, said so: "For the first time since I've been here, we've made a real effort at deficit reduction." In February 1991, President Bush, speaking, appropriately, before the Economic Club of New York, declared: "Thanks to the budget reforms that began last fall, the deficit will be virtually eliminated by 1995."

In truth, it was ever more Creative Math. Label it voodoo budgeting. The deficit for 1991—which Gramm-Rudman No. 1 of 1985 said absolutely would be zero, and which Gramm-Rudman No. 2 of 1987 said absolutely, positively would be no more than $64 billion, and which the Omnibus Budget Reconciliation Act of 1990 said would be certainly no more than $245 billion—set an all-time record: a whopping $269 billion.

That's the make-believe deficit. The one that's pared down because Congress and the president divert the surplus Social Security taxes that you pay to other purposes. Remember, the Social Security taxes withheld from your paycheck are not being set aside for your retirement. That money is paid out immediately to currently retired people. That means that when the government collects more Social Security taxes than it needs to pay today's retirees, the leftover sum is considered surplus.

When Congress raised the Social Security rates some years ago, lawmakers and the president promised that that surplus would be set aside for your retirement. The reason: The retired ranks are swelling faster than the workforce. As a result, there may not be enough workers to support Social Security payments to those who retire early in the next century.

When the 1991 Social Security surplus is subtracted from the government spending books, the real deficit totaled $321 billion. That's more money than the federal government spent for all its programs and services in 1979. The outlook for 1992, when everyone, Congress and presidents, Democrats and Republicans, once projected the beginning of budget surpluses: a real deficit of $400 billion. Or more.

The number may be more meaningful if you compare the federal government's spending practices with the way you manage your own or your family budget. Suppose that two decades ago, in 1972, you earned $11,000. That was the income of the average family that year. Suppose, also, that each year since then your income grew to keep pace with the average family, so that in 1991 you earned $36,000. Suppose, further, that the relationship between your income and the amount of money you spent each year was proportional to the income and spending of the U.S. government.

If you spent at that pace, the outstanding charges on your Visa or MasterCard charge account in 1992 would total about $184,000. Every month, you would write a check for $2,800 to cover the interest costs alone.

After paying Social Security and federal income taxes, you would have no money left. No money for food. No money for housing.

No money for clothing. In fact, you would have to borrow money for all those purposes. In a few more years, as the deficits continue to pile up, you would not have enough money to pay your income and Social Security taxes. And a few years after that, you would have to borrow money just to pay the interest.

That's the way Congress and presidents manage the national family budget. Is it possible, you might ask, that Congress one day will do what it has promised to do for years—eliminate the deficit and thereby reduce the amount of money collected from weekly paychecks to cover the interest payments on its trillions of dollars in borrowed money?

Not if experience is any guide.

Amid much fanfare and self-praise, Congress enacted the Congressional Budget and Impoundment Control Act of 1974. It was intended to give Congress greater control over federal spending. The measure created budget committees in the House and Senate and established a Congressional Budget Office to provide lawmakers with the expert advice they said they needed to manage the government's fiscal policy.

Alan Cranston, the Democratic senator from California, called the budget act "probably the most important bill that has been passed or considered by Congress during the time I have been in the Senate." Rep. Bill Frenzel, Minnesota Republican, said the act "will set up procedures that will tend to force us to establish our own spending priorities, to control our overspending more sensibly, and to strike a better balance between our income and our expenses."

And Rep. Al Ullman, Oregon Democrat, said the act "will make Congress a more respected institution and a more effective partner in our federal government. I believe it will be recognized as the major fiscal reform of the 20th century, and a fundamental new element in the framework of our democratic structure."

In the 18 years following passage of the legislation crafted to give Congress the sophisticated advice and legislative machinery to regulate government spending, lawmakers compiled 18 consecutive annual deficits—10 of them all-time record-breakers. That's far short of what Rep. Frank Annunzio, Democrat from Illinois, had promised on June 18, 1974, when the House passed the Congressional

The federal debt

Interest payments on U.S. government debt are nearly equal to all our spending on education...

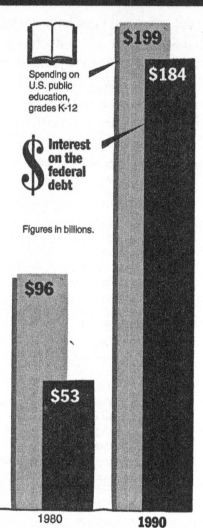

Spending on U.S. public education, grades K-12

$ **Interest on the federal debt**

Figures in billions.

$199
$184
$96
$53
$41
$14
$16
$7

1960   1970   1980   **1990**

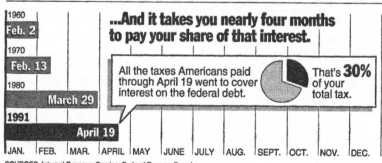

	Date
1960	Feb. 2
1970	Feb. 13
1980	March 29
1991	April 19

...And it takes you nearly four months to pay your share of that interest.

All the taxes Americans paid through April 19 went to cover interest on the federal debt.

That's **30%** of your total tax.

JAN. FEB. MAR. APRIL MAY JUNE JULY AUG. SEPT. OCT. NOV. DEC.

SOURCES: Internal Revenue Service, Federal Reserve Board

The interest charges on the national debt, which were soaring when we wrote about it in 1992, are rocketing toward $1 trillion dollars a year in the next decade – five times greater than the 1980s. At this rate, this taxpayer-paid cost will become the single largest item in the federal budget. Interest charges borne by taxpayers will even surpass defense spending by 2025.

Source: Congressional Budget Office

Budget and Impoundment Control Act. "...This landmark legislation will enable the Congress to be responsible for devising the budget and for meeting our obligations, with no deficit spending, and in the event that we collect more money than we spend, this money will be used to pay off our national debt."

 ## UPDATE

One of the most enduring pipe dreams spouted in Congress is the call to pay off the national debt—or, short of that, to eliminate deficit spending. The amount of time spent debating this issue on the floors of Congress and passing legislation that supposedly would achieve those goals is staggering. And what is the result?

In 1992, after a decade of furious lawmaking to rein in deficit spending, the national debt stood at $4 trillion.

In 2019, the federal deficit passed $22 trillion.

The national debt is growing at a rate of $1 trillion a year. From our nation's founding it took us nearly 200 years to run up $1 trillion in national debt.

The single greatest surge in deficit spending has come under Trump, largely as a result of the massive tax cuts in 2017 that rewarded corporations and wealthy individuals. Like politicians before him, Trump the candidate promised to "eliminate the national debt..." and then did otherwise.

The U.S. will never pay off the debt but reducing deficits has long been acknowledged as a crucial public policy goal.

Why does this matter?

"A growing Federal debt could place a high burden on future generations and hinder economic growth," according to the Congressional Research Service. "Rapid growth of Federal debt could also increase the probability of a financial crisis or fears of a sovereign default."

Adding to the debt is a constant of Washington, but one thing has changed. There's little discussion in Congress any more about reducing the deficit. The action is all on passing legislation that adds to the debt.

Runaway Write-offs

Long ago, businesses borrowed money to build plants, to buy equipment and to make new products, thereby creating jobs. In those times, there was a certain logic to allowing companies to write off the full interest expense on their tax returns. But in the 1980s, the interest deduction became an instrument to dismantle America — not to build it.

Businesses borrowed money to raid other businesses and sell off their assets. That led to the closing of factories, the elimination of middle-income jobs, and the paying of astronomical sums to owners, investors and corporate executives who brought it all about. All this was subsidized by taxpayers through the deduction for interest payments.

Like the takeover of RJR Nabisco Inc., the company that makes such diverse products as Winston cigarettes, Oreo cookies, Shredded Wheat, Camel cigarettes, Ritz crackers and Grey Poupon mustard. Kohlberg Kravis Roberts & Co., the Wall Street investment banking and buyout firm, acquired RJR Nabisco in April 1989 after winning a bitter bidding war with a company management team headed by President F. Ross Johnson. To pull off the deal, Kohlberg Kravis saddled RJR Nabisco with more than $20 billion in long-term debt, including $5 billion in junk bonds sold by Drexel Burnham Lambert.

The *New York Times*, quoting Wall Street investment bankers, described Drexel Burnham's sale of securities variously as "awe-inspiring" and as evidence that "the (Drexel) machine functions very well." In truth, the Drexel "machine" was headed for bankruptcy court, but in the interim the RJR deal produced awe-inspiring fees of hundreds of millions of dollars for its partners, Kohlberg Kravis, assorted lawyers and other professionals.

Taxpayers, on the other hand, are losing billions. During the last nine months of 1989 and all of 1990, RJR Nabisco wrote off more than $3 billion in cash interest payments, according to documents filed with the SEC. That allowed the new owners to avoid payment of $1 billion or more in corporate income taxes.

You might think of that $1 billion-plus this way. If you are a middle-class individual or family living in Fort Wayne, Ind., or Sioux City, Iowa, every dollar you paid in federal income taxes in 1989 and 1990 went to offset the lost tax revenue from the RJR Nabisco buyout. Actually, every dollar you pay in income taxes for a decade will go for that purpose.

While middle-class taxpayers everywhere must make up the lost corporate tax revenue, the executives who arrange the deals are profiting handsomely from them. At the same time, they personally are paying U.S. income taxes at the lowest rate in decades. In 1992, the maximum rate for individuals will be 31 percent. In 1990 and prior years it was 28 percent. Back in 1960, it was 91 percent.

Take Steven J. Ross, chairman of the board and co-chief executive officer of Time Warner Inc., then the world's largest media and entertainment company. Time Warner was created in July 1989 when the former Time Inc., publisher of *Time* magazine, acquired a majority of the stock of Warner Communications Inc., the motion picture, television and entertainment company.

As was the case with RJR Nabisco, the acquisition left the new company heavily in debt. In 1989 and 1990, according to reports filed with the SEC, Time Warner deducted $2.1 billion in interest payments. The write-off allowed the company to avoid payment of $700 million in federal income taxes. In fact, the SEC reports show that Time Warner, with total revenue of more than $19 billion over the two years, did not pay any federal income taxes.

For his services in 1990, Ross received regular cash compensation amounting to $3.3 million. Then there was a special $74.9 million bonus, bringing his total Time Warner income for the year to $78.2 million.

While RJR Nabisco and Time Warner may be exceptions in terms of the dollars involved, similar stories on a smaller scale are recurring across corporate America.

Beyond corporations that do not pay their fair share of taxes because of a preferential government rule book, there is yet a darker side to the story, one with bleaker implications for the American middle class. The expenditure of those hundreds of millions of dollars borrowed, and the hundreds of millions of dollars that were—and will be—paid in interest do not create new jobs.

In fact, to meet their interest payments, companies whose debt grows out of the corporate restructuring slash their workforces. And they receive a tax break for doing it.

What's more, the very deduction that wipes out current tax bills—the interest write-off—creates yet another tax-avoidance mechanism to shelter future profits: the net operating loss deduction—the magic wand that makes taxes disappear.

As with so many sections of the tax law, Congress originally agreed to the net operating loss deduction as an "emergency" measure to promote fairness. It was enacted in 1919 specifically to help ease business recovery from World War I.

Rep. Claude Kitchin, a North Carolina Democrat who was chairman of the House Ways and Means Committee, explained what he called the "net loss relief provision" during debate on a pending tax measure in February 1919. Kitchin said that the tax writers "agreed that it was wiser and safer" to limit the deduction to one year, "for the transition period from war conditions to peace conditions..." The provision, he asserted, would be "just for this year, 1919."

Time passed.

A hundred years, to be precise, and Kitchin's "loss relief" amendment is embedded in the Internal Revenue Code. For most of those years, the net operating loss deduction was not widely used by businesses and thus did not represent a significant loss of tax revenue. That changed in the 1980s, when investors, speculators and takeover artists saw an opportunity to turn the tax code into instant profits for themselves.

One company charted the course. In 1970, the Penn Central Transportation Co., which had been formed two years earlier with the merger of the old Pennsylvania Railroad and New York Central, collapsed into bankruptcy court. When it finally emerged from bankruptcy proceedings in 1978, the reorganized company, called the Penn Central Corp., bore scant resemblance to the railroad of old. Gone were the rail cars, freight yards and train stations. In their place were diversified holdings in housing, recreation and energy.

But the new Penn Central kept one "asset" from its dying days as a railroad: two billion dollars in net operating losses—thanks to that temporary 1919 "emergency" provision. To make full use of it, Penn Central acquired profitable companies and began using the old Penn Central's losses to reduce taxes owed by the newly acquired companies. While the operating income mounted, adding up to $1.8 billion from 1978 to 1984, the company paid no federal income taxes.

"Our income stream is not subject to current federal income tax as a result of our loss carryforwards," the company said in its 1983 annual report.

Since coming out of bankruptcy in 1978, Penn Central has written off more than $1 billion of the net operating losses, avoiding payment of hundreds of millions of dollars in federal income taxes. By 1990, Penn Central still had about $1 billion in net operating losses left over. Making use of them remained one of the company's primary objectives. As its officers told stockholders in 1989: "We must invest Penn Central's substantial cash resources and make use of its debt capacity ... and, at the same time, fully utilize the value of the company's remaining $1 billion in net operating loss carryforwards."

Then there is the Chicago-based Itel Corp. The company generated annual revenue of $2 billion from its interests in railcar and marine-container leasing, dredging, and the distribution of wiring and cable systems.

It also generated hefty tax-free profits, courtesy of the net oper-

Corporations discover the NOL, a tax write-off bonanza worth billions

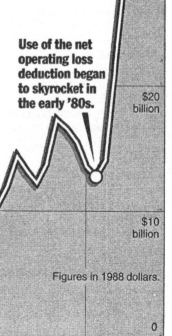

$50 billion

By 1988, U.S. corporations were getting $51.4 billion in tax write-offs from the NOL deduction.

$40 billion

Cost of NOL deductions

Companies escaped paying the 34% corporate income tax on $51.4 billion in write-offs in 1988, costing the U.S. Treasury $17.5 billion.

Use of the net operating loss deduction began to skyrocket in the early '80s.

$30 billion

$20 billion

A little-used rule: Only $1.6 billion in net operating loss tax write-offs in 1950.

$10 billion

Figures in 1988 dollars.

0

| 1950 | 1960 | 1970 | 1980 | '88 |

SOURCE: Internal Revenue Service

The corporate tax deduction for net operating losses (NOL) is more popular than ever: today, companies deduct on average $200 billion a year and save billions in income taxes. This obscure deduction zoomed into the news during the 2016 presidential campaign when it surfaced that Donald Trump had taken a $915 million net operating loss deduction on his 1995 tax return.

Source: Internal Revenue Service

ating loss deduction. Those profits helped secure a spot on the *Forbes* directory of 400 richest Americans for Samuel Zell, the Chicago investor who controlled the business.

From 1984 to 1989, according to SEC reports, Itel recorded $563 million in operating income—that's income before interest payments and taxes. Its federal income tax payments: zero.

"Federal income tax is not accruable or payable by Itel," the company's 1988 annual report said, "because income that would otherwise be taxable is offset by the utilization of its substantial ... tax loss carryforwards."

So what's the bottom line for the net operating loss deduction, which proponents defend as necessary to help start-up companies through their early money-losing years and to even out the tax bills of companies whose income fluctuates from one year to the next? At best, it has evolved into a device to transfer payment for a corporation's ill fortune from its stockholders and managers to individual taxpayers. In many cases, it also has become a lucrative tax-avoidance scheme enabling shrewd investors to use others' losses to cut their own corporate tax bills.

Actually, with the net operating loss deduction, a company can do more than avoid payment of future taxes. It also can go back in time and collect a refund of taxes paid. Losses incurred in on year, for example, can be subtracted from taxable income for three previous years, enabling a company to obtain a refund check from the U.S. Treasury for taxes paid in those years.

By now you may be wondering how you can do the same. Thumb

through the pages of the Internal Revenue Code and see if you can find a similar provision for workers whose income is derived from a daily job. A provision that says if you paid $3,000 in income taxes last year, but lost your job this year and are living off your savings and unemployment benefits that are about to expire, that you can obtain a refund of the $3,000 you paid. What? You can't find anything like that? Of course not.

But your loss is someone else's gain. In 1969, corporations wrote off $2.5 billion in net operating losses, or 3 percent of their taxable income. By 1988, those deductions had soared to $51.4 billion, or 13 percent of their taxable income. Thus, net operating loss deductions increased 1,956 percent during those years.

This is just the beginning. Absent a change in the rule book, the deduction will grow larger in years to come because more corporations are winding up in bankruptcy court, creating yet more net operating loss deductions for future use. This means middle-class individuals and families will continue to subsidize the failed business practices of the 1980s—practices that produced massive profits for corporate managers and investors, and bankruptcy, unemployment and reduced wages for workers.

Even unlawful business dealings that produced net operating losses are being converted to tax savings for the favored few. The new owners of Guaranty Federal, the failed Texas savings and loan, for example, benefitted from the fraudulent losses of their predecessors, who went to jail.

Tax Breaks for Fraud

The story begins with Guaranty's former owners, Paul Sau-Ki Cheng and Simon Edward Heath, Dallas real estate promoters. One-time classmates at Southern Methodist University in Dallas, Cheng and Heath had gone into the real estate business after graduation from college in 1977.

They began by building single-family homes in the Dallas area. In 1984, their real estate company, Pacific Realty Corp., acquired Guaranty Federal Savings & Loan, a savings bank in Galveston that dated from 1938. After moving the thrift's headquarters to Dallas, Cheng and Heath began doing business with Drexel Burnham Lambert's Beverly Hills office, presided over by junk-bond king Michael R. Milken.

Early in 1986, Cheng and Heath were "advised and encouraged by personnel" at Milken's office to launch a takeover, according to a federal complaint later filed against them. The target was U.S. Home Corp., a Houston-based builder of single-family, modular and mobile homes. The advice seemed invaluable, since Drexel Burnham was the homebuilder's investment banker and had underwritten a $50-million junk bond issue for the company the year before. Now Drexel Burnham was advising another party to make a run at one of its own clients—a client crippled by debt that Drexel Burnham had arranged.

With Drexel Burnham's encouragement, Cheng and Heath, through their real estate company, began acquiring U.S. Home's stock. The cash came mostly through loans from other Texas savings and loans. After picking up 9 percent of U.S. Home's shares, they offered in July 1986 to buy the remaining stock for $367 million. U.S. Home's board of directors rejected the deal and the takeover bid collapsed. That was good news for U.S. Home.

It was bad news for Cheng and Heath. They had paid nearly $30 million, mostly borrowed money, to acquire shares of U.S. Home that were worth only $23 million when the deal fell through. They were $7 million in the hole. As the value of their stock holdings declined, they were confronted with hefty interest payments on the money borrowed to buy the shares.

A solution soon appeared. According to a Federal Deposit Insurance Corp. (FDIC) lawsuit, it was a "fraudulent bond-trading" scheme involving speculation in U.S. Treasury bonds that worked like this: The two businesses that Cheng and Heath controlled—Guaranty Federal, their government-insured thrift, and Pacific Realty, their real estate company—opened brokerage accounts with Drexel Burnham and E.F. Hutton to handle buy-and-sell orders for U.S. Treasury bonds.

The crux of the scheme was to manipulate Treasury bond trading between the two accounts at each brokerage house—assigning losses to the federally insured savings and loan association, and profits to Cheng and Heath's private real estate subsidiary. Drexel and Hutton installed special phone lines in Cheng's Dallas office and home connecting him directly to their trading desks. From September 1986 to April 1987, Cheng made nearly 1,500 transactions, buying and selling more than $21 billion in Treasury bonds for Guaranty Federal and an additional $16.8 billion for Pacific Realty.

"From the very beginning of the trading scheme period," the FDIC contended, "the excessive trading resulted in significant and constant losses to Guaranty Federal, the insured institution, while Pacific Realty consistently realized significant gains." Guaranty Federal lost money every month and Pacific Realty made money every month through what the FDIC described as "unsafe and unsound speculation."

The strategy worked nicely for Cheng and Heath. According to the FDIC complaint, they earned $11.1 million for Pacific Realty and two family trusts. Drexel Burnham and E.F. Hutton also prospered, earning an estimated $49.6 million in commissions and markups from the nearly 1,500 trades. Individual brokers collected between $7.5 million and $15 million for their services.

The big loser was Guaranty Federal. The savings and loan lost $28.5 million on the trades and an additional $40 million later when it sold bonds at depressed prices, bringing the overall loss to $68.5 million. In a civil lawsuit, the FDIC sought judgments against Cheng, Heath and the brokerage firms for $130 million in actual damages and an additional $390 million in punitive damages. Drexel Burnham and Hutton contested the FDIC allegations.

On Aug. 6, 1990, both men filed for protection from creditors under the U.S. Bankruptcy Code.

Cheng, who listed his occupation as "real estate investment advisor" on the bankruptcy petition, said his income the previous year was $1.8 million. Nonetheless, he reported that he had only $55,000 in cash and bank deposits and that he owed an estimated $150,000 in federal income taxes. Heath was in even more dire straits, it seemed. He said his income the previous year was $1.5 million but that he had only $2,200 in cash and bank deposits.

In any event, on Aug. 15, 1990, a U.S. District Court jury in Dallas convicted Cheng and Heath of defrauding Guaranty Federal in transactions unrelated to the bond-trading scheme. They were found guilty of bank fraud, wire fraud, misapplying Guaranty Federal money and making false entries in the thrift's books in connection with a $10-million loan on a Florida property. Cheng subsequently was sentenced to 30 years in prison, Heath to 20 years.

All these transactions helped to undermine Guaranty Federal, adding it to the growing list of savings and loans that have collapsed and that are being bailed out by the federal government at a projected cost to taxpayers of a half-trillion dollars.

On Sept. 30, 1988, the Federal Home Loan Bank Board declared the thrift insolvent. That same day, the federal agency merged Guaranty Federal with two smaller failed Texas thrifts. The surviving entity was renamed Guaranty Federal Savings Bank and sold to Temple-Inland Inc.

As part of the federal rescue plan, Temple-Inland agreed to put in $75 million in cash and to buy $50 million worth of Guaranty Federal preferred stock in 1990 and 1991. The Federal Savings and Loan Insurance Corp. (FSLIC), in turn, agreed to cover any losses on Guaranty Federal assets, which had a book value of just under $1.7 billion. That meant if Guaranty Federal owned an office building that was worth, according to its books, $10 million, but could be sold for only $5 million, the FSLIC would kick in the $5 million difference.

Better still, to make the sale of the failed thrift more attractive, the government gave a note to Guaranty Federal's buyers promising to pay $700 million—and to pay interest on that note. Even better, the interest income is tax-free.

To summarize: Temple-Inland put up $125 million. The FSLIC—courtesy of the taxpayers—put up $700 million, plus a promise to make up any losses suffered on assets valued at $1.7 billion. And Temple-Inland collects interest on a $700-million promissory note—but is excused from paying taxes on that interest.

You can't do that. If you could, it would be like collecting the interest on $10,000 in your savings account—and then not having to report the money as taxable income. So: You pay taxes on the interest you receive on your passbook savings account. Some of your tax money is given to Guaranty Federal as interest on the government's promissory notes, but that interest is tax-free to the owners of Guaranty Federal.

And then there is, of course, the magic wand, as explained in the report to the Resolution Trust Corp.: "The Internal Revenue Code also permits the consolidated entity to use accumulated net operating loss carryovers and other loss carryovers of the failed institutions to offset taxable income of the acquiring association following the acquisition." Translation: The losses suffered by Guaranty Federal, due, at least in part, to the criminal conduct and the bond-trading activities of its former owners, may be used to reduce the taxes owed by its new owners.

From the beginning, Wall Street liked the deal. Prudential Bache Securities, in a report issued in October 1988, offered this observation on the advantages of Temple-Inland's new savings and loan business: "Temple-Inland should derive nearly $15 million to $20 million of tax benefits, according to management, from this investment in the current quarter. Next year, the benefit could be anywhere from $20 million to $50 million, followed by approximately $13 million to $15 million per year."

Donaldson, Lufkin & Jenrette, another Wall Street brokerage firm, in a report issued in May 1989, commented on why Temple-Inland's stock was selling below what the investment house believed the price should be: "We attribute the market's hesitancy in valuing the transaction to date to management's reluctance to advertise just how lucrative the deal is ... Temple-Inland will not have to pay taxes on S&L earnings until after 2000. The three units are currently carrying over $550 million in operating loss carryforwards."

So how much is this going to cost you? The meter is still running, but an August 1990 report to the Resolution Trust Corp. placed the estimated total cost of the Guaranty Federal bailout—cash and tax breaks—at $4.5 billion.

That means that the equivalent of every penny paid in federal income taxes by all the residents of Portland, Ore., for several years would go to rescue Guaranty Federal and to reimburse its new owners for losses.

Lest you believe that the people responsible for the government rule book—and who make all this possible—are troubled by the consequences of their handiwork, ponder the words of Ronald A. Pearlman, one of those rule writers. Pearlman was assistant secretary for tax policy in the Treasury Department for the Reagan administration. That's the executive-branch office that recommends the tax contents of the government rule book. Later, Pearlman became chief of staff of Congress's Joint Committee on Taxation. That's the committee with overall responsibility for the rule book's tax contents. Later, he became a member of Covington & Burling, a Washington law firm that often succeeds in influencing the rewriting of the U.S. government rule book for the benefit of its clients.

During a 1991 interview with *Tax Notes*, a Washington publication, Pearlman was questioned about the net operating loss deduction. Echoing the views of many members of Congress, Pearlman said: "Others may say the tax system is too generous in the way it deals with loss carryovers. That's not a concern I share."

UPDATE

Thanks to Congress, estate lawyers have good news for their wealthy clients: Death is certain, but taxes aren't.

Congress has lowered the federal estate tax so drastically over the past generation that it now applies to less than 1 percent of taxpayers. Even in years when the rate was higher, virtually no one in the heart of the middle class had to pay the federal estate tax, which was always intended to tax the estates of upper-income people. By 2019, a couple with an estate of $22.4 million left no federal estate tax bill.

And legal loopholes allow billionaires such as the Walton family of Walmart fame to avoid paying estate taxes that would otherwise apply to any American with such immense wealth. By creating Grantor Retained Annuity Trusts (GRATs), the Waltons have over the years avoided paying estate and gift taxes in excess of $100 billion, according to Americans for Tax Fairness.

Only about 1 in every 700 people who die leaves an estate that owes any federal tax, but that's too many for some in Congress. In 2019 a coalition of Republican senators introduced legislation to repeal the estate tax: Sen. John Thune, a Republican senator from South Dakota, made the ridiculous claim that it "remains an onerous and unfair tax that punishes hard-working families."

Chapter Four

THE LUCRATIVE BUSINESS OF BANKRUPTCY

INTRODUCTION

Bankruptcy has become a sure-fire way for corporations to get rid of employees. In 2018 and 2019, when the economy was said to be booming, a record 73,610 employees lost their jobs when their companies went bankrupt. More workers were let go due to bankruptcy in that two-year period than in the previous seven years combined, even more than at the height of the 2008-2009 financial crisis.

Some of these job losses were offset by growth in another sector— the bankruptcy industry, made up of so-called turnaround specialists and lawyers who feast on the remains of ailing companies by firing employees and liquidating assets. The Turnaround Management Association, the industry's trade group, says business is thriving.

But for individuals who need help to reorganize their financial affairs and get back on their feet, bankruptcy is increasingly out of reach. After lobbying by banks and credit card companies that falsely claimed that there were widespread abuses under existing bankruptcy law, Congress amended the law in 2005. Even though data indicated that the largest single group of bankruptcy filers were single mothers raising families or widows crushed by health-care costs, Congress bowed to pressure from the financial industry and passed a law that makes it much more difficult and expensive for an individual to file for bankruptcy.

Not surprisingly, the number of personal bankruptcies has declined, but not because there is less need. It's simply too costly for many debtors who have little or no money and few if any assets. Another reason for the decline: The 2005 bankruptcy bill made it virtually impossible for anyone with student debt to receive bankruptcy protection. Thus, student debt, held by 44 million Americans in 2019, is the only debt that cannot be discharged in bankruptcy court.

$500-an-Hour Jobs

It was May 22, 1990, Rosalind Webb's last day of work after more than 30 years at the Bonwit Teller store in downtown Philadelphia. The store was one of 14 Bonwit branches that were closing after Bonwit's parent company filed for bankruptcy protection.

That morning, Rosalind Webb did what she customarily did—she boarded the No. 48 bus near her home in North Philadelphia and rode 25 minutes to her job in the shipping department of the store.

Somewhere aloft, Wilhelm Mallory, Steven Hochberg and Peter Dealy did what they customarily do, too. Mallory flew from San Diego to New York and billed a client $250 an hour for his travel. His associate, Dealy, flew from Los Angeles to Las Vegas, and billed $300 an hour. Hochberg flew from New York to Atlanta and charged $150 an hour for his time in the air.

What kind of work warrants such fees for sitting in an airplane? The same kind that charges $225 an hour for Richard Schmid to pack and unpack boxes.

Mallory, Dealy, Hochberg, Schmid—they are all in a business that reorganizes companies and puts people like Rosalind Webb out of work. The bankruptcy business. It pays well.

Mallory billed $1,250 that day for his five-hour flight. That money—more than Rosalind Webb earned in three weeks—came out of the dwindling cash reserves of a floundering business that was eliminating Webb's job to save money.

With the surge in bankruptcies growing out of the excessive debt load that crushed many companies in the 1980s, there are more jobs than ever like those of Mallory, Dealy, Hochberg and Schmid. But there are many millions more people like Rosalind Webb who have been thrown out of work. They are, overwhelmingly, middle-income employees who are being forced into lower-paying jobs, part-time employment, premature retirement or unemployment. In the process, they are losing all or part of their pensions and having to settle for reduced benefits, or no benefits at all.

So it is with Webb, who became unemployed and had to pay $181 a month for medical insurance. "All those years I had health insurance and didn't need it," she said. "Now I need it and don't have it."

Rosalind Webb, like millions of Americans, became snared in an economic shift in the United States in which the middle class is being squeezed and the ranks of the working poor are growing, while new jobs paying up to $500 an hour are being created for a select group of professionals—lawyers, accountants, bankers, investment advisers, brokers and management specialists.

For all this, you can thank a series of Congresses, presidents and the heads of regulatory and administrative agencies who, during the 1970s and 1980s, rewrote the rules governing the federal tax and bankruptcy systems. These changes, along with Congress's failure to enact measures correcting growing inequities in the economy, benefited special interests at the expense of everyone else.

Consider Congress's handling of two issues—corporate debt and bankruptcy. While making sweeping revisions of the Internal Revenue Code throughout the 1980s, lawmakers agreed to leave intact a provision that allows corporations a virtually unlimited tax write-off of interest paid on borrowed money. This, even though corporate debt was ballooning and was being used increasingly to buy and then dismantle companies, not to build them.

That decision followed an overhaul of the U.S. Bankruptcy Code in 1978—the first revision in 40 years—that made bankruptcy easier for troubled businesses. Companies were given more flexibility to stay in business while they attempted to resolve their financial problems. The result: a bankruptcy code that encouraged an explosion in corporate bankruptcies brought on, in part, by an explosion in corporate debt that Congress failed to discourage through tax law revisions.

All this is incorporated in the government rule book, that agglomeration of laws and regulations that, through incentives and disincentives, sanctions and prohibitions, determines the course of the U.S. economy.

In the case of bankruptcy, a few numbers compiled from an analysis of a half-century of bankruptcy data tell the story. During the 1980s, businesses filed, on average, 63,500 bankruptcy petitions a year nationwide. That was up 155 percent over the 24,900 petitions a year filed in the 1970s, and up 302 percent over the 15,800 filed in the 1960s. The 1980s, in fact, produced the largest growth in bankruptcy cases since the Great Depression of the 1930s.

Corporate bankruptcy filings continue to proliferate. On average, 50,000 a year were filed in the 1990s and 43,000 a year in the 2000s. It wasn't until 2013-2016 that annual filings registered a significant decline at roughly 25,000 a year—fewer than recent decades, but still more than historical averages.

Not only is the number of bankruptcies spiraling; so, too, is the size of the companies flocking into bankruptcy court. When the Penn Central Transportation Co., parent company of the old Pennsylvania Railroad and New York Central Railroad, sought protection from its creditors in 1970, it was the largest bankruptcy in U.S. history—the first ever to exceed a billion dollars. For years, it was the bankruptcy against which all others were measured.

No more. Since 1985, more than 50 companies with assets of more than $1 billion each have filed bankruptcy petitions—including nearly a dozen with assets that exceeded Penn Central's $6.9 billion. The combined assets of large companies seeking bankruptcy court protection swelled to more than $70 billion in 1990.

Big-business bankruptcy has become so brisk that a new trend has emerged: the repeat bankruptcy customer. Braniff Inc., the airline, first sought protection in bankruptcy court in May 1982. It emerged two years later, in March 1984, but made a return appearance in September 1989. It emerged again in July 1991 and returned for a third time the following month. Continental Airlines went into bankruptcy court in 1983. And again in 1990.

UPDATE

The big bankruptcies of the past have been eclipsed by a new generation of spectacular failures. Among them: Lehman Brothers (with assets of $691 billion), Washington Mutual ($328 billion), World Com ($104 billion) and Enron ($66 billion).

As in the 1980s, some companies are making repeat visits to bankruptcy court. In 2001 the California utility PG&E filed for bankruptcy, listing assets of $36 billion. After a series of catastrophic fires caused in part by PG&E's failure to maintain transmission lines, the company filed for bankruptcy again in January 2019, listing its assets once more at $36 billion.

All this has been a bonanza for the burgeoning bankruptcy industry—the lawyers, accountants and other specialists who charge up to $500 an hour for their time.

They get paid to fly about the country, from courthouse to courthouse, from business to business. They get paid to talk for a few minutes on the telephone. They get paid to pack files. They get paid to unpack files. They get paid to pick up their mail. They get paid to sort their mail. They get paid to schedule conferences. They get paid to attend conferences. They get paid to keep a list of the conferences. They get paid to keep track of the way they spend their time. They get paid to fill out expense reports. And they get paid to eliminate the jobs of people who work for two weeks to earn what they charge for one hour.

Meet Ming the Merciless, otherwise known as Sanford C. Sigoloff, a Los Angeles businessman who described himself as "internationally renowned for his work in corporate turnarounds and restructurings." Indeed, newspaper, magazine and television reports praised his work as a doctor of ailing companies. The *New York Times* called him one of the "masters of the corporate turnaround." The *Los Angeles Times* described him as a "corporate savior."

But employees of companies that Sigoloff managed remember him better as "Ming the Merciless." Ming, the evil ruler of the planet Mongo in the Flash Gordon serial, is one of the more unsavory characters in science fiction. It is a nickname that Sigoloff relished. In fact, he gave it to himself to signify his single-minded dedication to cost-cutting.

Sigoloff and a small group of longtime allies directed Sigoloff & Associates, a "crisis management" firm in Santa Monica, Calif., whose clients have fallen on hard times. Its biggest client: L.J. Hooker Corp., the U.S. subsidiary of an Australian real estate company that once had annual revenue of more than $1 billion.

Beginning in 1987, Australian Hooker went on an American buying spree, snapping up such well-known department store chains as Bonwit Teller and B. Altman & Co. These and other acquisitions were made, naturally, with borrowed money. So much borrowed money that Hooker quickly collapsed under the weight of its debt and entered bankruptcy court on Aug. 9, 1989.

That same day, Sigoloff, who had been retained to guide the company and its subsidiaries through bankruptcy reorganization, distributed a news release: "Daily operations will continue as usual, stores will remain open and transactions ... will go on just as before the filing. Paychecks will be issued at the same time as if no proceeding had been filed."

Four months later, the paychecks began to stop. First, Sigoloff closed B. Altman, the 124-year-old New York-based department store chain with seven stores in New York, New Jersey and Pennsylvania. About 1,700 jobs were lost. Next, he liquidated all but two of Bonwit Teller's 16 stores, eliminating about 2,500 jobs in a department store empire that dated back 94 years. He closed all six stores of Sakowitz, the upscale Houston-based retailer that had been in business for 88 years, eliminating 450 jobs. He sold off most of Hooker's real estate holdings, throwing more employees out of work.

Hooker employed about 12,000 full- and part-time people in August 1989 when Sigoloff took over. When a Hooker spokesman was asked in late 1991—two years later—about the number then employed, he answered:

"Today the number is 62."

Author: "6,200?"

Hooker spokesman: "No, 62."

Author: "62 people?"

Hooker spokesman: "People. Exactly."

While the 1980s corporate restructuring boom resulted in the loss of 12,000 Hooker jobs, for Sigoloff & Associates, it produced $6.5 million in fees in the first year alone. And the fees continued—such as the ones charged for riding in airplanes.

Sigoloff and his colleagues flew often from Los Angeles, near their Santa Monica home base, to New York, Atlanta and other Eastern cities where Hooker had operations. On Feb. 12, 1990, Sigoloff flew

BANKRUPTCIES RISE, JOBS DISAPPEAR

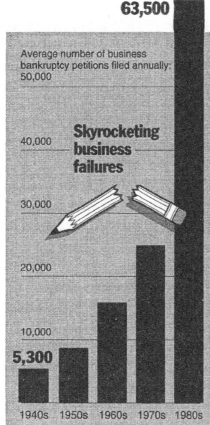

63,500

Average number of business bankruptcy petitions filed annually:

50,000

40,000

Skyrocketing business failures

30,000

20,000

10,000

5,300

1940s 1950s 1960s 1970s 1980s

SOURCE: Administrative office of U.S. Courts

WHAT WENT WRONG

Congress streamlined the Bankruptcy Code in 1978, making it easier for shaky companies to keep operating. Then came the heavy corporate borrowing and leveraged buyouts of the 1980s.

Result of that combination: Bankruptcy petitions filed in the 1980s soared — four times as many as in the **1960s.**

... WHAT WE'VE FOUND NOW

Corporate bankruptcy filings now average 35,000 a year and are a main cause of job losses. In 2019, depite a booming stock market, 62,100 workers lost their jobs when their companies filed for bankruptcy - more than in any year in the previous ten years.

Source: Challenger, Gray & Christmas Inc.

first class from Los Angeles to New York and billed $500 an hour for the five-hour trip. He also billed two hours' time for a conference that day on Bonwit Teller. Three days later, on Feb. 15, Sigoloff billed $500 an hour for three hours of phone calls, a one-hour meeting and five hours for "Travel: New York to Los Angeles." For the round trip, he collected $5,000.

In the first year that Hooker was in bankruptcy, Sigoloff logged about 175 hours in the air, charging more than $90,000 in fees for riding on airplanes. First class. Peter Dealy, a senior associate, logged 200 hours in the air. Fees collected for travel: $55,000. James M. Van Tatenhove: 250 hours in planes, collecting fees of more than $75,000. Seymour Strasberg spent 212 hours aloft and billed $60,000.

The charges are fees billed by Sigoloff & Associates, not necessarily paid directly to those doing the work. Overall, Sigoloff & Associates received more than $500,000 for time the associates spent in planes during the first 12 months that Hooker operated under the bankruptcy court's protection.

The Sigoloff firm is by no means unique. It is part of a growing fraternity that manages ailing companies and charges such fees. In fact, so many management consultants have entered the field that they have formed their own group. It is called, appropriately, the Turnaround Management Association. The association, composed of more than 400 managers, consultants, bankers, lawyers and accountants, holds an annual conference and bestows awards on companies deemed the most successful turnarounds of the year.

James A. Schuping, then the association's executive vice-president, foresaw a bright future: "The misfortune of the economy and a great many of the companies that are suffering right now are to the advantage of our people because that's their specialty. We look for this business failure phenomena to continue well throughout the decade."

A look at the billing practices of Sigoloff & Associates offers a glimpse at that future. Packing and unpacking files, for example. That chore led to several thousand dollars in billings by Sigoloff associate Richard F. Schmid, who managed Hooker's real estate operations in Washington, D.C. Schmid accumulated the file-packing fees as he prepared to move Hooker's offices in May 1990 from one suburban Washington location to another.

A sampling from his billing logs:

» May 14, 1990—"Worked on packing files for office move." Schmid billed four hours at $225 an hour, collecting $900.

» May 15, 1990—"Monitored removal of certain items of furniture, files and equipment..." Four hours, $900.

» May 17, 1990—"Continued selective packing of files for ... move." Two hours, $450.

» May 22, 1990—"Pack desk files for Chantilly move. Empty credenza and bookcases—sort files for storage." Three and one-half hours, $787.50.

» May 23, 1990—"Packing for Chantilly move." Four hours, $900.

» Finally, on May 24, the move took place, with the Hooker office relocating from Vienna, Va., to nearby Chantilly, Va. After the move, Schmid began a new series of entries on his expense reports:

» May 24, 1990—"Unpack boxes and set up at Chantilly." Four hours, $900.

» May 29, 1990—"Unpack files for use at new office." Two hours, $450.

» May 31, 1990—"Continue unpacking boxes and set up office space." Three and one-half hours, $787.50.

A Sigoloff spokesman, Michael Sitrick, said the firm's fees are reviewed and approved by bankruptcy court. As for flying time: "Sandy said they work while they're on airplanes. His comment was: 'They don't sit and watch movies.'"

When Sigoloff initially applied for fees for travel time in 1989, the U.S. Trustee who was monitoring bankruptcy court fees, expressed concern about the "substantial time" spent traveling, according to papers filed in U.S. Bankruptcy Court in New York. But the objection was later dropped after consultations with Hooker's lawyers. Hooker's counsel, Alan B. Hyman of the New York law firm of Proskauer Rose Goetz & Mendelsohn, told the court the travel time fees were necessary because Hooker's operations were "all over the country."

"We've been advised by Sigoloff," Hyman said, "that the way they keep the time records, and charge, they charge travel time for the exact time of the flight." Sigoloff later wrote that the travel fees were justified because "we are working on Hooker business ... we bill only for the scheduled time of the flight, not the actual time, which is often significantly longer on a cross-country flight."

As for entries such as "packing" and "unpacking" boxes, Sitrick, the Sigoloff spokesman, said that Richard Schmid might have been searching for financial records. "Dick is a terrific financial guy but maybe not a real good time-slip keeper," Sitrick said. "I know Dick Schmid. Dick is a very senior guy. He would have one of his subordinates packing and unpacking boxes. He wouldn't be packing and unpacking." Schmid later wrote that his decision to move Hooker's Washington operations and to lay off most of its staff saved creditors a substantial amount of money.

"This move saved the creditors $13,000 per month in rent, over $80,000 in payroll and benefits for the 20 employees who were terminated, and at least another $10,000 per month on telephone, supplies and other costs," Schmid wrote. "And, yes, the five key employees and myself who remained did indeed sort, evaluate and pack the files with critical documentation pertaining to ongoing lawsuits, as well as proprietary L.J. Hooker business records which were essential to an orderly liquidation."

Sigoloff himself later confirmed the need for Schmid to personally handle the packing and unpacking of the boxes: "In this particular circumstance, the files involved were highly sensitive payroll, termination and other management information requiring strict confidentiality."

Schmid's billing practices were in keeping with those of his coworkers, who collected fees for performing seemingly routine tasks. Richard A. Stemm, who was handling creditors' claims against Hooker, billed $90 an hour to "return car to airport" and "to make travel arrangements" and to "rearrange flight, hotel checkout, car return and standby" for a flight.

And then there was the "master calendar." That's the schedule of forthcoming meetings, court appearances and other dates affecting the business of L.J. Hooker. Sigoloff & Associates collected thousands of dollars in fees to revise, update and delete information from this schedule.

Excerpts from bankruptcy court records: On June 14, 1990, long-time Sigoloff associate Wilhelm Mallory, who was overseeing Hooker's retail properties, billed 6-3/4 hours, or $1,688, for "master calendar task review." Sigoloff, the highest-paid member of the firm, billed $500 an hour every time he worked on the calendar.

On Jan. 5, 1990, he spent an hour on "master calendar assignments." The next day, he billed three hours for work on the "professional master calendar." The day after that he collected $3,000 in fees for the "review of corporate master calendar/professional master calendar ..." On Jan. 9, it was two hours of fees for "review of master calendar draft II." Then on Jan. 31, after all the work on the master calendar that month, it was time for what Sigoloff described as "master calendar cleansing."

Sigoloff collected fees for working on the master calendar wherever he happened to be. On July 30, 1990, while on the French Riviera, Sigoloff phoned his office to "review Hooker master calendar." For the call, he billed his usual hourly rate—$500.

As is so often the case in bankruptcy proceedings, some of the most detailed work is keeping track of fees. And there are fees for keeping track of fees. Sigoloff & Associates staff billed thousands of dollars in fees to record their expenses, to fill out time sheets, to prepare an application to bankruptcy court for their fees, to appear in court to answer any questions the judge might have about the fee requests. Every three months, Sigoloff & Associates petitioned bankruptcy court in New York for payment of its fees.

The compiling, writing, revising and drafting of the final fee application generated yet another round of fees. On Nov. 17, 1989, Arthur Cayley billed three hours at $175 an hour for work on the "fee application." Three days later, he billed five more hours for work on the fee application. The day after that, he billed four more hours for work on the application. On Dec. 14, Cayley billed three hours and 50 minutes for giving "support for fee application."

After the application was completed, Sigoloff filed it with bankruptcy court in New York, seeking $1.8 million in fees and expenses for August through October 1989.

Bankrupted by Debt

Not everyone does so well off the bankruptcy boom. Ask Joyce Buckner, who lost her job as a $6.05-an-hour meat slicer at the Toppers Meat Co. in Sedalia, Mo. The plant was closed in 1990 after Doskocil Cos., a Midwestern meat processor that owned Toppers, entered bankruptcy.

"I went to school for a while but financially that wasn't working," she said. "I did try to find work but some of the jobs were at night, and when you have children, it's just not possible. It took about seven or eight months before I found a job."

Buckner eventually found work packaging bullets in a plant that manufactures ammunition. "I'm just there," she said, "because I need the money. The hourly wage isn't that great. It's $5 an hour. Less than what I was making but a little bit above minimum wage."

Doskocil was an American success story until, like so many other businesses, it got caught up in the takeover and debt revolution of the 1980s. The Hutchinson, Kan., company had carved out a niche in the highly competitive world of meatpacking by making pizza toppings for some of the largest fast-food chains. Doskocil grew by adding plants, employees and products until 1987, when it decided it wanted to really grow. Not slowly by selling more products and building more plants, but by acquiring a competitor.

With the help of Drexel Burnham Lambert Inc., Doskocil sold $50 million in high-risk, high-yield junk bonds to finance an acquisition. The next year it launched a hostile takeover of Wilson Foods, an Oklahoma City meatpacker that was six times larger than Doskocil. Doskocil had sales of $215 million, compared with Wilson's $1.3 billion. Doskocil had 900 employees, compared with Wilson's 5,000. Doskocil had five plants, compared with Wilson's 12.

Wilson had a corporate history dating to 1853, when it was one of the first of the great national meatpackers. Doskocil dated to 1963, when founder Larry Doskocil slaughtered a hog in a former chicken coop on the outskirts of Hutchinson and sold the parts. Nevertheless, the times were such that a small company with access to the easy money of Wall Street could take on larger prey.

Although Wilson initially rejected the bid, the Doskocil company eventually won out after a bitter three-month battle. The takeover fight generated millions of dollars in fees for lawyers, investment bankers and accountants. For Wilson, the price was steep, creating a loss in the last quarter of 1988 for "costs and expenses" to fight the Doskocil raid.

"These charges of approximately $11.8 million," Wilson reported to the SEC, "consisted primarily of financial, legal and bank commitment fees which were incurred by Wilson in its defense of the unsolicited tender offer."

The Doskocil company formally took control of Wilson in January 1989, firing the president, chief executive officer and more than 100 salaried employees at Wilson's corporate headquarters in Oklahoma City. Just 15 months later, the deal that took millions of dollars in fees to put together came apart. Unable to sell off parts of Wilson as planned, Doskocil could not pay the interest on the huge debt it took on to buy Wilson. Citing a "liquidity crisis," Doskocil filed for bankruptcy protection on March 5, 1990. Squeezed for cash, Doskocil sought to lower costs by closing plants or imposing layoffs or wage cuts at other plants.

Carol Jean Smith was one of the casualties. For more than six years, she had made meatballs for pizza toppings at the Doskocil-owned Toppers plant in Sedalia, 70 miles east of Kansas City. She earned $6.25 an hour. Then in May 1990, two months after Doskocil filed for bankruptcy, she lost her job. The Sedalia plant closed. Permanently.

To Carol Jean Smith and her coworkers, the shutdown came as a shock. "We thought the plant was doing OK," she said. "Everyone was always telling us what a good plant it was. Then they began laying off people and we began to wonder if they were going to close the plant. But they said no. They had no plans to do that.

"But then before it happened, we knew something was up. They began calling people in for a meeting. Even those who were on vacation got a call and were told to come to the plant. The meeting was in the cafeteria. The manager read a letter saying they were going to close the plant in two weeks. We were all shocked. We couldn't believe it."

After that, Carol Jean Smith looked for a job. Meantime, she cleaned houses—at $5 an hour.

If the Doskocil bankruptcy was a financial hardship for Carol Jean Smith, Joyce Buckner and others who lost jobs that paid $6 an hour, it was a windfall for another group of workers. Lawyers, accountants and consultants from across the country swarmed to bankruptcy court in Topeka, Kan., to grab a share of the fees for representing a variety of interests.

Nightingale & Associates Inc. of New Canaan, Conn., billed at a rate of $250 an hour as management consultant for the Official Committee of Unsecured Creditors of Doskocil. Andrews & Kurth, a Houston law firm, billed $250 an hour as counsel for the Official Committee of Unsecured Creditors of Doskocil. Stutman, Treister & Glatt, a Los Angeles law firm, collected up to $400 an hour as Doskocil's lead bankruptcy counsel.

Paul, Weiss, Rifkind, Wharton & Garrison, a New York law firm, billed $435 an hour as special counsel for the Official Unsecured Creditors' Committee of Wilson Foods. Price Waterhouse, the national accounting firm, collected up to $300 an hour as accountants for the Official Unsecured Creditors' Committee of Wilson Foods. Pepper, Hamilton & Scheetz, a Philadelphia law firm, billed $260 an hour as attorney for the Official Committee of Unsecured Creditors' of Wilson Foods. Kensington & Ressler, a New York law firm, billed $220 an hour as counsel for Doskocil.

In the past, such cross-country travel in the pursuit of bankruptcy business was rare. That's because such fees were rare. Until Congress rewrote the bankruptcy section of the government rule book in 1978, bankruptcy cases were processed in U.S. district courts, along with other civil cases. But most of the daily work in bankruptcy was presided over at a lower level by so-called referees, who were appointed by district court judges. Fees were comparatively modest. So was the number of bankruptcy lawyers.

When Congress revised the code, it created a separate bankruptcy court to deal solely with bankruptcy cases. Fees closer to the going corporate rate could then be charged. The result was predictable: Cases, fees and the number of lawyers specializing in bankruptcy soared. So much so that *Working Woman* magazine singled out bankruptcy practice as one of the 25 best career choices for women.

"Just a few years ago," the magazine said in July 1990, "corporate bankruptcy law, like real estate law before it, was the poor sister of the bar ... but the Bankruptcy Reform Act of 1978 allowed judges to award fees in line with regular corporate rates. Bankruptcy law suddenly became more lucrative, and large law firms that previously had farmed out bankruptcy work to smaller firms began to develop in-house departments."

Bankruptcy court judges in many jurisdictions routinely approve the fees. Sometimes they explain their reasons. Like the charges for "word processing expenses" billed in 1990 by the New York law firm of Debevoise & Plimpton, which represents L.J. Hooker Corp.'s creditors. These were not stenographic fees, but fees for the use of the firm's computers. The law firm billed $25 an hour for its own staff to use its own computers during regular working hours to prepare letters and legal documents, and $50 an hour outside of the normal workday.

Arthur H. Amron, a member of the firm, explained the procedure to the court: "There's a usage charge that is an hourly fee for the use of the system. There's an overtime usage by the word processing department outside of the normal hours. That is a charge added on to the usual charge for overtime use."

Replied Judge Tina L. Brozman: "I think that billing practices citywide have changed. I am not sure that I necessarily agree with them, but if it's standard, I think my mandate is to compensate firms as they are compensated in other matters and not to be niggardly."

During that hearing, at which Judge Brozman approved the awarding of millions of dollars in fees, she did reject one expense item—a $16 tip on an $88 taxi bill turned in by an Australian bank.

"Take out the tip," said Judge Brozman, "we will deal with it at ..." Attorney Alan Hyman interrupted with a little bankruptcy court levity: "It's expensive to take a cab to Australia."

As might be expected, the generous fees have prompted strong reactions from creditors, who get only what's left. Consider those with a stake in the reorganization of American Continental Corp. in Phoenix. American Continental was the parent company of Lincoln Savings & Loan Association, a California thrift controlled by Charles H. Keating Jr. that was seized by federal regulators in April 1989.

The American Continental bankruptcy case and related litigation became a perpetual money machine for scores of lawyers, accountants and other professionals. One law firm alone, Wyman, Bautzer, Kuchel & Silbert of Los Angeles, estimated in February 1991 that it had "devoted approximately 40,000 hours, the equivalent of 20 lawyer years, of professional services" to the American Continental case. When another law firm filed petitions in bankruptcy court in Phoenix, seeking payment of more than $1.5 million in interim fees in the case, a man and woman from Riverside, Calif., wrote the court complaining that the lawyers were "asking for money faster than the U.S. Mint can make money."

They were among the thousands of investors, many of them retirees, who had purchased American Continental bonds and who stood to lose most of their money. They argued that if American Continental had "this kind of money in the bank to pay attorneys, then the investors should be paid off first and the attorneys afterwards." A Westminster, Calif., investor, adding up the fee requests from several law firms, told the court: "All the available monies will be discharged to counsels and the creditors will be left holding the bag; again."

To be sure, not all bankruptcy court judges are so liberal in dispensing fees. Judge Joseph L. Cosetti, who presides over bankruptcy proceedings in Pittsburgh, rejected fees for some expenses that New York judges approved. Among them: the charges for word-processing, or computer use, during the bankruptcy reorganization of Allegheny International Inc., a Pittsburgh-based conglomerate, whose interests ranged from steel to Sunbeam appliances.

In an opinion dealing with fees, Judge Cosetti took special note of the billings for computer time: "Secretarial time, both regular and overtime, as well as charges for word-processing, are clearly overhead ... Therefore, those entries are disallowed." He also disallowed charges for meals and local cab fares. He cut the hourly fees charged by lawyers, saying they were too high. And he complained that lawyers from the same firm were billing for too much time in office meetings, and that multiple lawyers from the same firm appeared in court.

Nonetheless, the fee petitions were so voluminous—as they are in many cases—that Judge Cosetti conceded it was impossible to go over every claim. He wrote: "Unfortunately, the court lacks the resources because of its other cases to review, line-by-line, every fee petition filed in this case. The fee petitions which are the subject of this opinion, when stacked together, are over two feet high."

Law firms spend many hours preparing fee applications that even the most conscientious judges lack the time to sift through.

How many hours?

Well, in one month, a couple of lawyers and legal assistants in the Atlanta law firm of Trotter, Smith & Jacobs billed 150 hours—at rates up to $215 an hour—to prepare one fee application in the bankruptcy reorganization of Southmark Corp., a Dallas real estate and financial services firm.

Herewith a sampling from Trotter, Smith reports for April 1990:

"Review ... of court's Dec. 18, 1989, order to determine date next fee application by Trotter Smith & Jacobs must be filed."

"Drafting ... of memorandum ... regarding filing date for next fee application by Trotter Smith & Jacobs."

"Preparation ... of file containing prior fee application information."

"Conference ... regarding need to assign legal assistant to begin collecting documents and information for third application by Trotter Smith & Jacobs for interim award of attorneys' fees and reimbursement of expenses."

"Conference ... regarding assignments to individual attorneys for writing narrative summaries to include in application by Trotter Smith & Jacobs for interim award of attorneys' fees."

"Preparation, assembly and review ... of distribution packets to thirteen billing attorneys ... regarding the preparation

of summaries to be used in connection with the preparation
... of the third fee application ... for interim awards and
reimbursement expenses."

UPDATE

As employees lose benefits and some creditors receive pennies on
the dollar for their claims in bankruptcy court, those who manage
the bankruptcy process continue to profit richly. In the Lehman
Brothers bankruptcy, fees collected by lawyers and consultants
exceeded $2 billion; for Enron, fees topped $740 million. PG&E's
bankruptcy practitioners collected $400 million from their 2001
filing. At the time of this writing, fees for PG&E's 2019 filing are still
being tallied.

Paper Jobs

Not too surprisingly, the nation's bankruptcy courts are choking on
paper. Keeping track of hearings attended, hearings rescheduled, letters sent, letters not received, expense reports compiled and expense
reports filed, obviously requires a massive amount of record-keep-
ing. When the paperwork goes astray, as it is wont to do when lawyers and judges and courts process tens of millions of pieces of paper,
one result is ever more fees as everyone debates the legal subtleties of
errant legal documents.

Consider the events of a single day in a single bankruptcy court
proceeding and keep in mind that similar debates are taking place in
courtrooms across America. Again, at $100 to $500 an hour.

The city is Pittsburgh. The company is Allegheny International, a
once high-flying conglomerate. The date is Aug. 11, 1988. The place
is a 16th-floor courtroom in the federal building in downtown Pittsburgh.

A dozen lawyers are engaged in an animated discussion with
bankruptcy court judge Cosetti. The issue: whether one of thousands
of notices Allegheny mailed to potential creditors was properly sent.
The creditor, Equibank, Pittsburgh's third-largest bank, argues that
the notice was incorrectly addressed.

The notice was mailed from Allegheny's corporate headquarters, in the Equibank building in Pittsburgh, to Equibank's corporate headquarters, which are in the same building. The bank's lawyer contends that the notice was sent to Equibank's "mail room department and a gentleman or person by the name of D. Miller," rather than to the bank's corporate trust department.

Equibank's lawyer: "I have witnesses here today who will be testifying that there is no current D. Miller as an employee of Equibank, nor has there ever been a D. Miller in the employ of the corporate trust department for the last fifteen years." Because of Allegheny's error, he says, Equibank missed the deadline to file its claim.

"It's our position," he continues, "that we did not receive the notice, that this constitutes excusable neglect under Rule 9006 (B) (1) that we should be permitted to file the late proof of claim."

The judge: "Now, this is being opposed, as you know, by all the other committees and every party who can get their hands on a typewriter."

Equibank's lawyer: "Yes, your honor."

Creditors' lawyer: "It was addressed to a Mr. Miller, but in our response we also cite case law which indicates that as long as it's sent to the right firm and the right place and, in fact, it was sent to two places." He leafs through his papers and notes that in addition to the notice to D. Miller in Equibank's mail room, another was sent to the attention of William Barnum, also at Equibank's corporate offices.

The judge: "So there were two notices?"

Creditors' lawyer: "Yes."

Equibank's lawyer: "Well, your honor, if I may interpose here … Mr. Barnum is, in fact, the chef at Equibank's dining room. And how he could be expected to provide notice to the corporate trust department is quite frankly beyond me."

Laughter fills the courtroom.

Creditors' lawyer: "This request does clearly come after the expiration of the May 31st time period. So I don't even think we need to get to the question of excusable neglect because the request was made late."

The judge is familiar with the legal doctrine of "excusable neglect." But he notes he is not certain it can be invoked in the Equibank situation.

"My view is that the ... cases don't give much excusable neglect merit to slightly wrong addresses," he says.

In any event, the judge will think it over. If he agrees to allow the claim, he will inform the parties. Then they will have another hearing. The reason: to decide the value of the claim.

Cases like Allegheny International are so complex and so voluminous that they have forced bankruptcy courts to take special steps to handle the flow. Around the country, bankruptcy courts have limited hours, rented additional space, hired more clerks, contracted with private firms to take over tasks once performed by court employees, restricted access to records, installed telephone answering machines to route the flow of requests, and invoked other emergency measures to try to manage what one bankruptcy court official described as a "tidal wave" of paper.

In St. Louis, 10 additional clerks were hired to deal with the largest bankruptcy in the city's history, Interco Inc., whose holdings include such familiar names as Florsheim shoes and Broyhill furniture. In Phoenix, the bankruptcy case of American Continental Corp. became so gargantuan that the clerk's office retained a legal-services management firm, which rented an entire warehouse to store documents that fill nearly 10,000 boxes. That's for just one case. In Los Angeles, the influx of documents grew so great that the clerk's office in Room 906 began to resemble a supermarket, with specialized lanes to handle specific requests.

Inside the main door are these signs above the public counter: "Advanced Request Here," "Return Files Here," "Request Files

Here," "Photo Copying" and "Cashier." Unlike most supermarkets, however, there are no express lanes in bankruptcy court.

In Manhattan, the bankruptcy court clerk's office created a special division to try to manage the volume of paper produced by a series of massive bankruptcies stemming from the era of easy debt. Years ago, most bankruptcies—however large or small—were filed in one fifth-floor of the historic U.S. Custom House at the foot of Manhattan—except L.J. Hooker, Eastern Airlines, Ames Department Stores, Drexel Burnham Lambert, Integrated Resources, Pan American Airways, Best Products and other mega-bankruptcies. These were sent to a new office down the hall.

Until the summer of 1989, Room 510 was a dark, unused storage area, piled high with old furniture from the days that the building was New York's principal custom house. Within two years it began to look much like a typical clerk's office found in bankruptcy courts across America. Except that it handled fewer than three dozen cases. They are so enormous they required a section all their own.

"The purpose of that room was because we simply could not deal with the public otherwise," said Cecilia Lewis, the bankruptcy court clerk. After the large cases began to be filed, she said, the court discovered that "there were not enough telephone lines, not enough people, not enough copies of the petition available to give to people."

The bankruptcy court operation in Manhattan moved to its present location from cramped quarters in the U.S. Courthouse at Foley Square.

"We have only been in this building since 1987 and we are totally out of space," said Lewis. "At the time we moved in, this was a large expansion."

What accounts for the runaway growth of paperwork—In four words: the government rule book.

When Congress rewrote the rule book in 1978 to revise the bankruptcy law, it opened the floodgates to a specialized proceeding called Chapter 11. Under the old law, companies in trouble tended to file petitions under a section of the code called Chapter 7. That section provides for the liquidation of the company. Its assets are sold and the proceeds distributed to creditors. The business ceases to exist.

Chapter 11 is different. It allows a company to continue operations and existing management to stay in control. The company reorganizes under court supervision, protected from its creditors. Chapter 11 had existed previously, but the new law made it a more appealing option.

The change came at a time of shifting values in the world of business, when bankruptcy began to lose the stigma once attached to it. Those same shifting values permitted corporate managers to engage in practices—such as unrestrained borrowing—that they once would have avoided out of fear of bankruptcy. And they permitted executives whose faulty judgments resulted in the failure of their businesses to seek sanctuary in bankruptcy court and, perhaps more important, retain their jobs.

So it was that corporate debt surged to record levels in the 1980s as a result of the new attitude toward borrowing. In the past corporate managers saw debt as a necessary tool for corporate growth, but one to be used cautiously. But in the 1980s, fueled by the virtually unlimited tax deduction for interest paid on corporate borrowings, debt was seen as a positive force, a way to impose discipline on a company's operations.

Steven N. Kaplan, an assistant professor of finance at the University of Chicago, summed up this attitude in testimony before a Congressional committee in 1989: "The large debt service payments force managers to find ways to generate cash and prevent managers from spending money unproductively." The results of that trend have become painfully evident. The very factor that was supposed to impose discipline—the high debt service payments—instead became a liability that drove many into bankruptcy court.

An analysis of a half-century of bankruptcy caseloads shows what happened: From 1976 to 1979, businesses filed, on average, 3,700 bankruptcy petitions each year under Chapter 11. During the 1980s, with the new law in effect, businesses filed, on average, 15,200 petitions each year under Chapter 11. That was an increase of 313 percent. By contrast, Chapter 7 petitions rose just 43 percent, from an average of 28,200 to 40,300.

Viewed from a different perspective, in the late 1970s only one of every nine businesses that went into bankruptcy court sought to reorganize. In the 1980s, it was one of every three.

The dramatic growth in Chapter 11 proceedings—in which a business conducts its affairs under the supervision of the courts and an army of lawyers, accountants and management consultants—brought on the avalanche of paperwork.

As with so many legislative actions involving the government rule book, lawmakers failed to understand the consequences of their bankruptcy code revisions in 1978. Malcolm Wallop, a Republican senator from Wyoming, promised that "no longer will needless litigation in several courts be required to determine all the matters involved in a bankruptcy case." Don Edwards, a Democratic congressman from California, hailed the Bankruptcy Reform Act, saying that it "encourages business reorganizations by a streamlined new commercial reorganization chapter."

No more needless litigation? Streamlined?

As for the end of litigation, take a look at the bankruptcy proceedings of Integrated Resources Inc., the New York financial services company that collapsed in February 1990. There has been litigation involving unpaid merchandise, breach of contract, unpaid rent, default on promissory notes, fraud and misrepresentation in the sale of partnership interests, securities law violations, fraud and negligence in the sale of investment programs, conspiracy and fraud in the marketing of partnerships, nonpayment of notes, and a class-action lawsuit by stockholders.

There is so much litigation overall that in 1990 Andrews Publications of Westtown, Penn., began publishing a twice-monthly newsletter, the *Failed LBO Litigation Reporter*, just to report on cases in state and federal courts. Frank Reynolds of Andrews Publications said that the *Failed LBO Litigation Reporter* follows major bankruptcy cases with an eye on "who might be liable for the mess and who is going to sue who and what is the proportion of the liability among various parties."

As for streamlined, take a look at the number of law firms representing some of the interests in the Hooker bankruptcy case. There are Attorneys for the Creditors Committee, General Counsel to the Debtor, Special Counsel for Debtor, Attorneys for Debtor, Co-counsel to Debtor, Special Labor Counsel, Attorneys for the Official Committee of Unsecured Creditors, Special Local Counsel, Attorneys for

The 30 biggest bankruptcies in U.S. history

Assets, in billions of dollars, the year before bankruptcy filing.

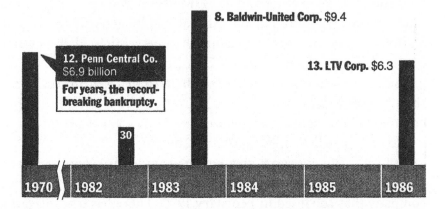

8. Baldwin-United Corp. $9.4

12. Penn Central Co. $6.9 billion

For years, the record-breaking bankruptcy.

13. LTV Corp. $6.3

30

| 1970 | 1982 | 1983 | 1984 | 1985 | 1986 |

... WHAT WE'VE FOUND NOW

We thought the largest bankruptcies of late '80s and early '90s were big. The largest corporate bankruptcies in the 21st century dwarf most of those in the past even when adjusted for inflation.

Lehman Brothers	$691 (Figures are in billions)
Washington Mutual	$327.9
Worldcom	$103.9
General Motors	$82.3
CIT Group	$71
Enron	$65.5
Conseco	$61.4
MF Global	$41
Chrysler	$39.3
Thornburg Mortgage	$36.5

Source: Administrative Office of the U.S. Courts

1. Financial Corp. of America $33.9

2. MCorp $20.2

3. First Exec. Corp. $15.2

4. Gibraltar Financial Corp. $15.0

5. Imperial Corp. of America $12.3

6. Allied-Federated Dept. Stores $11.4

7. First Capital Holdings Corp. $ 9.7

9. Southmark $9.1

10. Integrated Resources Inc. $7.9

11. Continental Airlines $7.7

14. Columbia Gas Systems .... $ 6.2
15. Enstar Group .... $ 5.6
16. American Cont'l Corp............ $ 5.1
17. Fin. Corp. of Santa Barbara ... $ 4.7
18. Texas American Bancshares.. $ 4.4
19. Lomas Financial Corp........... $ 4.3
20. Eastern Air Lines .... $ 4.0
21. Drexel Burnham Lambert Inc. . $ 3.7
22. Hillsborough Holdings .... $ 3.5
23. Southland Corp................... $ 3.4
24. First Columbia Financial........ $ 2.8
25. Rothschild Holdings............. $ 2.8
26. Public Service Co.–N.H......... $ 2.6
27. Pan Am Corp. .... $ 2.4
28. Landmark Land Co. .... $ 2.4
29. United States Lines .... $ 2.3
30. Manville Corp..................... $ 2.3

1987   1988   1989   1990   1991

Plaintiff, Special Corporate Counsel, Special Counsel for the Debtors Trade Creditors, Consultants for Debtors and Accountants to the Official Creditors' Committee. All those committees beget a prodigious volume of paperwork, which, in turn, begets prodigious fees.

When the L.J. Hooker Corp., the U.S. division of the Australian real estate company, filed for bankruptcy in New York in August 1989, it submitted one petition for Hooker Corp.—and 14 separate petitions for 14 Hooker subsidiaries. Consequently, each time Hooker filed an accounting, it submitted 15 separate statements covering operations and liabilities. One such statement, Document No. 47, was 1,510 pages long, seven inches thick, weighed 10 pounds, and contained the names of 15,000 potential creditors of one Hooker subsidiary— Bonwit Teller.

At the bankruptcy court in Dallas, there was the Southmark Corp., the real estate combine. Instead of fifteen subsidiaries, Southmark had 550 subsidiaries and 350 public and private real estate partnerships. The collapse of hundreds of those entities in turn spawned about 850 lawsuits. In Phoenix, the bankruptcy cases grew so large that the bankruptcy court was compelled to retain a private firm, Ameriscribe Management Services Inc., to handle the flood of legal documents.

So it is with the reorganization of Circle K Corp., a convenience store chain based in Phoenix that in 1990 had annual sales approaching $4 billion. By late 1991, Circle K had produced nearly 5,000 legal documents—some of which were thousands of pages long—that have been submitted to the court and Ameriscribe.

It is "generating huge, huge amounts of paper," said Mark A. Scipione, an Ameriscribe official. When the company filed its list of assets and liabilities, Scipione said, they were "25 volumes long. There were 40,000 pages of creditors.

"We had some people call and say, 'I want that list of assets and liabilities.' "And I said, 'Sure, do you want to pick them up with a truck or should I send them air freight?'"

Corporate bankruptcy lawyers can depend on a steady stream of business from private equity deals gone bad. Most of the companies that wind up in bankruptcy court after private equity companies have bled them with high management fees, debt charges and flawed business plans aren't household names. But one is.

Toys R Us had 1,500 stores, $11.5 billion in annual sales, and one of the best-known consumer brand names in the country when a private equity firm bought the company in 2005. Investors led by the KKR Group, Bain Capital and Vornado Realty Trust paid $6.6 billion with mostly borrowed money, and the company never got out from under the weight of the resulting debt heaped on it. When the company filed for bankruptcy in 2017, citing "expensive debt service" among other factors, store workers and creditors said the only winners would be the lawyers.

A bankruptcy judge confirmed that when he awarded Kirkland & Ellis, the largest law firm in the U.S., $55.7 million in fees as the company's bankruptcy lawyer. Creditors received on average 22 cents on the dollar. Employees who sought severance pay received even less. In 2018, the company shut down all its remaining stores.

Chapter Five

THE FOREIGN CONNECTION

INTRODUCTION

It was one of America's most historic years: In 1976 thousands of fairs and festive ceremonies were organized to celebrate the 200th birthday of the world's first modern democracy.

Though no one knew it at the time—nor would they have celebrated if they had—the year was historic in one other way.

In 1976 the U.S. bought more manufactured goods from abroad than it exported. It was a modest trade deficit—$9.4 billion—but it was the start of a trend that has continued unrelentingly, growing larger with each year, and in so doing eroding the economic well-being of millions of middle-class Americans.

The U.S. cumulative trade deficit reached $11 trillion in 2019. And the deficit is getting bigger every year—usually running at an increase of $1 trillion annually.

What difference does it make? It matters a lot if you have lost your job or can't find a job or are paid a low wage because low-cost foreign competition threatens to take your job.

For much of the nation's history, the U.S. enjoyed a trade surplus or recorded an occasional small deficit. Our trade ledger was generally in balance; imports and exports were roughly equal.

As industry after industry—apparel, tools, cars—came under pressure from imports, policymakers from both parties tried to assure workers that the worst was over. It wasn't. The number of U. S. manufacturing jobs stayed relatively constant from 1960 to 2000, though manufacturing as a percentage of total jobs in the economy dropped significantly. But after 2000 the bottom fell out of manufacturing and five million jobs vanished—a decline of 28 percent.

Economists debate the pros and cons of the impact of a large trade deficit on the nation's overall economy, but one fact is not debatable: The flood of imports has taken a bitter toll on millions of American workers who lost good-paying jobs making products that imports priced out of the market.

After years of false assurances that they would find new jobs to replace their old paychecks they feel betrayed. Which is one reason that millions voted for Donald Trump.

As for Trump, he's following the same path as those before him. In the China trade deal negotiated in 2019, the U.S. agreed to a pact calling for China to import billions of agricultural products in exchange for reducing tariffs on many China imports—which will almost certainly eliminate even more American manufacturing jobs.

Global Economy

Want to take advantage of the stew of rules, regulations and laws that govern the U.S. economy and the conduct of business in America? And maybe make a few million dollars and cut your taxes along the way?

Here are a few tips.

» Become a fugitive from justice and set up operations in a foreign country to conduct business, even to deal with government agencies back home.

» Become a citizen of a foreign country in order to play American stock and bond markets, or even to buy and sell American businesses, at lower tax rates than you'd get staying at home in the United States.

» Form an American subsidiary of a foreign-owned company so you can pay lower taxes than your U.S.-owned competitors.

» Start an American company, and then move your factory, jobs and investment dollars overseas.

Any one of those setups is now to your advantage because of the way the rules that govern business in this country have been written and rewritten.

Why would the U.S. government rig the game that way? In part because of the influence exercised by special interests in Congress and in federal agencies. In part because of good intentions gone awry.

One of the consequences: American companies, and companies worldwide, are conducting a replay on a global scale of a business practice that became common in the 1960s. That was the decade that U.S. companies began playing off one region of the United States against another, one state against another, one city against another. The objective was to locate a new plant or relocate an existing one in whatever area would offer the greatest tax incentives—so the company would have to pay the smallest amount of local and state taxes—and where employee wages and fringe benefits could be held down the most.

That practice has since gone global, as corporations and financiers play off one country against another, one national tax system against another, one country against its possessions. President Bush put a glowing light on it in 1991 in his annual report on the state of the economy that he delivered to Congress: "The benefits of global economic integration and expanded international trade have been enormous, at home and abroad.

"U.S. firms gain from access to global markets; U.S. workers benefit from foreign investment in America ... Competition and innovation have been stimulated, and businesses have increased their efficiency by locating operations around the globe."

The aptly named Marc Rich quite likely felt the same way. You may not recognize his name. But you quite likely have used one of his products. Rich, once a member of *Forbes* magazine's directory of the 400 richest Americans, operated a highly secretive and successful commodities business around the world. Through a maze of closely controlled companies, he bought and sold billions of dollars' worth of oil, copper, nickel, wheat, alumina and other commodities.

Back in 1983, Rich, two associates, and one of his companies, Clarendon Ltd., were accused by the federal government of failing to pay taxes on profits from rigging the price of crude oil during the 1979-

1980 energy shortage, then hustling the money out of the country. To continue doing business, Clarendon pleaded guilty to the charges and paid $172 million in taxes and penalties.

Rich fled the country, apparently unwilling to risk the possibility of a trial, conviction and a sentence that could add up to more than 300 years in prison. After the indictment, Rich began operating from Zug, Switzerland, where he settled into a multimillion-dollar mansion. Except, of course, when he was relaxing at his multimillion-dollar estate at Marbella on the coast of Spain. That's the estate, according to published accounts, with the swimming pool carved into a cliff overlooking the Mediterranean.

Whether in Switzerland or Spain, Rich directed the buying and selling of assorted commodities—he virtually controlled the aluminum market—in the United States and around the world.

He also had an impact on the jobs of American aluminum workers. People like Joseph Gladden of Ravenswood, W.Va. who, along with 1,700 other employees, was locked out of the aluminum smelting plant owned by a company called Ravenswood Aluminum Corp. Gladden began working at the plant in 1971 when it was owned by Kaiser Aluminum & Chemical Corp. Those were the days when American business operated in a way that came to seem hopelessly antiquated and naive to the wheeler-dealers who moved in during the 1980s, with the federal government paving every step of the way. The days when a company actually built a plant and ran it for the long term.

For Gladden, those days ended in 1986. That's when the first of a dizzying series of changes ensued. Joseph Gladden was about to meet the global economy. It began that year when British takeover artist Alan E. Clore seized control of the company. Clore lasted until the stock market crash of October 1987, when he defaulted on bank loans. The next buyer was an American takeover artist, Charles E. Hurwitz of Houston. To pay down the debt incurred when he bought Kaiser Aluminum, Hurwitz sold off pieces of the old company, including the Ravenswood plant.

Enter the third set of new owners in three years—bankrolled by a mysterious company with multiple ties to Marc Rich.

How is it possible for a fugitive to conduct business as usual in the United States?

The answer, once again, is the government rule book, the handiwork of a succession of lawmakers and presidents, regulators and administrators, who have chosen to write the rules to favor special interests—from wealthy individuals such as Marc Rich to influential businesses—rather than create a level economic playing field for everyone.

Nowhere is the imbalance more evident than in the rules—or, more accurately, the absence of rules—relating to foreign investment in the United States, foreign trade, the conduct of U.S. businesses abroad, unrestrained imports, and the global economy.

The transformation of once-American-owned businesses such as the Ravenswood plant into outposts controlled from abroad is part of a larger picture that is unfolding across America.

The most famous beer in America—Budweiser—the staple of corner bars, family cookouts and sports advertising, is owned by the mammoth Belgian-Brazilian beveridge conglomerate, InBev, headquartered in Leuven, Belgium. Those appliances in your kitchen or laundry room that bear one of the most familiar names in American consumer history—GE—are manufactured in Louisville, Ky., but the company is majority-owned by a Chinese multinational, Haier, headquartered in Qingdao, China.

The television game show "Jeopardy" is produced by Columbia Pictures Entertainment, which is owned by Japan's Sony Corp., the global electronic and media company. The 7-11 around the corner is owned by a Japanese-American conglomerate whose corporate parent is based in Tokyo.

That bestseller that you read, Stephen King's *The Stand: The Complete and Uncut Edition*, was published by Doubleday & Co., which is owned by Germany's Bertelsmann AG, a global communications company.

The deep-heating ointment you use to ease your aches and pains is made by the Mentholatum Co. Inc., which is owned by Japan's Rohto Pharmaceutical Co. Those tires on your car were made by the iconic American tire-maker BF Goodrich, which is owned by France's Michelin.

The Stroehmann bread you like so much is made by Stroehmann Bakeries, which is owned by Mexico's Bimbo Bakeries.

The locks on your doors are made by Yale, which is owned by Sweden's Assa Abloy, a Swedish conglomerate.

Once, all were American-owned.

To be sure, foreign-controlled corporations in America are still a comparatively small slice—7 percent—of total U.S. business receipts. But from 1979 to 1987, the revenue of foreign-controlled corporations rose from $242 billion to $685 billion—an increase of 183 percent. The revenue of U.S.-owned companies went up only 52 percent.

The growing presence of foreign goods and foreign-owned properties in the United Sates has been accompanied by generous tax breaks that the people in Washington have extended to foreign corporations and foreign investors. Internal Revenue Service data show that companies owned by the Japanese, Germans, British and other foreign interests are claiming far larger deductions on their U.S. tax returns than American companies do.

The oversized write-offs mean that foreign-owned companies are more likely than American companies to file a tax return showing little or no profit. This allows them to pay little or no U.S. income tax. In 1987, only 41 percent of foreign-owned companies reported a profit on their U.S. tax returns. By comparison, 55 percent of U.S. companies showed a profit.

That means that 59 of every 100 foreign-owned companies doing business in the United States reported—for federal income tax purposes—that they lost money. In the case of U.S. businesses, 45 of every 100 said they lost money. A House Ways and Means subcommittee investigation of 36 foreign-owned businesses, including electronics and automobile companies, showed that more than half "paid little or no federal income tax."

One tax break that has proved popular is the net operating loss deduction, which, you may recall, began to grow dramatically in the 1980s. The Ways and Means subcommittee reported that, in one case, an electronics company reported total sales of $4 billion over seven years, but only $15 million in tax liabilities. It turned out that "the company always had net operating losses available to zero out any tax. In 10 years, the company ultimately paid no federal income tax," according to Patrick G. Heck, assistant counsel for the committee.

Revenues of foreign-controlled companies in the United States rose 50 percent from 1984 to 1987. Their taxes went up 2 percent. Japanese-controlled companies in this country have done well, both in boosting their sales and avoiding U.S. income taxes. Their revenue rose 64 percent from 1984 to 1987, from $113 billion to $185 billion. Yet the federal income taxes paid by these Japanese-controlled companies went down rather than up—falling 14 percent, from $1.1 billion in 1984 to $951 million in 1987.

If you enjoyed the same increase in income that the Japanese companies achieved, your annual salary would have gone from, say, $30,000 to $49,200 in those three years. Simultaneously, the federal income taxes you paid would have dropped from $2,729 to $2,347.

Residents of foreign countries who buy and sell stocks, bonds and government securities in this country do even better.

In 1988, residents of Japan collected $8.4 billion from their investments in this country, mostly in interest and dividends. They paid $510.6 million in U.S. income taxes on that money. That is a tax rate of 6.1 percent.

By contrast, American workers with incomes between $40,000 and $50,000 paid taxes at an 11.6 percent rate.

Residents of the United Arab Emirates fared even better. They collected $312.9 million from their American investments. They paid $443,000 in U.S. income taxes. Their tax rate: One-tenth of 1 percent. American workers struggling to achieve a middle-class lifestyle, on the other hand, were taxed at 53 times that rate.

But take a closer look at the deal the U.S. government has arranged with the United Arab Emirates and other countries. In theory, foreigners are taxed lightly on their income in the United States because it is assumed that they pay income taxes in their home countries. That's the theory. Reality is quite different.

The United Arab Emirates, for example, imposes no income taxes on its citizens. It does levy a religious tax. But, as one U.S. government tax official explained: "They have no enforcement mechanism. No reporting. You're just supposed to pay it because (of) your conscience. My understanding is it's a rather modest tax in terms of collection."

Let us review: If you have $1,000 in your passbook savings account, you must pay income tax on the interest you receive. If a resident of the United Arab Emirates has $1 million in the same bank, that person pays no U.S. income tax on the interest.

Overall, wealthy residents and corporations in foreign countries collected $31.8 billion, mostly in interest and dividends, from their U.S. investments in 1988. They paid $1.7 billion in U.S. income taxes. That's a tax rate of 5.3 percent—less than the 5.8 percent rate paid by Americans who earn $7,000 to $9,000 a year.

Viewed another way: American workers who earned between $30,000 and $40,000 in 1987 paid, on average, $3,710 in income tax. If they had been taxed at the same rate that Congress granted residents of the United Arab Emirates, their average tax bill would have totaled $49.

UPDATE

The trend we spotted in 1992—provisions that allow wealthy foreigners to pay income taxes at a lower rate on dividends and interest from U.S. stocks and bonds than middle-income families pay on wages—persists.

Residents of countries with which the U.S. does not have a tax treaty earned $128.7 billion in income from U.S. sources in 2012, according to IRS data. On that income they paid taxes of $4.3 billion—a tax rate of 3.3 percent. Middle-class individuals and families earning from $75,000 to $100,000 paid taxes at a rate of 13.5 percent that year.

How is all this possible? There are a number of interwoven reasons, all related to the government rule book:

Enactment of laws and regulations to encourage an uncontrolled global economy. Outdated tax-treaty concepts. The State Department's long practice of catering to special foreign interests. The

FOREIGN COMPANIES GET LOW TAX BILLS

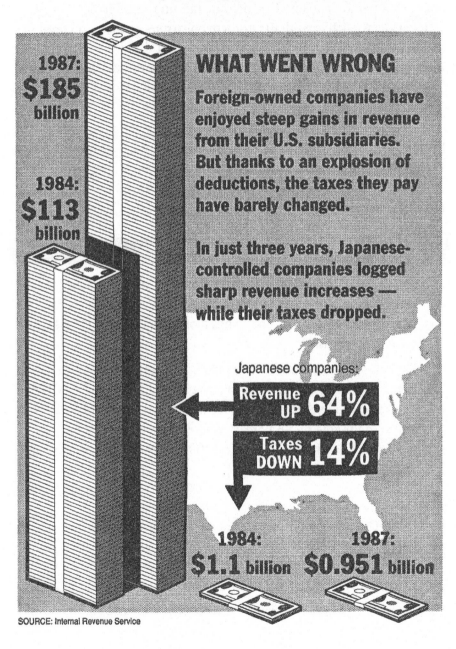

1987:
$185
billion

1984:
$113
billion

WHAT WENT WRONG

Foreign-owned companies have enjoyed steep gains in revenue from their U.S. subsidiaries. But thanks to an explosion of deductions, the taxes they pay have barely changed.

In just three years, Japanese-controlled companies logged sharp revenue increases — while their taxes dropped.

Japanese companies:

Revenue UP **64%**

Taxes DOWN **14%**

1984:
$1.1 billion

1987:
$0.951 billion

SOURCE: Internal Revenue Service

> We spotlighted how foreign-owned companies operating in the
> U.S. made a lot of money in the '80s but barely paid taxes. That's
> continued. Foreign-owned companies operating in the U.S. reported
> revenue of $4.9 trillion in 2015, but paid taxes on only about
> 1 percent of their revenue – $51 billion. With revenues of $800
> billion, Japanese companies paid taxes at a rate of even less than 1
> percent that year.
>
> Source: Internal Revenue Service

IRS's inability to commit sufficient resources to audit corporate tax returns in general and foreign-owned corporations in particular. And the complexity of the Internal Revenue Code.

For some measure of that complexity, consider one aspect of a business that operates globally—the pricing and sale of products among affiliated companies. Let's say the Global Widget Co. manufactures a part used in making widgets at a factory in a country with a low corporate tax rate, say 10 percent. It costs Global Widget $5 to make the part, which it sells to its U.S. subsidiary for $50. The U.S. subsidiary, in turn, sells the part to the American public for $55.

The United States subsidiary books a profit of $5 on the widget part and pays taxes, after deduction of expenses, at a 34 percent rate.

Global Widget's plant reports a profit of $45 in the low-tax country, where the part is produced, and pays taxes, after deduction of expenses, at a 10 percent rate.

So it is that corporations constantly shift their costs to countries with high tax rates, in order to maximize their deductions, while they shift their profits to low-tax havens to keep tax payments down.

UPDATE

The big 2017 tax bill richly rewarded U.S. corporations that
earn profits overseas. For decades, to avoid federal taxes, many
corporations had parked profits from their foreign operations in

offshore bank accounts out of reach of the IRS. As long as the money stayed offshore it wasn't taxed. It was all perfectly legal.

But as time passed and overseas profits began to pile up in ever greater amounts, reaching the astronomical sum of $2.5 trillion—an amount greater than the budgets of all the states combined—the companies began to lobby Congress for special treatment. Claiming they were victims of an unfair tax, they lobbied to bring the money back to the U.S. at a more favorable rate than the statutory 35 percent rate that corporations theoretically had to pay on domestic earnings.

In 2004, they struck gold. Congress approved a one-time tax break that let them bring $312 billion of this money into the U.S. at the miniscule tax rate of 5.25 percent, much lower than the prevailing corporate tax rate of 35 percent and even lower than the tax rate applying to individuals and families earning $30,000 to $40,000. In exchange, the companies promised to invest the repatriated money in plant and equipment to create jobs in the U.S.

But that didn't happen. A Senate subcommittee concluded in 2011 that the major beneficiaries of the tax forgiveness were a handful of corporations and their executives who pocketed tens of millions of dollars in stock options. There was no surge in new hires. There was no dramatic increase in plant construction. The subcommittee determined that the $312-billion tax gift provided no significant economic boost to the U.S. economy.

Guess what happened next? The money started piling up again in offshore accounts, and corporations again started complaining about the unfairness of the U.S. tax system that wouldn't let them bring that money back without a big tax bill, and how those offshore dollars, if brought back, could invigorate the U.S. economy.

Despite evidence that the previous tax holiday had done virtually nothing for the economy, Donald Trump campaigned in 2016 on behalf of another such tax break, claiming it would cause "all of this money to come back into our country" and "turn America into a magnet for new jobs."

In 2017, corporations struck gold again. The Tax Cuts and Jobs Act, with its myriad of corporate tax breaks and tax cuts for the wealthy, included a provision to allow corporations to bring back their offshore profits in existing accounts at a lower rate —15.5 percent— than the prevailing rate. Even better, the 2017 law set a new tax rate for all future foreign profits returned to the U.S.–zero.

A jubilant President Trump predicted: "We expect to have in excess of $4 trillion brought back very shortly. This is money that would never, ever be seen again by the workers and the people of our country."

A lot of that money did come back, but not to workers.

The Federal Reserve reported in 2019 that of the $777 billion repatriated, the bulk was "associated with a sharp increase in share buybacks." Translation: Companies spent their tax windfall buying their own stock. By reducing the number of shares in circulation, a buyback usually increases the value of the remaining shares and often leads to an increase in dividend payments as there are fewer shares to reward. One way or another, a stock buyback benefits the company's executives and shareholders—not its employees.

Exporting Jobs

Diverting operations and tax write-offs to the best possible locale was invented by U.S. companies, with the assistance of members of Congress who rewrote the government rule book in 1976 to encourage the practice. They did so when they amended the Internal Revenue Code to provide tax credits for American companies that established subsidiaries in U.S. possessions, notably Puerto Rico, where the islanders are U.S. citizens.

In essence, the provision allows subsidiaries to transfer profits from Puerto Rico to their parent companies in the United States without paying taxes on those profits. Thus, the U.S. government will provide a tax break to a company if it terminates the jobs, say, of 800 workers in Elkhart, Ind., who earn an average of $13 an hour. That is, the company will get the tax break if, at least in part, it replaces the $13-an-hour workers in Elkhart with $6-an-hour workers at a plant it builds in Puerto Rico.

Meet George Skelton. He was one of 800 production workers at the Whitehall Laboratories plant in Elkhart until April 1991. That was the month his job was eliminated. On Nov. 1, 1991, Whitehall Laboratories, a division of American Home Products Corp., closed the Elkhart plant permanently; the last of the 800 still on the job were thrown out of work.

Some of the products once manufactured there began coming from a new facility in Guayama, Puerto Rico. As for American Home Products, the Puerto Rican subsidiary allowed the company to escape payment of millions of dollars in U.S. income taxes, not to mention saving millions of dollars in salaries.

Said the 52-year-old Skelton: "All the companies that have moved down there, so far as I know, are good, healthy, rich companies. It's like giving welfare to the rich, the way I'm looking at it. Robbing from the poor and giving it to the rich."

For that, thank members of Congress and the 1976 Tax Reform Act that amended the tax code. While provisions in the Internal Revenue Code encouraging investment in Puerto Rico date to 1921, the 1976 law added a twist that led to a corporate stampede to the island.

Under the old law, the subsidiary of a U.S. company operating in Puerto Rico had to pay federal income taxes on its profits earned there when it transferred the profits back to this country. In other words, a company could accumulate its profits, year after year, on the island, and pay no U.S. income tax. But taxes had to be paid when the subsidiary paid dividends to its parent company. The new law exempted the dividends—or profits in Puerto Rico—from the U.S. income tax and allowed the profits to be shipped back to the United States tax-free.

There is no comparable tax provision for individual taxpayers. If there were, it would go something like this: If you had two jobs, one in Chicago and the other in Gary, Ind., you would pay federal income taxes only on the money you earned in Gary. The money you earned in Chicago would be tax-free.

Since passage of the 1976 tax act, corporations have terminated the jobs of tens of thousands of factory workers in the United States, replaced them with lower-paid workers in the possessions, mostly Puerto Rico, and escaped payment of billions of dollars in federal income and other taxes. Pharmaceutical companies in particular have embraced this provision. So much so that Puerto Rico boasts the world's largest concentration of drug companies.

The effect on U.S. mainland workers may be measured in announcements by pharmaceutical companies.

In 1987, Du Pont Co. announced that it planned to transfer production of prescription drugs from a plant in Garden City, N.Y., to a plant in Puerto Rico—and terminate the jobs of 168 Garden City workers.

In 1988, then-SmithKline Beckman Corp. announced that it would transfer production of prescription drugs from Philadelphia to Puerto Rico—and terminate the jobs of 800 Philadelphia production workers.

In 1990, Bristol-Myers Squibb Co. announced that it would transfer production of a cardiovascular drug from a plant in New Brunswick, N.J., to Puerto Rico—and terminate the jobs of 500 New Brunswick workers.

Let's look at one company, American Home Products, a New York-based health-care conglomerate that had sales of nearly $7 billion in 1990. Its Whitehall Laboratories division manufactures non-prescription products with such familiar names as Advil and Anacin-3, Preparation H and Dristan.

In February 1989, American Home Products told stockholders that "completion of a new facility in Puerto Rico in the fourth quarter of 1988 ... will enable Whitehall to achieve significant cost efficiencies while maintaining the highest manufacturing standards."

In October 1990, American Home Products announced that within one year it intended to close the Whitehall plant in Elkhart and transfer some of the work to its new plant in Puerto Rico. Among the products to be manufactured in Puerto Rico: Anacin, Dristan, Denorex and Advil.

The move exacted a heavy toll on the Elkhart workers, whose average length of service was 15 years. More than half the production workers were women. A survey showed that after one year, of 100 employees laid off only about half had found other work. In many cases, they were forced to accept part-time employment. Their average pay was $6 an hour. Before, it was $13.40. When they worked at Whitehall, they had good benefits, including company-paid health insurance. By one estimate, 70 percent of the Elkhart workers lost their medical insurance when the plant closed in November 1991.

George Skelton, who lost his job in 1991, is among those who can attest to the plummeting wages. It took five months before he found another manufacturing job, operating an injection-molding machine in a rubber company. At Whitehall Laboratories, he earned $13.40 an hour. In his new job, he earned $7 an hour. How many former coworkers does he know who were able to find new jobs that matched their Whitehall salaries?

"Basically," he said, "everybody that's found a job I know of is (making) half or less than what they were making (at Whitehall)."

Mary Soellinger, who worked at Whitehall eight years, did not even do that well. Laid off early in 1991, by year's end she still had not been able to find work.

"I suppose I could probably get in at McDonald's," she said, "but I really don't feel that it is fair to push people into minimum-wage jobs, because you can't live on minimum wages."

But Mary Soellinger and George Skelton's loss—and the loss of the other Elkhart workers—is American Home Products' gain. Listen to the words of Smith Barney, Harris Upham & Co., a Wall Street investment firm that reported in April 1990 on the tax good-fortunes of American Home Products: "In 1985, American Home Products initiated tax-sheltered manufacturing in Puerto Rico ... As a result, American Home Products' tax rate declined 13.9 percentage points from 1983 to 1988 ..."

For a personal comparison, if a family with income between $30,000 and $40,000 in 1988 had benefited from a comparable reduction, the taxes they paid would have fallen from $3,708 to $2,558—a savings of $1,150.

Companies long have called investors' attention to the reduced tax rates they enjoy on their Puerto Rican operations. In January 1990, the Rorer Group Inc., then known as Rhone-Poulenc S.A., a pharmaceutical manufacturer headquartered in Fort Washington, Penn., whose products include Maalox, reported that its profits were up and its tax rate was down: "Rorer's results were positively affected by a lower effective tax rate, which was 31 percent for 1989, compared with 35 percent in 1988. This reduction in rate was achieved primarily as a result of further tax benefits from manufacturing in Puerto Rico."

In 1991, the Upjohn Co., a pharmaceutical and health-care company headquartered in Kalamazoo, Mich., announced record second-quarter sales of $859 million, a profit before taxes of $175 million and a lower tax rate. Commenting on its tax outlook for the rest of the year, Upjohn reported: "The estimated annual effective tax rate for 1991 is 27 percent, compared to 32 percent a year ago. The lower rate resulted primarily from a greater proportion of total earnings from low-tax Puerto Rican operations and a lesser proportion of foreign income taxed at relatively higher rates."

George Skelton, whose annual income was sliced almost in half, had difficulty understanding the Washington wisdom underlying the tax break: "Everybody says, 'Well, they're (Puerto Rico) just like a state.' Well, they're not just like a state. Cause they don't pay taxes. And our states sure in hell don't get those kind of tax breaks.

"In my opinion, either you're in the game or you're out of the game. To me, they ought to be able to become a state, or else, if they're not a state, they ought to be treated like a foreign country. They ought to have tariffs put on them and they should have to pay taxes on their profits and everything.

"We're headed toward a $5-trillion national debt. And $350-billion-a-year deficits. And yet we're giving tax breaks to corporations like that to take jobs that would be paying toward that debt. It looks like a hell of a situation for our children and our grandchildren."

How much is the Puerto Rican tax rule costing you?

According to Treasury Department data, companies claiming the possessions tax credit escaped payment of $14 billion in income taxes during the 1980s. For the U.S. government to make up that lost revenue required every penny in tax paid by all middle-class taxpayers in Santa Rosa, Calif., Lakeland, Fla., and Portland, Maine, through the 1980s. And then some.

But what about all the new jobs created in Puerto Rico with that tax money?

Well, in the pharmaceutical industry alone, the lost tax revenue to the U.S. government adds up to $60,000 for every $6-an-hour job created. Thus, it would be cheaper for the U.S. government—and all American taxpayers—to send annual subsistence checks to those island residents who work for American drug companies, and keep the jobs here. In other words, Congress is spending $60,000 of taxpayers' money to eliminate one job in the United States that pays $28,000 a year and to create one job in Puerto Rico that pays $12,000.

While United States companies are exporting ever more jobs, the growing foreign influence in this country is showing up in other, more subtle ways. Take patents, for example.

For American business, the year 1986 represented a first. The first time a foreign-owned company, Hitachi Ltd., secured more patents from the U.S. Patent Office than an American-owned company. It has been downhill ever since.

In 1977, according to statistics compiled by the U.S. Patent and Trademark Office, the 10 corporations that received the largest number of patents broke down this way: Seven were American-owned. Three were foreign-owned. By 1989, those statistics were reversed. Seven of the top 10 corporate patent-holders were foreign-owned. Only three were American-owned.

In 1977, the top four companies were General Electric Co., ranked No. 1 with 822 patents for the year; followed by IBM, Westinghouse Electric Corp. and Xerox Corp.

In 1989, the four American companies were replaced at the top of the list by four foreign companies—all Japanese. Hitachi headed the list with 1,053 patents, followed by Toshiba Corp., Canon Inc. and Fuji Photo Film Co. Ltd. GE had fallen to the No. 5 slot, and IBM had dropped to No. 9. Between 1977 and 1989, four American companies disappeared from the ranks of the top 10: Westinghouse, Xerox, A.T.&T. and DuPont Co.

The makeup of the foreign companies on the list also had changed significantly. In 1977, two companies were German, one was Dutch.

There were no Japanese companies. By 1989, there were five Japanese companies among the top 10, one German, one Dutch.

While the Japanese and other foreign nations are churning out patents for new technologies and products, the United States, courtesy of the government rule book, is churning out something else: master of business administration degrees (MBAs).

All through the 1970s and 1980s, American colleges and universities turned out ever larger numbers of MBAs, a process that coincided with the steady erosion of the country's once-dominant manufacturing base. During the 1970s, MBA graduates outnumbered advanced-engineering graduates 36,600 to 16,100 a year. The opposite was true during the 1950s, a period of middle-class prosperity. On average, 4,700 advanced degrees in engineering were awarded each year, compared with 3,800 MBAs.

In the 1980s, the gap exploded as business schools turned out 64,200 graduates yearly while engineering schools produced only 20,000. Many of the 20,000 were foreign nationals who received their diplomas in this country and returned to their native lands.

Let's summarize the degrees and the numbers. Advanced engineering graduates do the kind of work that leads to new technologies and products, which in turn lead to the creation of new manufacturing jobs that pay middle-class wages.

MBAs do the kind of work that leads to new financial products—including assorted credit instruments like junk bonds—which in turn lead to the creation of a few high-paying professional positions, a lot of low-paying clerical jobs and, quite often, the elimination of manufacturing and other jobs.

So, from the 1950s to the 1980s, the number of advanced engineering graduates rose 326 percent, from an annual average of 4,700 to 20,000. During the same time, the number of MBAs spiraled 1,589 percent, from an annual average of 3,800 to 64,200.

It was a trend the Japanese did not rush to copy. In 1989, Japanese universities awarded nearly 12,000 advanced degrees in engineering, compared with 1,000 MBAs.

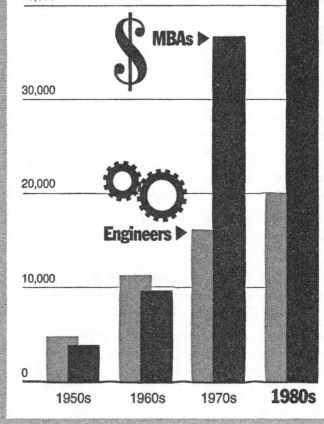

American academic emphasis: Money over engineering

In the 1950s, more graduates were awarded master's degrees in engineering than in business management.
In the 1980s, MBAs outnumbered engineers by more than 3 to 1.

Average number of degrees per year:

64,200

MBAs ▶

Engineers ▶

40,000

30,000

20,000

10,000

0

1950s 1960s 1970s **1980s**

SOURCE: National Education Association

MBA degrees continue to be awarded at a much greater rate than advanced engineering degrees. When we wrote about this issue in 1992, the U.S. was awarding roughly 40,000 more MBA degrees a year than advanced engineering. By 2018, the gap had grown to 125,000 more MBA degrees than engineering.

Source: National Center for Education Statistics

Akio Morita, the chairman of Sony Corp. and one of Japan's most innovative corporate leaders, understands the competition well: "Americans make money by playing 'money games,' namely, mergers and acquisitions, by simply moving money back and forth ... instead of creating and producing goods with some actual value."

 UPDATE

Wall Street continues to hatch risky schemes such as Credit Default Swaps which led to the Great Recession of 2008.

Global Moneymen—Beyond the Law

With the touch of a computer keyboard, an army of global moneymen move money, commodities and information around the world in the blink of an eye, erasing traditional boundaries among nations.

The crude oil in a supertanker bound from the Middle East to the United States, for example, may change owners a half-dozen times before it ends up as gas in your car. Each change in ownership is accompanied by a change in price—and the final price in the chain is the price you pay at the neighborhood gas station.

The electronic financiers have insulated themselves from regulation by the U.S. government and found ways to bend the rules to their benefit. From abroad, they have more opportunities than dealmakers on U.S. soil to escape payment of taxes either by legal or illegal means; engage in business practices that otherwise would be considered harmful to the best interests of American consumers and workers; avoid prosecution for financial crimes, and continue to do business with the U.S. government.

So it is that although Marc Rich most likely never set foot in Ravenswood, W.Va., he had a powerful impact on the town of 4,100, and its bitter labor dispute.

The trouble started in 1989 when the town's largest employer, the aluminum smelting plant, was purchased in a leveraged buyout—the third change of ownership in the 1980s. On Feb. 7, 1989, the plant was acquired by Ravenswood Aluminum Corp., a newly formed company whose stock was owned by Stanwich Partners Inc., a Stamford, Conn.-based investment company. Under Charles E. Bradley, Stanwich acquired interests in a wide range of companies in the 1980s, from steel distribution to metal fabrication.

But Ravenswood was not a typical leveraged buyout financed by junk bonds or bank loans. The money came from a mysterious source in Switzerland—Ridgeway Commercial AG. According to loan documents filed in a West Virginia courthouse, Ridgeway provided $260 million in loans for the buyout.

Ridgeway's official address was in Hergiswil, a scenic hamlet of 2,400 people on the shores of Lake Lucerne. Its U.S. address was "Clarendon, Ltd., Stamford, Conn."—the U.S. office of Marc Rich's international trading company, Clarendon Ltd., based in Zug, Switzerland.

The fine print of the loan documents disclosed yet another Rich connection. The preferred stock in Ravenswood Aluminum was held by a Dutch company whose president, Willy R. Strothotte, was one of Marc Rich's closest lieutenants, and whose office was in the same Zug office building where Rich and his companies were housed.

Just months after the Ravenswood plant was sold, Strothotte, the Rich executive, and another Rich associate acquired a majority of the stock in the company from Stanwich Partners, with Strothotte picking up the larger share. The ownership change set the stage for a labor dispute that would turn family member against family member in Ravenswood.

In the spring of 1990, months before negotiations were to begin on a new labor contract with the steelworkers union, the Ravenswood company implemented procedures that made a labor showdown seem inevitable. The plant was encircled with a 10-foot-high fence topped with barbed wire. Security cameras were installed. Office windows were boarded up. An armed security force was employed. Boxcars of food and mobile homes were brought into the plant, and salaried employees were drilled in security procedures. And ads began to appear in out-of-state newspapers for replacement workers. Not surprisingly, little progress was made toward a new contract that fall, and on Nov. 1, 1990, when the agreement expired, employees were turned away when they came to work. The company called it a strike; the aluminum workers call it a lockout.

The National Labor Relations Board (NLRB) agreed with the union and formally charged Ravenswood Aluminum on July 18, 1991, with refusing to bargain in good faith and for illegally locking out its employees. While the case worked its way through the administrative-hearing process, the company hired 1,100 workers to replace the locked-out employees, a move that led to scores of incidents of violence.

The shutdown was a financial disaster for the 1,700 employees of Ravenswood, many of whom, like Toby Johnson, had been employed there all their working lives. The son of a Ravenswood Aluminum retiree, Johnson went to work at the plant straight out of high school. He worked in the finishing department, where aluminum is cut into sheets for cans, automotive components or other products.

Like other Ravenswood workers, Johnson exhausted his unemployment benefits. After that, he and his wife and 13-year-old son existed largely on $35 a week in food vouchers from the United Steelworkers Union and provisions from the union-run food bank.

"Basically, we eat what they give you instead of going out to the store and buying what you want ... which you can't afford," Johnson said. "We have had to cut a lot of corners." When they need cash, they dipped into savings or were helped by relatives.

The hardest part for Johnson and other employees is what the shutdown has done to the community and to their own families. Ravenswood Aluminum hired many replacement workers from the town, putting neighbors and family members on opposite sides of a bitter issue.

"It's put a real strain on the community and individual families," Johnson said. "It's wrecked homes. There is brother out against brother. There is a father who's locked out and the son is working. It has worked on everybody emotionally and physically."

Johnson said the issue has touched his own family. A niece is married to a replacement worker. He said his father allows the man to visit the home.

"He keeps letting him come to his house, which I disapprove of," said Johnson. "He still comes there so I don't go there to my own parents' house. So it has really messed us up in our relationship."

 UPDATE

The Ravenswood lockout turned out to be a major victory for the United Steelworkers Union at a time when unions were winning few big victories on the picket line.

After locking out workers and cutting off their pay for 20 months, Ravenswood Aluminum Corp. capitulated, fired the CEO who it was felt had prolonged the dispute and signed a new contract with the plant's 1,700 workers.

After the strike, Marc Rich sold his interest amd ownership of the plant further changed hands in subsequent years.

While Rich's ties to Ravenswood Aluminum were shrouded in mystery during the strike, his ties to the broader economy were hiding in plain sight: the pennies and nickels found in most everyone's pockets, products of the U.S. Mint, which awarded millions of dollars worth of contracts for copper and nickel to Clarendon Metals over the years.

When we asked about the U.S. government's business relationship with Clarendon and Rich's association with the company, a spokesman for the Mint said. "The information that the United States Mint has on Clarendon comes from Clarendon. So what we would prefer you to do is to go to them and inquire. Is that fair? Because we would just be recounting to you what they have told us."

Let's make the Rich-U.S. government associations clear: Rich sold copper to the U.S. Mint, a branch of the Treasury Department, while the Internal Revenue Service, another branch of the Treasury Department, and the Department of Justice, in theory, sought to bring him to trial on tax-evasion charges—but not seeking too hard.

Rich gradually faded from the memories of law enforcement officials. When a telephone call was placed to the FBI in Washington to ask if there was a "Wanted" poster for Marc Rich, the following exchange took place in 1991 with a specialist on fugitives:

FBI representative: "I've heard the name before. I don't believe so. Is he wanted in this country?"

Author: "Yes."

FBI representative: "Are you trying to get a hold of the poster?"

Author: "Yes, exactly."

FBI representative: "I know the name. It's right on top of my head. It's not coming to me what he's been involved in and where he's wanted."

 UPDATE

Just hours before he left office, on Jan. 20, 2001, President Bill Clinton pardoned Marc Rich, a move that could have allowed Rich to return to the U.S. after years on the run. The pardon set off a firestorm of criticism and speculation as to why Clinton had done it. The most widely accepted explanation was that Denise Rich, the fugitive's former wife and a major Democratic party donor, had persuaded Clinton to grant the pardon.

Rich never returned to the U.S. He continued to live in Switzerland until he died from a stroke in 2013.

Chapter Six

THE HIGH COST OF DEREGULATION

INTRODUCTION

Washington's embrace of economic deregulation has inflicted dreadful consequences on middle-class Americans, costing them jobs, financial security, and in some cases their homes.

The idea sounded so good when this trend started in the late 1970s: Let's streamline government, cut red tape and let companies go about their business without those cumbersome rules from regulatory agencies.

But by retreating from oversight, government deregulation created chaos in industries from airlines to trucking to finance, killing jobs and sticking taxpayers with multi-billion-dollar rescue bills in the financial sector.

Overlooked in the frenzy to cut red tape was that there is a reason for regulations—to maintain stability in those industries and to guard against reckless practices.

What is most troubling is that we as a nation have learned nothing from the chaos of the past. The deregulation fever that started in Congress has spread to federal agencies. The FAA has stood by and allowed airlines to gradually shift major maintenance on their aircraft to low-wage foreign bases where the mechanics, working from English-language manuals, cannot read or speak the language. Whatever inspection is made is done almost solely by the airline's own personnel, not an FAA inspector.

The U.S. Department of Education, rather than monitoring the companies that service the $1.5-trillion student loan program, turned the job over to private companies that have gouged students with fees and fines and made it next to impossible for thousands to ever pay off their loans.

President Trump crows about the regulations he's scrapped, but deregulation is deeply ingrained in Washington, with agencies increasingly reluctant to use their regulatory powers. Rather than taking an active oversight role in approving Boeing's 737 Max, the FAA basically ceded that authority to Boeing, allowing the company to certify as airworthy its automated flight-control system that later was blamed for two crashes that killed 346 people.

One of the few bright spots on the regulatory front for consumers has been the Consumer Financial Protection Board. Conceived by Elizabeth Warren when she was a Harvard law professor, the CFPB was created by Congress in 2010 in response to widespread abuses by banks and other lenders that fueled the Great Recession of 2008.

Under Warren's early influence, the CFPB became an aggressive advocate for consumers who had been victimized by predatory lenders, ruthless debt collectors and unscrupulous mortgage companies. The CFPB cracked down on abusive practices and clawed back $12 billion for distribution to millions of consumers who'd been defrauded.

Bitterly opposed by bankers and conservatives from the start, the CFPB's proactive stance came under more fire when Donald Trump became president. The Trump administration sought to water down its activities and supported legal action to undercut the authority of the agency—renamed the Consumer Financial Protection Bureau—in a case pending in the U.S. Supreme Court at the time of this writing

Wrecking Industries and Lives

In the decade following deregulation of the trucking industry in 1980, more than 100 once-thriving trucking companies went out of business. More than 150,000 workers at those companies lost their jobs.

After deregulation of the airlines in 1978, a dozen airline companies merged or went out of business. More than 50,000 of their employees lost their jobs.

After deregulation of the savings and loan industry in 1982, about 650 thrifts folded, with hundreds more in serious trouble. The bailout left taxpayers stuck with a $125-billion tab.

Then the people who rewrote the government rule book to deregulate airlines, trucking and savings and loans decided to rewrite the rules on banks. They called it banking reform. President Bush spelled out the plans in 1991: "Regulatory reform is long overdue. Our banking reform proposals ... address the reality of the modern financial marketplace by creating a U.S. financial system that protects taxpayers, serves consumers and strengthens our economy."

Sound familiar? It should. The arguments for deregulating banks are much the same as those that were made in the 1970s and 1980s for the other industries: Removing government restrictions on the private sector would let free and open competition rule the marketplace. Getting rid of regulations would spur the growth of new companies. Existing companies would become more efficient or perish. Competition would create jobs, drive down prices and benefit consumers and businesses alike.

That's the theory. The gritty reality, as imposed on the daily lives of the men and women most directly affected, is a little different.

For Christopher E. Neimann of Fort Smith, Ark., deregulation meant the loss of health insurance as he was battling cancer. Neimann, who worked for a trucking company, was diagnosed with a rare bone cancer in November 1987. He went on medical leave two months later. In August 1988, his company, Smith's Transfer Corp., entered bankruptcy, a victim of deregulation's rate wars. Its checks began bouncing, including ones paying for Neimann's treatments at the M.D. Anderson Cancer Center in Houston.

On April 11, 1989, the hospital sent Neimann a stern letter asking him to pay his bill, which totaled $30,128. When the bedridden, gravely ill Neimann couldn't make payments, the hospital began pressuring his wife, Billie.

"The hospital called me one night and told me they were going to dip into the estate," she said. "And he wasn't dead. He was still alive. I knew he was going to die. And they knew he was going to die. I just cried and I said, 'I beg your pardon. Could I ask you what estate are you talking about?' And they said, 'Well, his estate.' And I said,

'Ma'am, at 31 years old, you don't have an estate. You don't have anything to go into an estate. At this age, we're just starting out.' I said, 'You can dip all you want. Dip right in and get some of the bills, too. Because there won't be anything left.'"

After a battle of a year and a half, Neimann died on June 6, 1989, age 31, leaving behind a young wife and an infant daughter. The calls from M.D. Anderson's collection department continued.

"They kept calling and told me that I was still liable," said his wife, who has since remarried. "I was so upset that eventually I talked to my lawyer and he told me to give them his name. I don't know what's happened, but lately they haven't called."

For Leslie Wagner of Flower Mound, Texas, deregulation meant seven years of relentlessly shrinking paychecks—and, ultimately, no paycheck. At 23, she went to work as a flight attendant for Braniff International Airlines. That was in 1969, when the Dallas-based carrier was the nation's eighth largest airline. By 1982, her base salary was $19,300 a year. That year, the fourth year of airline deregulation, Braniff asked workers to accept wage cuts and other concessions.

Even after employees agreed to reductions, Braniff still could not pay its bills and the airline was forced to seek protection in bankruptcy court in May 1982. The action grounded Braniff and put 9,000 employees, including Leslie Wagner, out of work. Two years later, a scaled-down Braniff Inc., under new owners, emerged from bankruptcy court and resumed service. Former employees were offered jobs, but at reduced pay. When Wagner returned to work in 1985, her new base pay was $15,600 a year—19 percent less than she earned in 1982.

By 1989, with Braniff still in financial trouble, employees were asked to take another pay cut. Wagner's base pay went down again—to $14,400. On Sept. 28, 1989, Braniff was forced into bankruptcy court for the second time in seven years. Its assets were auctioned off to pay creditors, and the airline's remaining 4,800 employees were let go. Leslie Wagner was out of work. The company resumed limited service in 1991, but Wagner was not recalled. It didn't matter. Braniff was back in bankruptcy court a month later, for the third time in a decade.

For Joyce D. Heyl of Sioux Falls, S.D., deregulation meant the loss

DEREGULATION'S VICTIMS

WHAT WENT WRONG

Thousands of firms gone. 200,000 jobs lost. Deregulation has been costly to workers and consumers alike.

In the case of the savings and loan industry, the cost to taxpayers will be staggering: the equivalent of every penny of tax paid by every resident of Ohio, Vermont, Washington, South Carolina and New Mexico earning up to $50,000 — for the next 33 years. That's until the year 2025.

THE YEAR
2025
2010
1999
1992

Now, the push is on to deregulate the banking industry.

SOURCE: Projections from U.S. government tax data

The government bailout of banks arising out of the 2008 recession cost taxpayers an estimated $500 billion, according to a Massachusetts Institute of Technology report.

of a job. Heyl worked 19 years in the accounting department of an interstate trucking company, American Freight System Inc., until it went out of business in 1988.

"When you work for a company a long time and you like your job, you always think it's going to be there and then suddenly one day it's not," she said. "I loved my job. I was very upset when the company went down."

Her standard of living went down with it. "I'm 59 years old and I thought to go back into the job market with a lot of young people was something I wouldn't be able to do," she said. To supplement the family income she worked part time at various jobs. At American Freight, she earned $410 a week, or $21,320 a year. Afterward, she was lucky if she earned half that.

For Barbara Joy Whitehouse of Salt Lake City, Utah, deregulation meant a devastating financial blow on top of a personal one. Her husband was killed in a 1986 Montana highway accident while driving a truck for a company called P-I-E Nationwide Inc. After his death, Whitehouse, 54, began receiving $299 a week under Montana's workers' compensation law, which makes payments to spouses of workers killed on the job.

Because P-I-E was a large company and appeared to have considerable assets, Montana authorities permitted it to pay claimants directly rather than contribute to the state's workers' compensation fund, which disburses benefits in most cases.

That was a mistake. P-I-E was not as solid as Montana officials thought. Deregulation was helping drive it, like many other interstate trucking companies, out of business. After huge losses, P-I-E filed for bankruptcy. After the bankruptcy filing, the company ran out of cash and Whitehouse's biweekly checks stopped. P-I-E's last check to her bounced.

Whitehouse filed a claim with the bankruptcy court for $466,440—the amount due her under Montana law if she lived to be 84 and didn't remarry. Her claim was one of more than 7,000 unsecured claims against P-I-E.

"P-I-E knew they owed me $299 per week for life and should have put aside a safe fund to meet this debt," Whitehouse wrote to the bankruptcy court. "They didn't, so now the court wants me to go at the bottom of the list to see if they can offer me what's left after the big guys get their fair share. I am as important as any big company ... This is wrong. My husband dies, the law says they pay me for life and now I have nothing."

UPDATE

Barbara Joy Whitehouse never received a dime from the bankruptcy court that denied her claim for $299 a week that she was counting on for her retirement.

She lived out her life in a mobile home park for seniors just outside Salt Lake City. Her only income, $942 a month from Social Security, was not enough to live on and pay for the expensive medications she needed to treat a variety of her ailments, including lung disease. To supplement her meager income, she scoured her neighborhood for old cans and every two weeks took them to a recycler who paid her $30 for the castoffs.

Barbara Joy Whitehouse died in 2007.

For you, the American taxpayer and consumer, deregulation has meant fewer airlines and higher air fares, more unsafe trucks on the highways, and more of your tax money diverted to pay for the savings and loan debacle. That last one is going to cost you for years to come.

For this, and all the other costs associated with deregulation, human and economic, you can thank the people in Washington who wrote the government rule book, the collection of laws and regulations that provide the framework for the U.S. economy. Changes in the economic rules by a succession of presidents and Congresses have propelled federal, state and local taxes ever higher while forcing middle-class job holders into lower-paying jobs. So it is with deregulation, which has meant lost jobs or pay cuts for employees in the airline and trucking industries and, ultimately, higher taxes for everyone to rescue the savings and loan industry.

Backers predicted a rosy future for airlines and trucking when those industries were deregulated. Few of the benefits they foresaw have come about. Advocates of airline deregulation claimed that it would stimulate competition, reduce fares, open up air travel to more Americans. And in the beginning it seemed as if that would happen.

Freed from government approval to set fares and schedules, the industry eagerly embraced deregulation. New airlines began service and existing carriers extended routes to new points. Fares went down. Service went up. Competition increased. It didn't last. In an unregulated market, those who had the financial muscle to dominate soon did. The big airlines gobbled up the little airlines. New airlines soon found they lacked the financial resources to compete.

As a result, there is less competition in the airline industry than before deregulation. In 1978, the 10 largest airlines accounted for 88 percent of passenger miles flown by U.S. flag carriers. By 1990, the 10 had increased their share of the miles flown to 94 percent. In many markets, there is virtually no competition, and prices reflect it

Even on routes where competition developed after deregulation, ticket prices soared. A one-way ticket on the Eastern shuttle from Washington to New York cost $38 in 1977. By 1991, a ticket cost $142—nearly four times what it did in 1977. If the price of a gallon of unleaded gasoline had gone up at the same rate, it would have cost $2.33 in 1991.

For many air travelers, ticket prices are irrelevant.

They are the people who live in small towns across America that were once served by airlines but no longer are. Paul Stephen Dempsey, a University of Denver law professor who has studied the impact, estimated that more than 130 small communities were dropped from scheduled air service after deregulation.

In summary, under airline deregulation, fares have gone up, not down. Competition became destructive, not productive. Service was cut back. The increase in air travelers was lower in the decade after deregulation than in the decade before it. Cities once served by multiple carriers are now served by one or none. And the airline industry is in shambles.

Nonetheless, the people in Washington have a different view.

Samuel K. Skinner, when he was Secretary of Transportation, offered this assessment in January 1991: "Airline deregulation ... ushered in a decade of competition and consumer savings unsurpassed in the history of the industry. With deregulation having accomplished so much throughout the 1980s, we must stay the course in the coming decade as the industry continues to restructure. Every credible analysis of airline competition in the 1980s has declared deregulation a success."

Judge for yourself.

The year 1990 was the worst financial year in American aviation history as airline losses soared to $3.9 billion.

By late 1991, Pan American, the flagship of U.S. carriers, founded in 1927, was in bankruptcy court and on the verge of liquidation. Eastern Air Lines, founded in 1927, was in bankruptcy court and was being liquidated. Braniff, founded in 1934, was in bankruptcy court for the third time and was on the verge of liquidation. Continental Air Lines, founded in 1937, was in bankruptcy court. Midway Airlines, founded in 1979, was in bankruptcy court and was being liquidated. Trans World Airlines, founded in 1928, couldn't pay its bills and was in bankruptcy court.

And then there's America West Airlines of Phoenix—once considered deregulation's success story. From a modest regional carrier with three jets and 280 employees in 1983, it grew into a nationwide airline with 92 planes and 12,000 employees. With revenues of $1 billion, it moved onto the list of the nation's top 10 airlines in 1990. In 1991 it moved into bankruptcy court.

UPDATE

Today, there is virtually no competition in the skies. Fewer major airlines operate in the U.S. than at any time in the modern history of the industry. Four carriers control 80 percent of the business in the U.S.—American Airlines, Delta Air Lines, Southwest and United Airlines. Gone are TWA, Eastern, Pan Am, Braniff, Continental, Midway and a dozen more. Contrary to claims that deregulation would spur competition from new airlines, no new airline has gone into business since 2007, and that airline, Western, failed the same year.

The consolidation has proven to be painful to many small and medium-sized cities that the federal government no longer requires to be served by airlines, as was the case before deregulation. Although total air traffic has increased, the number of departures from small and non-hub airports has declined by 31.5 percent from 2007 to 2016, according to a *Wall Street Journal* survey.

Hit hardest of all by deregulation have been airline employees, especially pilots and flight attendants, who've seen their earnings and benefits cut back sharply since 1980. Pilots earned a median salary of $67,000 in 1980, according to Labor Department data. If that salary had kept pace with inflation, it would have become $220,000 by 2018. Instead, median salaries of pilots in 2018 were $115,000—or 48 percent less. Flight attendants earned on average $57,000 in 2018 adjusted for inflation—or about 13 percent less than they earned in 1980.

Struggling to Survive

In trucking, it's been a similar story. Rather than making the industry stronger, as congressional backers predicted, deregulation triggered price wars and cutthroat discounting that have destroyed many of the largest companies and weakened others.

More trucking companies failed in the 1980s than in the entire 45 previous years that the Interstate Commerce Commission (ICC) regulated the industry.

Part of the reason, of course, was that there were many more companies scrambling for work. In 1979, the year before deregulation, 186 companies went out of business. Eleven years later, the number had soared to 1,581, the most trucking failures ever recorded in a single year. For the decade, a total of 11,496 failed.

A decade into deregulation, trucking was following a variation on the airline-industry pattern. That is, after an initial burst of competition came a shakeout, with widespread failures that eventually left control of the industry in fewer hands. Meanwhile, though, small, mom-and-pop operators continue to come in, keeping the pressure on.

Trucking industry data show that consolidation underway. Before deregulation, the three largest trucking companies accounted for one-third of the operating revenue of the top 25 companies. In 1991, those three—Roadway Express, Consolidated Freightways and Yellow Freight System Inc.—accounted for about one-half. Nevertheless, advocates of trucking deregulation, like their airline counterparts, contended that it was an unqualified success. "The trucking industry has saved millions of dollars through more efficient operations allowed and stimulated by deregulation ... The benefits to consumers from deregulation exceeded our fondest dreams," Darius W. Gaskins Jr., former chairman of the ICC, told a House committee in 1989.

A 1990 study by the Brookings Institution, a Washington, D.C., think tank, echoed this view: "Surface freight deregulation (trucking and rail) has been extremely beneficial to shippers and to their customers. Total annual benefits from rate and service changes amount to $20 billion." While companies that hire truckers profited from lower rates, there was no economic data showing that the cost savings were passed along to consumers. There is substantial economic data, however, showing that the cost savings to shippers have come at workers' expense.

Indeed, what happened to those workers provides a glimpse into the future for employees in other industries, both blue collar and white collar. Corporate restructuring and downsizing led to layoffs and the elimination of benefits. But the most pervasive trend—one that seems to be growing—is that which forces workers into lower-paying jobs.

Sometimes it happens across a broad industry. Three jobs that pay, say, $30,000, are eliminated and six jobs that pay $15,000 are created. The government statistics show a gain in jobs, but often fail to disclose the decline in wages. Similarly, workers in other companies are compelled to accept pay cuts in return for keeping their jobs.

Consider the pay of flight attendants. In 1983, according to data compiled by the Association of Flight Attendants, their average annual salary was $28,847. Six years later, in 1989, it had declined to $27,160. That represented an average pay cut of 6 percent at a time when living costs shot up 24 percent. Some, like Leslie Wagner, took even deeper pay cuts.

During those same years, the people who write the government rule book—and who revised the laws that ultimately led to lower salaries for airline employees—increased their own salaries 48 percent. The pay of members of Congress went from $60,662 in 1983 to $89,500 in 1989. The $28,838 increase alone exceeded the full salary of flight attendants.

For truckers, the 1980s were a dismal time. Between 1980 and 1990, the number of employees increased 248,000, rising from 1.242 million to 1.490 million. Average yearly earnings went from $18,400 to $23,400, the government says.

What those figures fail to disclose: During the years when total employment rose, more than 100 of the big, established trucking companies folded. With them went more than 150,000 jobs. These were the higher-paying trucking jobs—drivers with seniority and company-paid benefits, such as health insurance and pensions. Many of those truckers earned solid, middle-class wages—$30,000 or more.

Deregulation brought an influx of one-owner shoestring trucking operations, which cut into the business of those established companies. Jobs at these small operations paid less. So it was that deregulation eliminated two jobs that paid, say, $30,000, and created three jobs that paid $20,000 or less.

Just as misleading are the earnings reported by the government. In 1990, trucking industry workers earned, on average, $23,400 a year, according to the Bureau of Labor Statistics (BLS). But the government excludes one major category of truckers from its figures—self-employed drivers. And their earnings generally are lower than those for drivers employed by major companies.

"We don't really have any data on how many there are," said a BLS official. "An individual in business for himself is technically not covered by our study." A spokesman for the ICC said that the agency does not know how many owner-operators exist. "I'm not sure we have ever had an accurate count," he said.

The Owner-Operators Independent Drivers Association, the largest trade group representing individual drivers, estimates there are 350,000 to 400,000 owner-operators. Based on surveys by its magazine, *Landline*, the association estimated the annual income, after expenses, of owner-operators at $20,000 a year, or $385 a week, according to Sandi Laxson of the drivers' group.

"Deregulation has been a nightmare for our people," said Laxson. "I remember my uncle was a truck driver 20 years ago and, wow, he made a lot of money. He was on the road all the time. But his wife drove a nice car and they had a nice house. Now, drivers are struggling to survive."

The source of the upheaval in the trucking industry is the Motor Carrier Act of 1980, which changed the rules that had governed trucking for half a century. Responding to criticism that the ICC's rules had frustrated competition and discouraged new companies from entering the business, Congress scaled back the agency's powers, making entry easier and giving truckers more freedom to set rates.

President Jimmy Carter summed up the high hopes when he signed the law in July 1980: "The Motor Carrier Act of 1980 will eliminate the red tape and the senseless overregulation that have hampered the free growth and development of the American trucking industry."

Undoubtedly, the ICC, like its counterpart in the airline industry, the Civil Aeronautics Board (CAB), had stifled competition and discouraged innovation. Rather than correct the defects in the regulatory system, Congress chose instead to throw out the entire system, thereby ushering in an era of economic anarchy for which no one was prepared. It was somewhat akin to eliminating the referees in a football game because of flawed calls, instead of merely replacing them.

As promised, the law unleashed new competition—on a scale unforeseen and with an intensity that became destructive. New trucking companies surged into the industry by the thousands. Most were one-person operations. By 1979, the year before deregulation, the ICC had granted operating licenses to 17,000 interstate carriers. By 1990, that number stood at 45,000. The ICC granted more operating certificates in the 1980s than in the previous 45 years it regulated the industry. From being an agency that exercised tight control over truck licensing, the ICC essentially rubber-stamped applications.

Yet while the number of companies more than doubled, there was no corresponding increase in the volume of freight hauled. Too many trucks were suddenly chasing too little freight. Total inter-city tonnage increased just 11 percent, from 2.26 billion tons in 1980 to 2.5 billion tons in 1989. Thus, more than twice as many ICC-approved companies were competing for roughly the same amount of freight.

The trucking glut led to desperate rate wars as truckers scrambled to survive. With each round of rate cuts, many longtime companies found themselves awash in red ink. As losses mounted, companies whose trucks had long been familiar names on American highways began to vanish. Even companies that initially thought they would benefit from deregulation were destroyed by it.

When the parent corporation of American Freight System Inc., one of the nation's largest trucking companies, based in Overland Park, Kan., acquired another old-line interstate carrier, Smith's Transfer Corp. of Staunton, Va., in 1987, it sought to allay concerns of Smith employees about being absorbed by another company. In an Oct. 2, 1987, letter, American Freight welcomed the Smith workers into the new company, citing numerous fringe benefits—profit-sharing, pension and health and welfare plans—to which they would be entitled.

"Your economic security has been made more certain," the letter said. "American Freight System is a financially viable carrier with a secure future in the deregulated motor carrier industry." Nine months later, American Freight filed for bankruptcy court protection. The action threw 9,300 people out of work, closed 258 trucking terminals across the nation and idled 17,000 trucks and trailers. The company has since been liquidated.

For trucking companies still in business, the outlook is grim. Many that have survived deregulation's rate wars are just getting by. Profit margins have been squeezed. Equipment is neglected or pushed to the limit.

So many carriers are entering and leaving the industry that the Federal Highway Administration has been unable to keep pace with safety inspections of interstate carriers. The inspections are required by the Motor Carrier Safety Act of 1984, which was aimed at reducing trucking accidents. A 1991 report of the General Accounting Office noted: Federal Highway Administration "workload data show that the number of carriers entering the marketplace in any one month can exceed the number that underwent safety reviews."

For those vehicles that the highway agency did inspect, the GAO said, "70 percent ... received a less-than-satisfactory rating."

That comes as little surprise to DeWayne Snow. The owner of Snow's Welding & Truck Repair Inc. in Tyler, Texas, 100 miles east of Dallas, Snow does repair work for both large and small trucking companies.

"It's real tough on them right now," Snow said. "They don't fix anything they don't have to ... They'll bargain over everything. They even say to you, 'Can I bring in some used parts?'"

As companies fought to stay in business after deregulation, they struggled to cut costs. Usually that meant reducing the wages and benefits of workers. This sometimes was accomplished, curiously enough, through a program intended to broaden ownership— Employee Stock Ownership Plans, or ESOPs.

Created by Congress in 1974, ESOPs have become more and more popular with a wide spectrum of American corporations. Proponents say that ESOPs give workers a voice in their company's operations and make them feel committed to its success. In the trucking industry, though, ESOPs were used as a device to persuade employees to accept pay cuts. In return for wage reductions of up to 15 percent, workers received stock in the company. If the firm prospered, they were told, their stock would appreciate in value and they would earn back what they had given up. That was the theory, anyway.

Contrary to the image of American labor as uncompromising on bread-and-butter issues, trucking industry workers went along— usually overwhelmingly so—with virtually every request of financially strapped employers for wage cuts in exchange for ESOPs. Since 1980, more than two dozen ESOPs financed by worker wage cuts have been adopted by large trucking companies. With few exceptions, the companies failed anyway.

The first major trucking company to adopt an ESOP was Transcon Lines Inc. of Los Angeles, a carrier with terminals in 45 states. The plan, approved at Transcon in 1983, was widely hailed as an example of labor and management cooperation. A remarkable 88 percent of Transcon's 4,000 employees agreed to reduce their wages by 12 percent for five years in return for 49 percent of the company's stock.

Financial analysts loved the deal. Said William H. Legg, a transportation analyst with Alex Brown & Sons Inc. of Baltimore: "Without the ESOP, Transcon wouldn't have been able to put enough capital into the company to stay even with the more well-heeled carriers."

The Transcon example soon spread through trucking, as one carrier after another secured wage cutbacks from workers in return for stock in the company. In the spring of 1989, amid much fanfare, Transcon distributed 2.5 million shares of stock to its workers, signaling the successful conclusion of the plan. Calling the ESOP an "unqualified success," Orin Neiman, Transcon's chairman, paid tribute to the workers who now owned almost half of the company's stock.

"The ESOP helped the company through years of fierce price competition and saved Transcon and 4,000 jobs that otherwise would have been lost," Neiman said. One year later, Transcon was out of business.

With the ICC's approval, the company was sold in 1990 to a Florida-based real estate company. Later that year, Transcon closed its doors and entered federal bankruptcy court in Los Angeles. Its trucks, trailers and terminals were later sold.

Virginia Oates, who worked for Transcon in Charlotte, N.C., remembers the last day. "The company I worked for, Transcon Lines, was involved in a hostile takeover on April 20, 1990," she wrote the ICC. "The takeover transpired at 4:50 p.m., Friday, April 20, 1990, without any advance notice to the employees of Transcon Lines from anyone. All personnel, except the salesmen, were advised to take all their personal things with them as they left that day." A Transcon employee for 15 years, Oates—and 4,000 Transcon workers nationwide—were suddenly out of work. The stock they had bought with $50 million of their wages was virtually worthless.

"It is hard for me to believe that the ICC has done their public duty in this case," wrote Oates.

More than 800 trucking companies went out of business in 2019, throwing thousands of drivers out of work. Some companies shut down so abruptly that their drivers were still on the road. This failure rate reflects the chronic financial chaos that dominates the trucking industry thanks to Congress and previous administrations.

Since Congress deregulated the industry in 1980, literally tens of thousands of trucking companies have gone out of business. More bankruptcies may be on the horizon even for large companies; in 2019 one of trucking's largest carriers, the Celadon Group, filed the largest bankruptcy in the history of the industry.

The chaotic nature of deregulated trucking finds companies earning good profits one year, then verging on collapse the next. USA Truck, an Arkansas-based carrier, earned $2.5 million in one quarter of 2008, but squeaked out a mere $1,000 profit in the same quarter in 2009.

Trucking's instability, caused in part by excessive competition, has taken a toll on the earnings of workers who once held some of the most dependable, good-paying blue-collar jobs to be found in the middle class. If truck drivers in 2018 made on average what they did in 1980, they would have earned $87,000 adjusted for inflation. Instead, their earnings were $46,000, nearly 50 percent less.

The Deregulation Bandwagon— and Its Victims

Trucking deregulation was the product of a broad-based political movement for regulatory reform that gathered steam in the 1970s. While the perception exists that deregulation was Ronald Reagan's idea, it actually predated his arrival in the White House. In fact, airline and trucking deregulation was pushed through by Reagan's predecessor, Jimmy Carter.

The legislative coalition that brought about those changes and the subsequent deregulation of the savings and loan industry in 1982 had broad support in both parties.

It seemed that everyone in Washington was caught up in deregulatory fever from the mid-1970s on. It was a new concept that backers said would yield enormous economic benefits for the nation.

When President Carter signed the airline deregulation bill in 1978, he said: "It will also mean less government interference in the regulation of an increasingly prosperous airline industry."

When Congress adopted trucking deregulation in 1980, Herbert E. Harris II, a Democratic congressman from Virginia, hailed it as a victory over red tape: "The reform of trucking regulations will significantly reduce the current excesses of government regulation that prevent free market conditions from guiding the trucking industry toward more efficient pricing decisions that benefit shippers, carriers and consumers."

When President Reagan signed the law deregulating the savings and loan industry in 1982, he said it would make thrifts a "stronger, more effective force." He added: "This bill ... represents the first step in our administration's comprehensive program of financial deregulation. It provides a long-term solution for troubled thrift institutions."

Such political opposites as Sen. Jake Garn, the conservative Republican from Utah, and Senator Edward M. Kennedy, the liberal Democrat from Massachusetts, were both on the deregulation bandwagon. And it was Kennedy, more than any other senator, who led the charge for passage of the airline and trucking deregulation bills.

When Carter signed the Motor Carrier Reform Act on July 1, 1980, at a ceremony in the White House Rose Garden, he singled out Kennedy for special attention: "It's particularly gratifying to me to welcome Senator Kennedy ... because he's done such a tremendous job ... in helping the whole nation understand the advantages to be derived from this trucking deregulation bill."

Using language that sounded very much like the speeches that Reagan administration officials would make later in the 1980s, Kennedy described the Motor Carrier Act as "a significant victory" in the "ongoing battle to ... reform and reduce needless federal regulation of business ... It means less government interference with industry ... and more freedom for individual firms to conduct their business in the way they think best. It'll mean new opportunities, new jobs."

Kennedy was half right. New jobs were created—at low wages. But many jobs that paid middle-class wages were eliminated. Ask Charles D. Wright Jr.

For 12 years, Wright was a dock worker at a sprawling truck terminal in Hagerstown, Md., a distribution hub that received and rerouted freight across America. After completing high school in Hagerstown, Wright went to work at the terminal, on a plain north of the city where he had hunted groundhogs as a boy. He felt fortunate.

"Trucking was a good job in those days," he said. "The pay was good. It was steady work." And Ryder Truck Lines, which owned the terminal, was a good company, he said.

"I was proud to work there," he said. "People would ask you where you worked. I'd tell them, 'Ryder Truck Lines.' Big smile."

Ryder was one of the nation's oldest trucking companies. Founded in the 1930s, it was owned by IU International Inc., a Philadelphia-based conglomerate that had diversified into the interstate trucking business. In addition to Ryder, IU owned another old-line trucking company, Pacific Intermountain Express Inc. (P-I-E), based in the West. As separate divisions of IU, Ryder and P-I-E long were profitable operations. Deregulation turned the profits into losses.

To try to stem the losses, IU merged Ryder and P-I-E in 1983, creating Ryder/P-I-E Nationwide, the same company that employed Barbara Joy Whitehouse's husband as a driver. But despite the merger, the red ink still flowed. The trucking operations lost $42.5 million in 1984. Another change was also beginning. Charles Wright and fellow workers at the Hagerstown terminal watched the company, once a solid, well-run organization, gradually deteriorate into a chaotic operation.

"They kept on hiring more management, more supervisors," he said. "When it was Ryder, there were just two supervisors a shift, and some nights only one. And then after deregulation, we had more superintendents and more managers than we ever had before. There was a lot of turnover among those guys. When it was Ryder, the same guys were supervisors for years."

The Ryder/P-I-E merger didn't work. In 1985, the company lost $86.4 million—the largest one-year loss ever recorded by any trucking company. In the fall of 1985, to keep afloat, the company proposed an Employee Stock Ownership Plan. In exchange for giving up 15 percent of their wages for the ESOP, employees would receive stock in P-I-E. A prospectus spelling out the benefits was mailed to employees: "The purpose of the plan is to enable employees ... to acquire stock ownership in and thereby to share in the future of and to provide employees who participate with an opportunity to accumulate capital for their future economic security."

Over the five-year life of the ESOP, employees would give up about $250 million in wages in exchange for 49 percent of the company's stock.

Victor Anderson, another Hagerstown dock worker, recalled the day the ESOP was proposed: "They took everybody off the dock and brought us down to our break room and said, 'Hey, we've got this ESOP program. We're in financial difficulty and if you all don't decide to get into this—now we can't force you to get into this—but if you don't get into this, we're going to go out of business—next week.'"

Employees who signed up were sent buttons proclaiming: "I'M AN OWNER," which they were urged to wear on the docks. The more workers who supported the ESOP, the lower the company's wage costs, so IU kept up a steady drumbeat of promotions urging workers to "... keep those sign-up cards coming in" and to "get to 100 percent and top 'er off." Fearing that they would lose their jobs, more than 85 percent of P-I-E's 10,500 employees signed up. Charles Wright reluctantly agreed to go along, although he was convinced it was merely a device to get him to take a wage cut from $500 to $425 a week. In truth, most workers felt they had no choice.

"When you think about it, what are you going to do," asked Anderson. "Are you going to take a 15 percent cut in pay or are you going to go out and try to get a job when it was hard to find one? So the majority of the people decided to get into the ESOP ... You were under a lot of pressure."

Eighty-five days after the stock plan was adopted, IU sold the company that it had spent months persuading employees to save by forfeiting their wages. On December 31, 1985, the truck line, then renamed P-I-E Nationwide Inc., was sold to a privately held Chicago investment partnership, Maxitron Inc., which had no experience in the trucking industry.

Many employees were embittered by the sale, coming so soon after they had agreed to 15 percent wage cuts. "When they turned around and sold the company right after the ESOP, it left a bad taste in people's mouths," said Anderson. "They led us to believe that the company would not be sold, that it was going to turn around and that sometime our stock would go onto the open market."

Such was not the case. Under Maxitron, P-I-E continued to slide.

Top management changed with each season. In the 20 months after adoption of the ESOP, P-I-E had four different chief executive officers. The chaos at the top filtered down through the company.

"It seemed like anything that went wrong was your fault," said Wright, "and anything that went right was their idea."

"The equipment was neglected after deregulation," said Anderson. "Before, they had a regular program to replace so many tractors each year. That way you replaced your fleet every few years." But after deregulation they had to do everything to keep their customers. One of the big things that suffered was the equipment.

"One way they could cut expenses was, if the truck needed brakes or tires, to run it one more trip. Or if the clutch was slipping on a tow motor, use it another week before you fixed it. There was a lot of neglect."

In 1990, the company changed hands yet again. The new owner was from Miami Beach and, like Maxitron, had no experience in the trucking industry. Olympia Holding Corp., as it was called, had the same address and many of the same officers of a company that only three weeks earlier had acquired control of another old-line trucking firm, Transcon Lines of Los Angeles. Olympia's plan, its officers told the ICC, was to merge the troubled lines into one company. After applications were submitted, the ICC tentatively agreed to transfer the operating certificates to the new owners.

If the ICC had been guilty of overregulation in the past, its approval of the Transcon and P-I-E acquisitions showed just how far in the other direction the agency had swung. The central figure behind Olympia Holding and the Transcon and P-I-E deals was a controversial developer, Leonard A. Pelullo, who has operated from Chester County in Pennsylvania to Miami Beach. About the time that the ICC approved Pelullo's control of the two trucking companies, he and his businesses were the subject of civil complaints and criminal investigations. Disgruntled investors, banks, the IRS, other government agencies, and federal grand juries were suing or probing Pelullo's business activities, from Philadelphia to Miami, from Newark to Los Angeles.

Some of his difficulties grew out of his unsuccessful attempt to restore a collection of Miami Beach's historic art deco hotels. The real estate venture was undertaken by the Royale Group Ltd., a publicly traded company that Pelullo controlled. After the Royale Group attracted millions of dollars from investors and banks to restore the hotels, the company collapsed.

While the ICC was considering the transfer of P-I-E's and Transcon's operating certificates to Pelullo's companies, his business empire was reeling, as a summary of the litigation and complaints against him shows:

» His principal company, the Royale Group, and its affiliates were in bankruptcy court in Miami.

» A bankruptcy court trustee in that case reported to the judge that Pelullo had transferred assets to family-controlled entities, with the apparent intent to "deprive creditors" of assets.

» The Federal Deposit Insurance Corp. (FDIC) had filed a claim in Dade County, Fla. circuit court seeking to recover more than $30 million in principal and interest from a loan to a Pelullo company by a failed savings bank.

» The IRS had filed a claim of $697,000 against Royale and seized company documents in an attempt to collect unpaid federal taxes for various Pelullo corporations.

» A federal grand jury in Cincinnati had indicted Pelullo for allegedly bribing an officer of an Ohio savings and loan. A jury later acquitted him of the charge.

» A federal grand jury in Philadelphia was investigating charges that Pelullo had defrauded a savings and loan association in Stockton, Calif., from which the Royale Group had borrowed $13.5 million in 1984.

» A civil complaint filed in New Jersey accused Pelullo of raiding the pension fund of Compton Press Inc., a Morris Plains, N.J., printing company of which he acquired control in 1987, and of siphoning off millions of dollars from the company's retirement plan for his personal use. A federal judge in New Jersey later sent Pelullo to jail for three weeks when he failed to pay back the fund.

This, then, was the background of the new owner of two long-time trucking companies, whose certification the ICC approved in April 1990.

Pelullo's Growth Financial Corp. acquired Transcon for $12 on April 1, 1990. That's right. Twelve dollars.

In the next few weeks, liquid and real assets of Transcon were diverted to other Pelullo entities, according to a bankruptcy trustee. The trustee asserted in bankruptcy court in Los Angeles in 1990 that Growth Financial appropriated to itself $1.655 million in cash belonging to Transcon. The trustee said that transfers were only the first of many transactions that would reduce Transcon to a "debt-ridden shell, all in an attempt to move all of Transcon's assets beyond the reach of its creditors."

What happened to the cash that disappeared from Transcon's accounts remains a mystery, but the trustee contended that perhaps $400,000 was diverted to P-I-E, as were tractors and trailers owned by Transcon. If they were diverted to P-I-E, none of these assets helped that company either. It just prolonged the inevitable.

Victor Anderson and his fellow P-I-E workers at the Hagerstown terminal saw it coming. "It just became so obvious the last month they were going to go down," he said. "When you run out of toilet paper and soap, you know it's the end."

Then the company ran out of cash. "It got to the point none of the banks would cash our checks," Anderson recalled. "We had two or three checks bounce and ... after two weeks none of the banks would cash our checks because the company's checks were bouncing." To solve the problem, P-I-E issued the checks and cashed them in the office at the terminal.

The end came quickly. On October 16, 1990, P-I-E filed for protection from creditors in bankruptcy court in Jacksonville, Fla. Pledging to reorganize and stay in business, the company closed terminals and slashed its workforce. It was too late. In early December of that year, the bankruptcy reorganization was converted to a liquidation. P-I-E's few remaining assets were to be sold off.

December 17 was the last workday for Charles Wright at the Hagerstown terminal. After 12 years of steady employment, he was out of a job. To support his wife and two children, he began drawing $215 a week in unemployment compensation. Along with his wages, Wright lost his health benefits. The Teamsters Union offered to provide coverage, but he'd have to pay the cost. It was an offer he had to pass up.

"When we left, we were told we could pay into the health and welfare program for $432 a month," he said. "But who has $432 a month when you are laid off? How is anybody who's laid off going to afford that? So we don't have any health coverage."

And what of Leonard Pelullo, the man the ICC approved to take over P-I-E? In a criminal case involving events that occurred before Pelullo acquired Transcon and P-I-E, he was convicted in 1991 of defrauding a Stockton, Calif., savings and loan and the Royale Group, the company that he controlled, of $2.2 million. In that case, a U.S. district court jury in Philadelphia found him guilty on five counts of wire fraud and racketeering. Judge Robert F. Kelly sentenced Pelullo to 24 years in prison, jailed him immediately and ordered him to pay a fine of $4.4 million and restitution of $2.2 million.

At the sentencing hearing, Judge Kelly posed a rhetorical question concerning Pelullo's control of a public company—a question the ICC might easily have asked at the time of the P-I-E/Transcon merger:

"Why would any public corporation ask him—let him—ever get control of their assets?"

After rewriting the rules for the airline and trucking industries and driving down the earnings of their workers, the advocates of deregulation moved on to an even bigger target: banking.

In legislation subsequently adopted in the 1980s and 1990s, federal oversight of the mortgage industry was greatly loosened, setting the stage for the mortgage crisis that triggered the Great Recession of 2008 and nearly brought down the global economy. The capstone victory of the deregulation zealots was passage of the Financial Services Modernization Act of 1999. The law removed regulatory barriers between banks, securities companies, and insurers so that they could sell each other's financial products. In effect, it let banks become stockbrokers as well as bankers, and allowed stockbrokers to become bankers.

Together with earlier legislation, this revolutionized the mortgage industry and led banks and other financial houses to take greater risks than had been legally permitted in the past—risks that culminated in the mortgage meltdown of 2008.

The 2008 recession was a catastrophe for millions of Americans who lost their homes, their jobs and their retirement savings. Although the stock market recovered, many middle-class families never did.

Millennials, born between 1981 and 1996, may have been permanently left behind by the recession, according to a Federal Reserve report in 2018. "Millennials are less well off than members of earlier generations when they were young, with lower earnings, fewer assets, and less wealth," the Fed concluded, meaning that these young people approach middle age with less financial security than any generation since the Great Depression of the 1930s.

Chapter Seven

THE CHAOS OF HEALTH CARE

INTRODUCTION

Obamacare tried to fill one of the most gaping holes in the American health-care system by providing health insurance to millions of Americans who hadn't been able to afford it.

Though relatively modest in scope and the target of a relentless barrage of litigation and repeal efforts by conservatives since its passage, Obamacare partly accomplished its goal.

Yet now another, and in many respects more ominous, challenge has arisen to undermine the health of Americans—and not just those who are uninsured.

Companies and insurers are shifting more and more of the costs of employer-provided health plans to their employees through higher deductibles and out-of-pocket expenses. These costs are rising at an alarming rate that exceeds the rate of inflation.

Research has long shown that the more people have to pay in out-of-pocket medical expenses, the more likely they are to forgo medical care, especially those with modest incomes.

What's happening to average Americans is another chapter in the chronic turmoil within the American health system as it lurches from one crisis to the next.

This isn't likely to change. For decades Washington has promoted the notion that the free market and for-profit health care would hold down costs and bring high-quality health care to all. Not only has that policy failed, but in the meantime tens of billions of dollars— money that could have gone into patient care—has been drained from consumers and transferred to investors, executives and others who have a stake in perpetuating this myth.

End of the American Dream

Bobby Jean McLaughlin of Charleston, W.Va., mother of six and grandmother of six, is a multiple statistic in America's new economic order. McLaughlin lost it all.

She lost her job, her health insurance, her pension, her savings and, in the end, her husband. She lost her job as a $6.20-an-hour department store manager after 18 years as a result of the prevailing corporate financial craze. With it, she lost the health insurance that had paid the family medical bills. And she lost her pension when she took the lump sum payment set aside for her retirement and was obliged to use it instead to pay hospital and doctor bills.

She had little choice. Her husband of more than 35 years, Joseph, worked in a small bakery in Charleston that did not provide health insurance for its employees. He was suffering from emphysema, his condition deteriorating with each passing day. When he no longer could breathe without the aid of a ventilating machine, he was forced to quit.

Recalled McLaughlin: "It just wiped out my savings. I couldn't tell you the amount of money we put out. He was using those tanks of oxygen. And it was just breaking us up, cause they were $38.50 every time they came with one. I tried to get help with the medical bill, but they look at you like you are dirt under their feet. We were always kind of independent. He worked at the bakery 30 years. He worked even after the doctor told him his lungs were bad enough he could get disability."

In December 1990, Joseph McLaughlin died. No one, not in the federal government, not in private industry, keeps an accurate count of the Bobby Jean McLaughlins. But their numbers already are in the millions. They are the anonymous middle-class health-care casualties of high-stakes corporate finance in America, the victims of a government rule book that looks after the demands of dealmakers and ignores the needs of ordinary citizens.

They are not poor enough to qualify for state or federal health-assistance programs. They are not affluent enough to be able to afford the cost of private medical insurance.

And so they go without—joining the ranks of an estimated 40 million Americans who have no medical insurance. That does not take into account more millions who are underinsured.

UPDATE

About 27 million Americans had no health insurance in 2018, substantially fewer than the 46.5 million who had no health coverage when the Affordable Care Act (Obamacare) was enacted in 2010. Obamacare has helped millions who previously had no health insurance and shows the role the federal government can play, however modestly, to improve the lives of its citizens.

But Obamacare didn't cover all those without insurance. Many say that the cost is still too high; others have incomes just above the cutoff line to qualify.

A single-payer insurance system, like those in virtually every other developed nation that provides universal health coverage, would solve this problem by covering even the poorest Americans.

A trend toward reduced health-care benefits for employees and rising costs to workers has become clear. Consider:

» U.S. Labor Department surveys in 1990 of large and medium-size companies that offered health insurance for 31 million employees show that the percentage of those employees with fully paid coverage for themselves alone fell from 75 percent in 1982 to 48 percent in 1989. (Large and medium-size companies employ 100 or more employees.)

» At those same companies, the percentage of employees with fully paid coverage for themselves and members of their families fell from 50 percent in 1982 to 31 percent in 1989.

» The average monthly employee contribution for individual

health-care protection rose from $9 in 1982 to $25 in 1989—an increase of 178 percent. During that same period, the average weekly paycheck went up 25 percent.

» The average monthly employee contribution for combined individual and family health-care protection rose from $27 in 1982 to $72 in 1989—an increase of 167 percent.

» Part-time workers seldom receive fully paid fringe benefits such as health insurance and pensions, and their numbers are growing exponentially. Companies like this arrangement because it reduces costs.

» As a result of the largest increase in corporate bankruptcies since the Great Depression, millions have lost their health insurance protection.

» Faced with steadily rising expenditures for the health-care costs of retirees, companies are curtailing or eliminating a benefit once promised for life. Millions of future retirees will see their coverage disappear. The government's General Accounting Office estimates that companies paid $9 billion in retiree medical costs in 1988, but should have set aside $32 billion for future payments. They did not.

» The number of workers losing their health-care protection grows daily as one company after another dismisses employees to trim expenses, eliminates jobs while seeking to reorganize in bankruptcy court, or goes out of business.

For a lucky few workers facing rising health-care costs, the government rule book offers some relief. Call it the hospital legal lottery. If you win, your medical bills are paid. If you lose, you pay your own medical bills. But very few win.

Here is how it works: Let's say the company where you have been employed for so many years decides to restructure itself to cut its costs. As a part of the realignment, your job is terminated. Suddenly, you lose the health insurance that has been paying your medical bills. You hire a lawyer and sue the company. If you are like most workers, you will lose, which means you will be responsible for all those medical bills. If you are among the lucky few, you will win and recover, if not your health, at least the money you lost.

But the process can be expensive and time-consuming. Ask Roy Mahon Jr. In 1984, Mahon went to work as a salesman in Garden City, Kan., for Massey-Ferguson Ltd., the Canadian company that was one of the world's largest manufacturers of agricultural tractors, combine harvesters and other farm equipment.

"I was a salesman for six months," Mahon recalled, "then I was moved up to store manager."

A year later, Massey-Ferguson executives followed a course charted by so many U.S. corporations. They reorganized the business, as they put it at the time, to "achieve profitable growth through acquisition." First, they created a new company called Massey Combines Corp., which took over the money-losing combine operations, including the dealership that employed Mahon in Kansas. The rest of the business operations stayed with the old Massey-Ferguson, which gave itself a new name, Varity Corp., and sold stock. The proceeds were earmarked for the acquisition of businesses. To soften the impact of the change, Massey-Ferguson executives came up with a name to describe the corporate realignment. They called it "Project Sunshine."

The new Massey Combines got more than just the depressed combine business. It also got about $200 million in debt, about 1,500 employees, including Roy Mahon, and the financial obligation to pay the medical claims and other benefits of retirees and the widows of retirees of the original Massey-Ferguson.

The result was predictable. In 1988, Massey Combines Corp. went into receivership in Canada, the equivalent of bankruptcy court. The company fired all its employees and notified retirees that their health and other benefits were being terminated.

Roy Mahon remembers that time well. Earlier in the year, he said, "I was working on a new parts counter in our building. I stood up and I thought I had sprained something real bad. Turned out I had an aneurysm and it gave way. That night I was in the hospital. Two days later I had my leg taken off. Consequently, they found out I had an aneurysm in each groin and my aorta was about to blow ...

COMPANIES TRANSFER HEALTH COSTS TO WORKERS

WHAT WENT WRONG

The number of companies that provide fully paid medical insurance for their employees is steadily shrinking as American business transfers health-care costs to workers.

Plans for individuals

Percentage of workers with fully paid health insurance at companies employing 100 or more people.

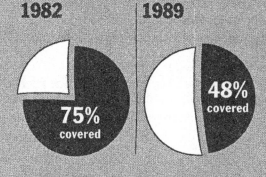

1982

75% covered

1989

48% covered

Plans for families

1982

50% covered

1989

31% covered

SOURCE: Bureau of Labor Statistics

The trends were unmistakable in the '80s – companies wanted to pay an ever-smaller share for employee health insurance. Sadly, it's gotten worse. The share of health care costs for the middle class has dramatically increased the last four decades. A total of 75 percent of companies providing health insurance in 1982 picked up all the costs. In 2019, that number had fallen to 14 percent. Even the best companies are taking away fully-paid health insurance from their employees. In a 2016 survey, Fortune found that of the 100 Best Companies to Work For only 9 percent still provided full health coverage.

Source: Bureau of Labor Statistics and Fortune

So basically the operations were the amputation of the left leg, then aorta surgery, and they went in and rebuilt the area on the right leg … The surgeon spent 7½ hours on that leg."

Soon after Mahon returned home to recuperate, he discovered something amiss at Massey Combines. "I was wondering what was happening because one of my claims went to the administrator and they sent it back not paid," he said.

"The next thing I knew I got a telephone call from my former boss who said the company went belly up. They were bankrupt and everything was gone … That was it. I was left hanging with about $65,000 to $75,000 in hospital bills."

Eventually, Mahon said, Kansas Medicaid paid all but $18,000 to $20,000 of the bills. He had to pay the rest. "I had to cash in my IRA account to survive," he said. "I sold one of my cars. I sold my house to get what I could get out of it because I had to have funds to live on. I had to get these bills down. But consequently I have absolutely no credit whatsoever … Financially, I'm now at the bottom."

A philosophical Mahon—the assets he accumulated over a lifetime parceled out to pay his bills—summed up his situation: "I found out very quickly if you are 56 and 57 and have one leg and are trying to get a job, forget it. I had an extensive sales background. But no one was interested after I had the leg removed. I am sorry to say it but it's the facts of life."

That was early in August 1991. Days later, his situation—at least his economic condition—had changed. He won the health-care legal lottery.

Not long after Mahon and the other Massey Combines employees and retirees lost their health insurance, they retained a law firm to file a class-action lawsuit against Varity Corp. They argued that the creation of Massey Combines was a sham transaction intended to allow the company to escape its obligations to provide health insurance for current and retired employees.

As the case was about to go to trial, Mahon and several other more severely disabled workers reached an out-of-court settlement. Mahon was uncertain of the exact amount of the settlement, but he said that his remaining hospital bills were to be paid and he was to be reimbursed for other expenses and losses.

He added: "I just wish this had never happened. If they had done what they said they were going to do, this would have been a lot easier on us. I would probably have come out in a lot better shape ... I have no credit. Nobody would probably give me credit now. If I went down to buy a house today they would laugh at me."

As for the other nearly 100 employees who were part of the class-action litigation, a jury found Varity liable for $10 million in actual damages and $36 million in punitive damages. Varity immediately announced its intention to appeal the verdict, saying that it would "move to set aside the verdict based on its view that the verdict is inconsistent with the law and facts and, if necessary, would vigorously pursue an appeal of the decision." Varity Corp., which was created out of the same Canadian parent company as Massey Combines, contended that it had no responsibility for Massey Combines' former workers.

The workers in the class-action lawsuit fell into several categories. Some, like Mahon, had incurred medical expenses after the new Massey Combines was established. Others had disabilities that went back to the old Massey-Ferguson. And then there were the retirees, who maintained that the old Massey-Ferguson had made a commitment to provide health insurance until they died, a commitment that workers in many businesses are led to believe is irrevocable. It is not.

In any event, the economics of it all puzzled Mahon. "Can you imagine," he asked, "what this whole thing is going to cost, all the lawyers' fees? It's unreal. The odd part of it is that Massey-Ferguson had a reputation for taking care of their people. If you said a bad word about Massey-Ferguson, the fight was on. They had that kind of loyalty. But you won't find that anymore."

Varity Corp., for its part, prospered. In March 1988, the same month that Massey Combines went into receivership, Varity reported that it "achieved its highest earnings from operations since 1976." That was $50.6 million.

The rising profits, though, had a down side: Corporate income taxes. But just as the old Massey-Ferguson came up with a solution for its failing combine business that was also a solution to its burdensome benefit commitments, Varity came up with a solution to its tax problem. In 1991, the Canadian company, which could trace its corporate ancestry back to the first Massey manufacturing plant in 1847, reincorporated in Delaware and became a U.S. company, relocating its world headquarters from Toronto to Buffalo.

So what's the tax advantage for a Canadian company to become a U.S. company? Remember the net operating loss deduction? That's the deduction that allows companies to subtract prior-year losses from their taxable income for 15 years into the future—and avoid paying corporate income taxes.

Listen to how Varity, in reports filed with the Securities and Exchange Commission, explained the benefit of its new American home: "The amount of the United States net operating loss is significantly larger than the net operating loss for Canadian tax purposes. The period that the net operating loss may be carried forward from the year of incurrence for Canadian tax purposes is seven years, whereas for United States tax purposes it is fifteen years."

What kind of money is at stake here? Varity had a net operating loss left over from past years of more than $1 billion. More than half that sum was in the United States, meaning the company could escape payment of $170 million or so in U.S. income taxes.

Let us summarize: A Canadian company divides in two, with the slumping business operations and the obligation to pay health-care benefits to one group of workers and retirees dumped into one company (Massey Combines Corp.) and the thriving business lines folded into another (Varity). After Massey Combines goes into receivership, leaving its American workers and retirees to fend for themselves, Varity moves to the United States to escape payment of U.S. income taxes by taking advantage of the net operating loss deduction.

UPDATE

To the crowded field of multiple and sometimes conflicting interests that make up the crazy-quilt pattern of companies clustered in the health-care industry has been added yet another player that does not bode well for consumers—hedge funds.

By 2019, hedge funds had more holdings in health care than in any other sector of the economy. After years of raiding established companies to gobble up their assets and spit out their liabilities—such as employee health plans—hedge funds have been aggressively investing in health-care companies since 2015.

In 2019 Trump targeted high drug prices for reform, and some Democrats proposed Medicare for All, but neither potential threat to the health-care industry's bottom line seems to have fazed investors who have dismissed the risk of health-care regulation. On Wall Street, health care is a business, not a public service, and the hedge funders are betting that it will stay that way.

Losing Health Benefits in Bankruptcy

For a growing number of retired people, and future retirees, the rulemakers are playing a kind of health-insurance roulette. It's a game of now-you're-covered, now-you're-not.

The supplemental coverage that companies provide their retired employees is growing in importance because the gap between what

Medicare pays and does not pay is steadily increasing. These rising out-of-pocket medical expenses are placing an added burden on people living on fixed incomes.

But corporate promises of lifetime health insurance are vanishing along with the corporations. Depending on the health of your company, you could, after you retire, lose your benefits if the company declares bankruptcy. This could happen the day the company folds, or months or years later. You may lose all of your medical-insurance protection or only a portion of it. You may have to pick up the full tab or only a portion of the bill. All this depends in part on the vagaries of bankruptcy law and whether the company you worked for is being reorganized or liquidated.

Under bankruptcy law, a company can cut off health benefits to retirees almost immediately after it files for bankruptcy protection, if it files under Chapter 7—the liquidation section—of the code. If, however, the company files under Chapter 11—the reorganization section—it must continue payment of benefits and can only terminate them with court approval. The distinction between the chapters stems from the Retiree Benefits Bankruptcy Protection Act, which was passed amid great fanfare in 1988 with lawmakers claiming that retiree health-care benefits would henceforth be protected when a company sought bankruptcy court protection.

As Sen. Howard Metzenbaum, the Ohio Democrat, told the Senate in 1988: "(This) legislation is a major reform of our bankruptcy laws. It protects retiree health and life insurance benefits when companies go into bankruptcy. This measure sends a strong and powerful message to companies which make promises to their workers—you cannot use the bankruptcy courts as a way of reneging on retiree promises."

But if the company is in weakened financial condition with few assets, the distinction between Chapter 7 and 11, and the protections which Senator Metzenbaum claimed the 1988 act afforded, are meaningless.

Retirees of Garfinckel's Inc., Washington, D.C.'s once-premier department store chain, learned the lesson the hard way. They also learned that however sincere the motives of lawmakers, there is a difference between Capitol Hill rhetoric and reality. Following a dizzying series of events in which Garfinckel's was bought and sold five times in 10 years, Garfinckel's entered bankruptcy court in 1990 under Chapter 11 and shortly afterward chose to liquidate rather than reorganize. In addition to putting 800 people out of work, the shutdown led to the cancellation of health benefits for retired employees.

For most of the retirees, cancellation of their benefits meant they went without the additional coverage provided by a lower-cost group plan such as Garfinckel's. "They had been part of a larger group so they benefitted from the costs associated with that," said John Noble, a lawyer who represented them. "For them to go out into the market and get coverage was simply impossible. Many were probably uninsurable because of pre-existing conditions."

Much the same kind of process was underway, though on a much wider scale, in the Eastern Airlines bankruptcy case. One group of Eastern retirees—those 65 years or older—lost its company-provided health care in 1991 after the airline filed for bankruptcy. Another group—those under 65—twice postponed the cutoff of their benefits. After Eastern sought bankruptcy court protection in 1989, it tried to reorganize, but when that failed, the airline shut down operations in January 1991 and began liquidating assets. Five months later, the trustee overseeing Eastern for bankruptcy court applied for permission to terminate the health benefits of 11,000 retirees.

"The trustee recognizes that numerous retirees will suffer hardship as a result of the termination of the retiree benefits," the trustee wrote in a petition to the court. "However, inasmuch as the liquidation of Eastern's estate will generate barely enough funds to satisfy the costs of liquidation and make a token distribution to creditors, the continued payment of retiree benefits can no longer be justified given the trustee's obligation as a fiduciary to Eastern's estate and its creditors."

When a committee of Eastern retirees asked the court to block the move, a compromise was struck in which coverage was dropped for those over 65 in return for providing benefits for the under 65 group until the end of 1991. William G. Bell, a lawyer representing the retirees, said the decision was made to give up the coverage of those over 65 and try to preserve benefits for those under 65, who were not covered by Medicare. Those under 65 also had to kick in $75 a month toward their own coverage. In December 1991, a bankruptcy court judge extended the coverage through 1992, instructing Eastern to pay an additional $20.4 million—an amount equal to the cost of providing the retiree health benefits program in 1991.

"We got a year's extension," said Bell. When Bell was asked the solution to the health benefits crisis affecting retirees at Eastern and other bankrupt corporations, he said: "I hope it's a Congress that gives us a national health plan. I told the judge in bankruptcy court 'Just give us two years.' Then maybe both parties are going to have to act on this."

The pattern is abundantly clear: Many corporations are systematically scaling back the health-care coverage they already provide. At large companies, workers are being forced to assume a growing share of the costs, through higher deductibles or increased co-payments. At small companies, the coverage is being eliminated.

Employers say they can't afford it. Neither could Bobby Jean McLaughlin, the West Virginia mother and grandmother who worked for Heck's, the discount department store chain based in Nitro, W. Va. Starting as a clerk, McLaughlin worked her way up over 18 years to become manager of the cosmetics department.

The retailer was prospering, growing from a single store in downtown Charleston to a regional chain with more than 120 stores scattered across the middle-Atlantic states. Then the new management took over. That was 1983. And the business went awry.

The layoffs came first. Next came individual store closings. And finally bankruptcy and the death of a retailer and more than 7,000 jobs.

McLaughlin remembered being summoned along with another employee to a meeting with the store manager and district manager. "They told me that my job was eliminated," she said. "They eliminated two department managers in each store ... You go all your life thinking something like this couldn't happen."

McLaughlin wondered whether she could work as a clerk instead of a department manager. "I even asked them if they had any kind of job in that store that I could do ..." she said. Their reply: "No, ma'am."

"And I said after all these years you can't find a job for me in this store?" The answer: "No, ma'am."

McLaughlin, 57 when she was forced out, described her years at Heck's: "I was at work every day and was never late ... was never disciplined. I received good evaluations ... I was never reprimanded or told that my work was unsatisfactory." Nevertheless, the firing was swift and immediate. She was told to get her things and "leave the store," she said. "They treated you like ... you done something wrong after working for them all those years ... It hurts you when you work in a place for years and they treat you like that."

Not only was McLaughlin out of work, but the health insurance that paid her husband's costly medical bills was gone. Private insurance was unaffordable. Eventually, he had to quit his bakery job and was hospitalized twice. On the second stay, he spent about five days in intensive care. "There was one test they run on him," she said, "it was close to $1,000."

When the couple was interviewed in their home in 1990, McLaughlin, who despite his serious illness was given to quiet witticisms, was tied to an oxygen machine by an umbilical-like cord. It was long enough that it allowed him to walk slowly through the rooms of their one-story house.

He was disconnected from the system only when his wife had to drive him to the doctor's office. "It's really hard on him," she said at the time. "It's just gotten that bad in the last year or two. I've been trying to pay the hospital a little at a time," she added. "The guy from the hospital calls every month if I'm late ..."

After McLaughlin died, Bobby Jean McLaughlin went to work full time at the same bakery where her husband spent his working life. The pay was minimum-wage. And she was confronted with a hospital bill that she said has "something like a balance of $24,000." It was turned over to a collection agency.

The bill collector "was calling me quite a bit," she said. "And he would call and ask to speak to Joe. After I told him my husband had died, he would still call me and ask to speak to Joe. I do OK, you know, just paying my utility bills and paying my property taxes and stuff like that. But I just can't pay this hospital bill."

She added: "It has made a nervous wreck out of me."

Health-care costs to American families with health insurance continue rising faster than their incomes.

The combined costs of premiums and deductibles for middle-class employees outpaced the growth of median income from 2008 to 2018 in every state, according to a Commonwealth Fund report. These workers spent on average 6.8 percent of their income on employer premium contributions plus 4.7 percent on per-person deductibles. Lower-income workers paid a much higher percentage of their income on employer coverage.

Death of a Department Store

In March 1987, Russell L. Isaacs, the chief executive officer of Heck's Inc., the discount department store chain where Bobby Jean McLaughlin had worked, received a singular honor. He was selected by the Horatio Alger Association as one of 10 people from across the country to receive its annual Distinguished American Award.

The 54-year-old Isaacs that month joined a prestigious roster of previous award-winners. They included Bernard M. Baruch, adviser to seven presidents; Raymond A. Kroc, the founder of McDonald's Corp.; Dr. Michael E. DeBakey, the pioneering heart transplant surgeon, and Sam Moore Walton, the co-founder of Walmart stores and one of America's 10 wealthiest individuals.

Intended to recognize rags-to-riches success stories, the awards are given, in the association's words, to show young people that "opportunity still knocks in America for anyone willing to work." The association and its awards are named for the author of the popular 19th-century novels—*Ragged Dick* and *Luck and Pluck* among others—that recounted the tales of young boys who achieved success, fame and wealth through hard work, perseverance, honesty and luck. The association described the winners as "role models who give others a different kind of inspiration to succeed."

In Isaacs' case, the association related his rise from an impoverished West Virginia family—his father was a coal miner and his

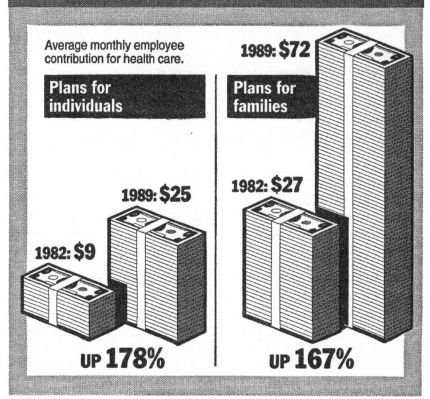

Employees are forced to pay more for their health insurance

Average monthly employee contribution for health care.

Plans for individuals

Plans for families

1989: **$72**

1982: **$27**

1989: **$25**

1982: **$9**

UP **178%**

UP **167%**

SOURCE: Bureau of Labor Statistics

... WHAT WE'VE FOUND NOW

If the cost of family health insurance had gone up at the rate of inflation in the last three decades, families would be paying $138 a month. Instead, they're paying $473.36 – more than six times the cost in 1992.

Source: Bureau of Labor Statistics

mother suffered an apparent stroke during the birth of her seventh child—to become chairman and chief executive officer of Heck's. The association said it was most fortuitous that Heck's directors had selected Isaacs, who once had been the company's chief financial officer, to run the entire operation: "Giving Isaacs free rein has proven to be a wise decision ... His previous knowledge of the company gave him an advantage in implementing changes he thought most beneficial to the company."

Actually, Russell Isaacs had just overseen three consecutive years of losses adding up to $31 million. He had directed the closing of three dozen stores scattered across several states. He had fired hundreds of employees, including Bobby Jean McLaughlin and many others who had worked at Heck's for 10 or 15 years or more. And he had presided over the company's relentless downhill decline—a decline that in time would lead to the elimination of thousands of jobs.

In fact, the week before Isaacs was inducted into the Horatio Alger Association at a dinner in Washington, Heck's Inc. filed for bankruptcy protection. The irony is not an isolated one. For Russell Isaacs, the $300,000-a-year chief executive, is little different than thousands of other executives and investors who have assumed control of American corporations—from retailing businesses to manufacturing plants.

He was a financial officer by training. And by all accounts a good one. But aside from a grasp of the numbers, his critics say, he had little understanding of the business he was running, or what made it work.

Listen to Douglas R. Cook, one of the founders of Heck's who left when Isaacs took over: "Russell is a certified public accountant and a good financial man. Unfortunately ... there's a difference between a financial man and a hands-on manager." Cook, who with three other men built Heck's from a single department store in Charleston into a chain of stores across the middle-Atlantic states, added: "I always tell people, if you started out to destroy a company, you couldn't have done as good a job as Russell Isaacs did ... He ... tried to make a lot of changes, tried to fix a lot of things that weren't broken."

Isaacs has a different explanation. When Kmart and Hills built stores "two or three times the size of ours, you know it doesn't take a rocket scientist to figure out you can't compete with that size store," he said. "Just picture a 40,000-square-foot store beside a 120,000-square-foot store. Where's the customer going to go? He's going to go where the selection is the greatest and prices are the best."

While Heck's no longer exists and thousands of employees lost their jobs, there were a few notable financial success stories. One was that of Russell Isaacs'. As was the case with many corporate executives and investors, Isaacs, his managers and those who followed him received millions of dollars, collectively, in generous compensation packages, pensions and severance contracts.

By contrast, Patsy J. Perry of Teays Valley, W.Va., one of the many longtime Heck's workers dismissed by Isaacs and his successors during a string of failed reorganization efforts, received little more than $1,000. The money represented her pension for 12 years' work. There was no severance pay for Perry, then 56, who lived alone and supported herself. There was no interim allowance to tide her over until she found another job.

More important for Perry, a diabetic who took insulin daily, the medical insurance that Heck's provided was terminated. For two years, Perry said, she could not afford regular medical checkups. Her vision deteriorated because of the diabetes.

Still, she recalled fondly the early years at Heck's. "We were just like one big family," she said. "In fact, that's what they called it—Heck's family." To understand how that family was born and prospered, and then withered and died, it is necessary to turn back the clock to 1959.

The place is downtown Charleston, in an empty building that had housed a Kaiser-Fraser auto dealership. It was there that Fred Haddad, brothers Tom and Lester Ellis, and Douglas Cook opened their first discount department store. Haddad and the Ellises had operated competing stores in nearby Madison, W.Va. Cook was working for a wholesale distributor.

The new store—called Heck's after the letters in the names of the founders and two friends—proved an instant success. A second was opened in 1960 in St. Albans, W.Va., Cook recalled, "and about a week or two later we opened our third store in Huntington." Fred Haddad was Heck's chairman of the board and president, a hands-on executive who wandered through the stores and knew his employees by name. Cook was in charge of merchandising and advertising.

Soon they expanded beyond West Virginia, opening stores in Kentucky, Maryland and Virginia. From the very beginning, according to Cook, the company was profitable: "We showed a good profit. And it was profitable every year up until, say, 1984."

By 1983, when Haddad retired and sold his Heck's stock, the company had grown to 122 stores with annual sales of $435 million. Although net income trailed off in 1983 to $10 million from a peak of $15 million in 1980, Heck's still had posted 24 consecutive years of profits. Then it all unraveled.

Haddad was replaced by Russell Isaacs, who had worked for Heck's in the 1960s and 1970s before becoming executive vice president of Wheat First Securities Inc., a Richmond, Va., brokerage firm. Haddad was a retailer by instinct. Isaacs was a trained certified public accountant. *Discount Store News*, a trade publication, related this account of the differences between the two men: "Unlike Fred Haddad, his predecessor, who was described by one Heck's executive as a hip-pocket entrepreneur, Isaacs is seen as a professional executive who has taken the entrepreneur's room at the top and made it big enough to hold a management team."

Isaacs recruited new managers, introduced new marketing concepts, redesigned store layouts, and added a new computer system. In a report to stockholders, Isaacs recited the achievements for his first full year in charge: "Cramming into one year an effort that normally requires three to five years to achieve, Heck's in 1984 reset, or relayed, the floor plans of 105 of the company's 125 discount department stores in nine states. Accompanied in many cases by partial or full remodeling, the reset stores were made to conform to highly successful prototype retail units tested over the past years."

As part of the sweeping overhaul, Isaacs told shareholders, "each store was planogrammed, a photo-optical process that allocates product space uniformly ... according to a master plan based upon sales. Hence, fast-moving products were given greater shelf space and a better position than slower-moving items. In addition, low-profit and marginal products were dropped from Heck's product mix, an important step in improving store productivity ..."

The rearranged layouts, Isaacs said, included "one or more race-track aisles leading shoppers to prominent departments through the store. The racetracks were dotted with tables featuring fast-moving and desirable merchandise to attract shoppers." Isaacs concluded that "though the overall effort was massive and frequently caused dislocation to shoppers, the initial results indicate a positive response."

Well, not too positive. Despite—or perhaps because of—the race-track aisles, photo-optical process and upscale merchandise, Heck's celebrated its silver anniversary in 1984 by recording its first loss ever: $8 million. Along the way, veteran Heck's employees heard a mounting chorus of complaints from customers who were irked when they were unable to buy products the chain had stocked for years but no longer carried.

Like Lucite paint. Perry said it was one of the biggest sellers in the store where she worked, but the new management "did away with it and went to another brand ... I know the other paint didn't sell."

Douglas Cook agreed. "We had a big following in that," he said. "We had regular customers ... We did a terrific amount of Lucite business ... The first thing that Russell Isaacs' new management team does is throw out Lucite paint ... That's a good example of why ... the customers get upset."

The ever-changing store layouts also caused confusion. "Every time you turned around," Perry said, "they were changing something. All the customers complained because they never could find anything..." But Russell Isaacs, fresh from the experiences of his own investment firm and a satellite Wall Street investment house, plunged ahead with more changes.

He next did what so many other executives do when confronted with an ailing business: He acquired other businesses. In 1985, he bought another retailer, Maloney Enterprises Inc., which operated 34 discount department stores in Heck's marketing area. Maloney's had filed for bankruptcy in 1982 and was just emerging from court protection. So the price was right. The acquisition brought the number of Heck's stores to 166.

That same month, Heck's picked up a quick $9 million from the IRS by applying its 1984 net operating loss against taxes paid in earlier years when the company was profitable. Even so, Heck's was sinking fast.

On September 4, 1985, the company borrowed $4 million from Algemene Bank Nederland N. V., a Netherlands bank. Two weeks later, it borrowed an additional $1 million. Next, it began firing dozens of workers. On October 11, Heck's management sat down to decide who would go. It later seemed to some that many employees selected for termination were those with the most experience—and the most pay and benefits.

There was S. Pearl Lovejoy, who was earning $6.61 an hour as a supervisor after 16 years with Heck's. That gave her a base salary of under $14,000 a year. There was Bobby Jean McLaughlin, who was earning $6.20 an hour as a department manager after 18 years with Heck's. That gave her a base salary of less than $13,000 a year. And there was Patsy Perry, who was earning $5.60 an hour as a supervisor after 12 years with Heck's. That gave her a base salary of under $12,000 a year.

All three women were in their fifties. Each worked at a different store in the Charleston area. Each got the word on her termination during individual meetings around lunch time on October 15. As Lovejoy later described her abrupt dismissal in a court document: "A district manager said there were going to be cutbacks in each store, that another employee and I were the two to go. He said the quicker you get to the unemployment office the quicker you will receive your checks. You will receive your vacation pay for 1986 plus any retirement due you in one lump sum. You can check out and leave now."

In an interview, Lovejoy recalled that "they told me they was paying me too much money."

Perry recounted her dismissal in an interview: "They just came in one morning, the store manager and the supervisor, and called me and another lady and told us as of today we were being laid off. And she had worked longer than I had ... She was in cosmetics ... I was over all the (cash) registers ...

"I was so upset. I asked them if we could work in a different part of the store if they were doing away with our jobs. And they said no, they weren't doing it that way ... They were just letting us go ...

I was 50 and I think Inez must have been about 57, the lady that got laid off when I did. They called it laid-off, but then later they called it terminated ... They had us go home as soon as they told us. They thought it would be better if we leave the store immediately, they said."

The employees were stunned. "It was a shock," Perry said. "My mother was here visiting ... When I came home, I cried and cried. She nearly thought I was going to have a stroke. That night, the girls from the store kept coming over to the house. It was like a funeral."

The timing of her firing had a bitter twist for Perry, who had lived for years in her own home in St. Albans, about 15 miles from the store. "I sold it in September," she said, "and bought me a little trailer and a lot ... so I'd be close to work and I could be here till I retired ... about five minutes away. And then I got laid off the next month."

40 Years Old and Out of Work

Other former Heck's employees, particularly those over 40, found themselves unable to obtain a job that paid comparable wages or benefits. Betty Jean Thompson, a widow, was terminated as a $6.09-an-hour department manager after 11 years. Thompson eventually was hired by another retailer, but for only 20 hours a week. Her new salary: $3.50 an hour. That represented a 43 percent pay cut. There was no health insurance. No life insurance. No pension.

For a brief time, the firings of people such as Betty Jean Thompson and Bobby Jean McLaughlin and Patsy Perry and Pearl Lovejoy appeared to stem the tide of red ink at Heck's. Indeed, company executives forecast a return to profitability by year's end.

The optimism was unfounded. As it turned out, Heck's new management team had failed to detect data errors in yet another of its fresh merchandising and cost-control innovations—a new computerized accounting system. The computer, it seemed, abetted by human error, ran amok. Price markdowns on merchandise went unrecorded, thereby creating fictitious profits. Invoices were incorrectly marked, which led to the reordering of unneeded goods. A company spokesman was quoted as saying: "When you have computers and people messing up, you have a big problem." By the time all the bookkeeping errors had been corrected, Heck's had posted a $5-million loss for 1985.

The longtime employees had seen it coming. Recalled Bobby Jean McLaughlin: "I would order six eyebrow pencils. Two or three dozen would come in ... They had people who didn't know what they were doing." That was none too surprising, given the stream of new management recruits. "That's all you saw," she said, "were people from different places. They brought people in to show us how to set the shelves and all that stuff, like we weren't smart enough. They brought all those big shots in."

Isaacs labeled the accounting breakdown nothing more than "a temporary setback in our efforts to return the company to a strong, profitable operation." Nevertheless, to shore up Heck's shaky finances, the board of directors embarked on another money-raising course: It voted to raid the company's pension fund.

In 1986, Heck's informed the Pension Benefit Guaranty Corp. that it intended to withdraw $4.6 million of the $7.4 million in the retirement fund. Heck's management was going to take 62 percent of the fund's assets and use them to help bail out the business. That would leave 38 percent of the assets, or $2.8 million, to be distributed among 3,251 employees with vested pensions.

That worked out to an average of $861 for each employee. Isaacs and Ray O. Darnall, who had served as president and later vice-chairman of the Heck's board, did a little better. According to records filed with the U.S. Securities and Exchange Commission, Isaacs collected $134,494 from the pension plan, and Darnall picked up $397,851.

The pension fund raid failed to shore up the company's shaky finances. Heck's ended 1986 with a loss of $18 million. Five months after Heck's submitted the pension plan termination to the PBGC, the company filed for protection in bankruptcy court. As the year wore on, however, Isaacs expressed continued confidence in the plan to restore Heck's to profitability. To that end, in 1987 he announced the appointment of a new president with a similar-sounding name. He was John R. Isaac Jr., who had worked for several retailers, including Service Merchandise Co. and a subsidiary of Federated Department Stores.

Russell Isaacs was enthusiastic about the new president: "We believe his extensive retailing background will be instrumental in helping Heck's effect the recovery it has been working so diligently to achieve. I'm just tickled to death with him."

John Isaac had been president of Tradevest Inc., a Florida mail-order company that attorneys general in several states had labeled a pyramid scheme. Tradevest peddled $789 subscriptions to a mail-order purchase club. Once people joined the club, they could sell subscriptions to others and collect a commission. In return for their fee, members were assured they could earn a rebate of 90 percent of what they spent buying products. The rebate would come as an annuity—to be paid 20 years after the purchase. Soon after John Isaac left the mail-order business to take over day-to-day operations at Heck's, Tradevest filed for bankruptcy protection.

But John Isaac was confident about Heck's. A discount store trade publication quoted him at the time as saying that "the company has been making good progress in redefining its basic core group of stores and in re-evaluating its future direction. I'm very optimistic about our prospects." Once more, the optimism proved unfounded. Heck's ended 1987 with another loss. In fact, the loss of $61 million was almost double the cumulative losses of the preceding three years.

John Isaac, who recruited new management, including former employees at Tradevest, ended the year by closing eight more stores and dismissing scores of employees. By June 1988, John Isaac had a new plan: He would sell off or close an additional 40 stores, fire hundreds more employees. A company news release used all the catch-phrases that have become so much a part of corporate jargon to justify eliminating businesses. John Isaac said "the restructuring would enable the company to dispose of assets which have not provided an adequate return on investment ... and which the company believes provide only limited growth potential for the future."

It was to no avail. The losses continued to pile up. Heck's stores continued to disappear. From a high of 166 stores, the retailer shrank to 55 stores. Employment plummeted from more than 7,000 workers to 1,700. By 1990 the name Heck's had vanished; the remaining stores were renamed the Take 10 Discount Club—as in pay $5 to become a member and take 10 percent off everything. Total Heck's losses for

1988 and 1989: $85.5 million. In February 1990 the management of Take 10 Discount Club sold the business to a subsidiary of Jordache Enterprises Inc. The sale price: $1 and the assumption of $22 million in debt. The remaining stores scattered across the hills of Appalachia were relabeled L.A. Joe Department Stores. One year later, L.A. Joe was in bankruptcy court. The stores later closed.

Two footnotes to the collapse of a once-successful regional retailer: John Isaac, who earned $360,000 a year in the top job at Heck's, and four associates who managed the final dismantling of the company, collected more than $1.5 million in severance pay. And about two dozen lawyers who oversaw the formal breakup of the company in bankruptcy court collected additional millions of dollars. The top lawyers, paid at the rate of $200 an hour, collected in less than four hours the amount of money the average Heck's employee—whose job was eventually terminated—received for his or her lifetime retirement.

By the way, the lawyers also got a piece of the proceeds from the terminated pension plan.

It happened this way: By the time Heck's completed the paperwork on ending the retirement system, the company already was in bankruptcy proceedings and the more than $4 million removed from the fund got tied up in the process.

The bankruptcy court eventually approved a plan that called for 20 percent of the money to go to Heck's for operating the business, and the remaining 80 percent to go into a cash pool. That cash pool was used to pay the administrative costs of bankruptcy, including attorney's fees, and creditors like Pittsburgh National Bank, Algemene Bank of Nederland N.V., General Electric Co., International Business Machines Corp., Black & Decker Corp. and Eveready Battery Co. Inc.

There were no million-dollar severance packages for employees who were thrown out of work when the stores closed, or who, like Patsy Perry, lost their jobs in the earlier failed restructuring.

Although she subsequently found work in a convenience store, Perry said that she did not make as much as she did at Heck's. What's more, two years went by before she qualified for medical insurance. During that time, her eyesight deteriorated and she had laser surgery on both eyes. She also underwent a hysterectomy. As for the medical bills run up during the time she had no health insurance, Perry said: "I still owe almost $4,000 to them people which I can't begin to pay. So I don't know what's going to happen."

When she was off work for an extended period, she lost her job at the convenience store. She later found another job working about 30 hours a week for minimum wage. It provides some insurance. The job is at a Value City discount store housed in an old Heck's building.

UPDATE

These days when some patients can't pay their hospital bills, the hospital steps in—and sues them.

Using a tactic that once was virtually unheard of, hospitals are suing patients by the thousands, many of them middle-class people with jobs and health insurance, who don't have the money to pay their medical bills because of soaring deductibles or costly out-of-network charges.

Teachers, managers, store clerks, public employees, stay-at-home moms, retirees—all have been targeted, their wages and bank accounts seized and liens placed on their houses. Some have been forced into bankruptcy by lawsuits. The litigation is being filed in courts from coast to coast by for-profit and nonprofit hospitals. The University of Virginia Health System, a public agency, has been an especially egregious offender, suing former patients—some of whom are its own employees—36,000 times in a six-year period ending in 2018, according to *Kaiser News*.

Only about half of employer-sponsored health plans required a deductible in 2006. By 2019, that number had swollen to 82 percent. On top of that, the dollar amount of the deductible rose sharply as well—from an average of $584 to $1,655, according to the Kaiser Foundation.

Chapter Eight

SIMPLICITY PATTERN— IRRESISTIBLE TO RAIDERS

INTRODUCTION

This is the the story of how a company that was long a household name in middle-class America was attacked by corporate raiders and wrecked through a strategy that has become a standard battle plan for an army of today's hedge funds and private equity moguls.

Backed by Wall Street banks, the raiders devised a cutthroat financial strategy: Borrow money to buy established companies, use the federal tax code to reduce those costs, sell off assets to pay down debt and raise cash to reward investors, and then sell the company in a sharply reduced condition with fewer employees—all the while collecting fees at every stage of the "restructuring."

The takedown of Simplicity Pattern and other hostile takeovers of the era were a prelude to what was to come. Then in its infancy, the private-equity industry grew by leaps and bounds in the following years, applying the rapacious formula of borrowed money and federal tax breaks that had enriched investors at Simplicity or resorting to bankruptcy court to stiff employees and creditors.

Proponents of hostile takeovers and leveraged buyouts claim that their work revitalizes corporate America by getting rid of corporate deadwood and rejuvenating underperformers. Whatever the merits or validity of that theory, the people who pay the highest price are employees of companies targeted by private equity.

A Harvard-University of Chicago study that examined outcomes of private-equity buyouts concluded in 2019 that employment in targeted companies fell by 4.4 percentage points and that earnings per employee, including managers, fell by 1.7 percent in those companies from 1980 to 2013.

The Raiders Attack

For more than half a century, Simplicity Pattern Co. was as much a part of the American home as the radio and the sewing machine. It helped dress generations of girls and boys, women and men, through the sale of billions of patterns for the home-sewing market. Decade after decade, the company's revenues grew. It enjoyed good relations with a loyal workforce at its plant in Niles, Mich. But, as with many mature companies, the earnings from Simplicity's major business—the sale of patterns—had begun to trail off in the late 1970s, a problem the company's management had yet to deal with.

Then came the moneymen. By the time they were finished, a company that once had $100 million in the bank was more than $100 million in the hole.

They were men like John Brooks Fuqua, an Atlanta investor who made so much money swapping corporations like cards in a poker game that he once earned a spot on *Forbes* magazine's list of the 400 richest Americans. And Victor Posner, another onetime member of the Forbes 400, a Miami Beach wheeler-dealer who led Sharon Steel Corp. into bankruptcy court and was convicted of filing false income tax returns to evade more than $1 million in taxes. There was Graham Ferguson Lacey, a British takeover artist and born-again evangelist who prayed with Jimmy Carter at the White House. And Charles E. Hurwitz, a Houston investor whose business associates included former President Gerald R. Ford and Michael R. Milken, who later went to prison for securities-law violations.

There were others, and throughout the 1980s they all worked their managerial and financial wizardry on Simplicity. When they were done, they had turned a venerable, money-making business, which paid federal income taxes, into a money-losing business that paid no federal income taxes. They had driven Simplicity to the edge of bankruptcy.

In that decade, the moneymen:

» Bought and sold the company four times and made tens of millions of dollars running up the price of Simplicity stock in threatened and actual takeovers.

» Drained $100 million that Simplicity had in its bank account and investment portfolio.

» Raided the company's pension funds on two occasions, taking out $10.7 million.

» Issued bonds and borrowed from banks, sending the company's debt soaring from near-nothing to $100 million.

» Sold off properties to raise badly needed cash after they had depleted the company's $100 million cushion.

» Created so much debt that Simplicity could no longer generate enough cash to make the interest payments.

» Defaulted on the interest payments on bonds and bank loans.

It was just one more American business success story—if you measure success by how much money assorted investors made buying and selling Simplicity stock, buying and selling the company itself. And they got help from the U.S. government rule book. Thanks to several provisions of the federal tax code, including the net operating loss deduction and the deduction for interest expense, they were able to build their empires on debt and write off the interest. So the raids that cost hundreds of Americans their jobs and made millions for the raiders were, in effect, subsidized by the American taxpayer.

Consider John Brooks Fuqua, who accumulated enough of a fortune that he earned the ultimate accolade, a business school named in his honor—the Fuqua School of Business at Duke University. Fuqua was the third of the four moneymen who acquired Simplicity in the 1980s. Fuqua was chairman of Triton Group Ltd., a Los Angeles company that in an earlier incarnation, under a different name and management, had been a failed real estate investment trust. In 1983, three years after the company emerged from bankruptcy proceedings, Fuqua and several associates took control of Triton, which was little more than a corporate shell.

For investors, Triton painted a cheery picture of a Fuqua-led future. In a report to stockholders, the company said: "The objective of the Fuqua group investors is to create value for all Triton stockholders ... Several years ago Fuqua took over the management of a

A PATTERN OF GREED

WHAT WENT WRONG

Simplicity Pattern Co. was sitting on tens of millions in cash and investments in 1981. It was too good to pass up.

Over a decade, six moneymen made runs at the dowager company. When they were done, the money was gone. And Simplicity was drowning in debt.

... WHAT WE'VE FOUND NOW

The corporate raiding strategy that drove the Simplicity takeover became a pattern for private-equity companies to follow from then on.

similar publicly owned former real estate investment trust. Fuqua undertook a corporate restructuring comparable to that underway at Triton and in five years that company's stock increased fifteen times in value."

Triton purchased Simplicity Pattern Co. for $65 million in 1984 and sold it three years later for a profit of $52 million before taxes. That was good for Triton. It was not so good for Simplicity Pattern. The company, bought with borrowed money, was burdened with so much debt that it couldn't sell patterns fast enough to pay the interest on its bonds and loans.

And it definitely wasn't good for Simplicity's employees—people such as Charlotte L. Mitchell, a secretary at the plant since 1970. On June 8, 1988, six months after Fuqua's group sold Simplicity to Wesray Capital Corp., Mitchell got a big surprise. It was on her birthday. "They (her coworkers) had a big party for me in the office," she remembered. During the party, "my boss got back and he said, 'Charlotte, I've just been told you are going to be let go.'"

Others got the news equally abruptly. Mitchell told of a secretary who had been on sick leave. Her bosses called her at home and said they'd like to take her to breakfast. "After breakfast was over, they told her she didn't have a job to come back to," Mitchell said. However the notification, the reasons were the same: debt and declining sales.

That was the explanation given to Edgar C. Stanley, manager of the bindery and finishing department, who'd been at the plant since 1971. He was dismissed the same day as Mitchell. In a "Dear Ed" letter, Charles E. DeWitt, a vice president and plant director, wrote: "As you know, the performance of the home sewing market has been weak and sales trends in the industry for the first five months of 1988 have been soft. These unit sales declines and our outstanding debt have created the need for Simplicity to reduce costs ... The decision was made that Simplicity must reduce its workforce ... Thus, effective today, your employment with Simplicity will end."

At 62, after more than 17 years at Simplicity, Stanley was out on the street. His medical insurance was paid for three months, after which he was on his own. His life insurance was paid for two months, after which he was on his own. And he got a reduced pension. The new

Simplicity executives had handled the layoffs with about as much skill as their predecessors had dealt with the company's underlying problems. Which is to say that Simplicity Pattern was hardly a model of a well-managed company.

UPDATE

Following the pattern that shredded Simplicity, a succession of private-equity companies took over the discount shoe retailer Payless Shoes, starting in 2012 when it had 4,000 stores and 15,000 employees, mostly in the U.S. The financiers loaded Payless with debt, paid themselves hefty dividends and drove the company into bankruptcy—not once, but twice.

There isn't a Payless Shoe store left in America, and only a handful of employees remained in 2019 at the company's headquarters in Topeka, Kan., where 800 once worked.

A Vulnerable Target

Simplicity had been founded in New York City in 1927 by an advertising man, Joseph M. Shapiro, and his son, James. It opened the Niles plant in 1931 and, through low prices and solid marketing, became the world's largest pattern maker. But in the mid-1970s a disturbing trend began to emerge.

Although the company was financially healthy, it was making more and more of its money from its investments, less and less from the sale of patterns. Between 1976 and 1980, income from patterns dropped from $24 million to $9 million. During those years, income from investments rose from $3 million to $9 million. The explanation was simple enough. As more women left the home and moved into the workforce, they had less time for sewing. Fewer women making clothes for their families meant the sale of fewer patterns.

While that trend had been clear for some years, Simplicity's long-time management seemed unable to develop other business lines to take advantage of the company's equipment and expertise. In short, Simplicity Pattern Co. was a Harvard Business School case study of a stagnating company—an entrenched management unable to meet the challenges of a changing market. Simplicity was also a company ready-made for the corporate raiders.

By the early 1980s, the raiders were being glorified as the saviors of American business: MBAs flying about the country buying up companies, ousting unimaginative managers, installing tight spending controls, selling off or shutting down peripheral operations, restructuring businesses and putting them back on a solid foundation. That, anyway, was the image.

As Drexel Burnham Lambert Inc., the Wall Street investment house, explained to a congressional committee in 1985: "Drexel believes that corporations that have undergone restructuring as a result of acquisition activity or strategic change have evolved into stronger companies better equipped to compete in today's domestic and international markets. An unsolicited acquisition can also result in the replacement of management with a new team better able to realize the full potential of a target company ... Merger and acquisition activity results in a shifting of assets to more productive uses."

Not really. Drexel Burnham itself proved that. It filed for bankruptcy court protection in 1990, a victim of its own philosophy. Simplicity Pattern was another victim of that philosophy. Its story, with variations, has been repeated at hundreds of businesses, with the same consequences for tens of thousands of workers.

It began in 1979, when corporate raiders started poring over Simplicity's financial documents, taking note of the more than $100 million parked in investments and pension funds. Among the early arrivals was Victor Posner, an investor described by one newspaper as a "corporation empire-builder." While empire building, Posner arranged for the publicly owned corporations that he controlled to pay personal and living expenses of himself and his family. Securities and Exchange Commission (SEC) records show that corporate funds were used to redecorate his apartment, to buy jewelry, to pay for groceries and for the yachts that his Sharon Steel Corp.—based in the landlocked western Pennsylvania community of Sharon—owned and docked next to Posner's home in Miami Beach.

Posner began acquiring Simplicity stock in earnest in August 1979. Over the next four months, his holdings grew to more than one million shares, or 7 percent of the stock. The four-month cost: $7.1 million. Drexel Burnham fanned the speculative fever after Simplicity postponed its annual shareholders' meeting in 1980. In a report to its clients, the investment firm suggested that Simplicity management had delayed the meeting because it feared it might lose control of the company. That fear was good reason to speculate in Simplicity stock. As Drexel Burnham put it: "Such a change in management is, in our judgment, a valid reason for speculating in the shares for those who are inclined to a short-term philosophy."

Meanwhile, Posner continued to add to his Simplicity holdings. By the end of 1980, he owned nearly 9 percent of the company.

In Niles, Simplicity's management was trying to cut costs and threatening to move the company to a part of the country where wages and costs would be lower. Under the headline, "Simplicity considers abandoning Niles plant," the *South Bend (Ind.) Tribune* on Nov. 8, 1980, quoted Kenneth James, the company's director of employee relations, as saying: "We've got to look at the alternatives of getting out of here."

Company officials kept the pressure on in the weeks that followed, saying at one point that they were looking at possible sites in Kansas where the Niles plant could be moved. Simplicity's unions agreed to concessions that would cut the manufacturing payroll by 10 percent over the next four years and the company agreed to stay in Niles, at least through September 1985. With the labor concessions in hand in Niles, the takeover action began to heat up on Wall Street.

In a friendly deal initiated by Simplicity's management, NCC Energy Ltd., a little-known oil and gas company out of London, bought up 15 percent of Simplicity's stock in the spring of 1981. NCC Energy was controlled by British financier Graham Ferguson Lacey and boasted of having oil, gas and mineral properties in Australia, Asia, Ireland and the United States. Its investment adviser was Drexel Burnham Lambert, and among those touting the deal was Peter Ackerman, the right-hand man of Drexel's junk-bond creator, Michael Milken.

Drexel liked the deal so much that it picked up 5 percent of Simplicity's stock for itself—a transaction it kept secret. Additional Simplicity stock had been acquired by another member of the Milken-Drexel family of investors, an inner circle of financiers that traded stocks, bonds and companies among themselves. That was First Executive Corp., a Beverly Hills life insurance holding company that later sought protection from its creditors by going into bankruptcy court in 1991.

NCC Energy bought out Posner, paying him $22 million for his holdings. That gave Posner a profit of $10 million. This set the stage for the world's largest pattern maker, which had no experience in the oil and gas business, to go into the oil and gas business. NCC Energy's intention, a Simplicity spokesman said at the time, was to use millions of dollars of Simplicity's reserves to explore for oil and gas. This would be good for Simplicity, the spokesman said, because NCC's oil and gas exploration was thriving, and pattern-making was declining.

But before the NCC-Simplicity business combination could be finalized, another raider appeared on the scene. In August 1981, companies controlled by Carl C. Icahn reported they had acquired 1.6 million shares of Simplicity, or 11.2 percent of the stock outstanding. By November, Icahn controlled 13.3 percent and had made a tender offer to buy an additional 18 percent—effectively blocking the NCC-Simplicity deal. To fend off Icahn, NCC Energy enlisted the help of an Australian company, Waltons Bond Ltd., to make a counteroffer for Icahn's holdings. A month later, Waltons Bond paid Icahn's companies $26.5 million for their shares.

That transaction was especially lucrative for Icahn, whose businesses picked up a quick $15-million profit on the turnaround in Simplicity stock. Now the scorecard read: Investors Posner and Icahn: $25 million. Simplicity, its employees and customers: reduced earnings and higher pattern prices.

While Icahn was selling his stock to Waltons Bond, another company, Cook International, was buying Drexel Burnham's 5 percent of Simplicity shares for $6.8 million. Cook later sold the stock to NCC Energy. There was but one problem with the roughly $60 million in Simplicity stock purchases made by NCC Energy, Waltons Bond and Cook International: None of the companies had the cash to pay for the securities. Not to worry. Once NCC Energy assumed control, it would merely take the money out of Simplicity to pay for buying Simplicity.

A new management team took over in January 1982. Lacey, NCC Energy's chairman and chief executive officer, took on the same titles at Simplicity. Six of Lacey's allies also joined the board of directors. Among them was R. Cecil McBride, an aging Ulster millionaire who had bankrolled a teenage Lacey in his first ventures.

Lacey brought to his new job as chief executive of a venerable American business a reputation—at least in the British news media—for having carved out a "phenomenal business career." It began with McBride and real estate dealings in Northern Ireland during the 1970s and was followed by trading in large blocks of stock in British companies and finally the acquisition of companies. There were some setbacks along the way. A structural engineering company that he headed collapsed in 1978. A textile company that he headed went into receivership in 1980.

But, befitting his growing reputation as a fast-moving entrepreneur, Lacey began making acquisitions as soon as he assumed control. Interestingly, Lacey's Simplicity made the acquisitions from Lacey's NCC Energy. There were a pair of buildings in New York City, including a townhouse in which Lacey lived; an interest in a regional airline that had yet to get off the ground; oil and gas exploration, and common stock in an unidentified company—$10 million in all. This was good for NCC Energy, because its parent company back in England, Birmingham & Midland Counties Trust—also controlled by Lacey—was on the verge of bankruptcy. It was not so good for Simplicity.

Lacey's Simplicity also decided to pour cash into a gold-mining project in Australia—a Waltons Bond venture—and to buy $25 million of notes issued by a Waltons Bond-controlled mining company. This would be good for Waltons Bond, which needed cash. It would not be so good for Simplicity.

Simplicity's top officers spoke enthusiastically about the acquisitions and its future as an energy producer. In an April 1982 report to stockholders, Lacey and two members of the old Simplicity management, Harold Cooper, vice chairman of the board, and Lilyan H. Affinito, president, wrote:

"The board has embarked on a program designed to provide the company with both capital and earnings growth through ... acquisitions in oil and gas opportunities in the United States; acquisitions in energy and mineral opportunities in Australia, and other acquisitions, primarily in the United States, that will not be energy-related."

Then the deals unraveled. Simplicity's small stockholders, worried about the drain of assets, filed a lawsuit to block the board's actions. The lawsuit alleged that NCC Energy, Waltons Bond and Cook International had "failed to disclose that they intended to use the cash assets of Simplicity in order to finance their acquisition of Simplicity stock" and that they "intended to use the cash assets of Simplicity to prevent Birmingham [NCC's parent company] from being forced into receivership." This was self-dealing, serving only the personal interests of the defendants and constituted fraud, the lawsuit said. The board had been checkmated.

NCC Energy's parent company could no longer meet its debts. Birmingham & Midland Counties Trust was forced into receivership in England.

Waltons Bond announced it was severing ties with NCC Energy and Simplicity and was returning a $10-million Simplicity mining deposit. And four months after gaining control of Simplicity, NCC Energy announced it would sell its 20 percent interest.

No problem. Another moneyman, Charles Hurwitz, a Houston financier, was standing by. In May 1982, a pair of Hurwitz companies, MCO Holdings Inc. and Federated Development Co., announced the purchase of Simplicity's stock from NCC Energy and an agreement to buy the Simplicity stock held by Waltons Bond. Total purchase price for the 33 percent interest: $48 million.

MCO Holdings, based in Los Angeles, had investments in oil, gas and geothermal resources. Federated was a New York holding company. Perhaps more important, Hurwitz had access to an unlimited supply of cash. His banker was Michael Milken.

Simplicity also had a new chairman and chief executive officer—Charles E. Hurwitz. And Hurwitz's allies, naturally, joined him on the Simplicity board. They included George Kozmetsky, a director of the Institute for Constructive Capitalism and immediate past dean of the College and Graduate School of Business of the University of Texas, and Barry Munitz, former chancellor and professor of business administration at the University of Houston.

In the beginning, Hurwitz's Simplicity abandoned the oil and gas business and gold-mining ventures. Instead, the pattern maker began buying stock in a New York company called Twin Fair Holdings Inc., which owned properties that it leased to major retail chains, such as Gold Circle and Hills department stores. By the end of 1983, Simplicity Pattern owned 96 percent of Twin Fair. Simplicity also began buying stock in Amstar Inc., a century-old company best known for its Domino brand sugar. While Simplicity's new managers were spending money to buy sugar refineries and real estate, they were seeking to cut the pay and benefits of employees in Niles.

Hurwitz also initiated the paperwork required by the Internal Revenue Service that would lead to the removal of $2.9 million of $7 million from one of the pension funds covering Simplicity workers in Niles. Federal law allows companies to remove money from a pension fund if they certify that there are sufficient assets to meet pension obligations.

Simplicity's management continued to look for business investments unrelated to its pattern-making and pattern-printing operations. In 1984, Twin Fair Holdings Inc., a subsidiary of Simplicity Pattern, began buying stock in another sugar refiner, Holly Sugar Corp., and acquired a golf and tennis development in Naples, Fla.

Hurwitz also decided to change the name of the business to Maxxam Group Inc., and stockholders agreed. The proposal was put to the stockholders this way: "The name Simplicity Pattern Co. Inc. was chosen at a time when the company was engaged exclusively in the manufacture and sale of paper patterns for home sewing to retail merchants.

"The company's pattern business is now conducted primarily through the company's wholly owned Delaware subsidiary, Simplicity Pattern Co. Inc. With the acquisition of Twin Fair Inc., the company is now also engaged in real estate development ... By reason of these changes, management believes that the proposed new name will more appropriately identify the company."

Simplicity management renewed the pressure on the unions to reduce wages and benefits. A headline in the *South Bend Tribune* for May 30, 1984, said: "Simplicity wants pay cut to '82-'83 levels." The *Niles Star* reported that if the company could not reduce its labor costs by about $1.9 million a year it would leave the city it had called home since 1931. The newspaper quoted Charles DeWitt, the manager of the facility, as saying: "Simplicity has already identified a plant site in the South where taxes, utilities, and labor costs are lower and where local communities are aggressively soliciting new manufacturing operations with whole packages of special incentives."

Both the city of Niles and Simplicity's workers responded. The city promised to help arrange financing for more modern equipment and to give Simplicity, the area's second-largest employer, a 50 percent property tax break on plant improvements. Working against a deadline set by the company, Simplicity's five unions agreed to trim 3 percent off wages, which averaged about $9.90 an hour. They also agreed to give up two paid holidays and to eliminate the jobs of about 70 workers. Some of those who were terminated had been at Simplicity for more than three decades. The savings added up to $1.5 million, or 79 percent of the $1.9 million the company sought.

Bruce Bracken, director of employee relations, was quoted in an area newspaper as saying: "We fell short of our goal, but management was willing to stay here anyway because of the proven workforce and high risk of starting off fresh somewhere else."

In reality, management was about to move on. Now that Hurwitz had invested Simplicity money in sugar and real estate; now that the company name had been changed to Maxxam; now that Niles taxpayers were going to subsidize the purchase of equipment; now that workers had agreed to pay cuts, he decided to unload the business. For a hefty profit. Less than two weeks after the labor agreements had been sealed, Hurwitz announced that Simplicity would be sold to Triton Group Ltd., a holding company controlled by John Brooks Fuqua.

The board of directors of Maxxam, Simplicity's most recent parent, explained the decision in documents filed with the U.S. Securities and Exchange Commission: "The primary goal of the board is to broaden Maxxam Group Inc.'s economic base and enhance its potential earning power and underlying asset value. The board believes that the sale of Simplicity to Triton on the terms provided in the sale agreement provides an excellent opportunity to further this objective.

"As previously reported by Maxxam Group Inc., Simplicity has experienced continuing decreases in net sales and income from operations since the mid 1970s, reflecting the decline in pattern unit sales, although Simplicity continues to be a profitable business producing substantial cash flow."

Maxxam also said that Simplicity would prosper under its new owners as a result of "Simplicity's recently strengthened management team and by the experience of Triton's principal shareholder, Fuqua Industries Inc., in managing consumer product based businesses."

The moneymen loved the idea. Especially the dealmakers at Drexel Burnham Lambert. "Simplicity Pattern is a cash cow," Drexel Burnham told its clients in a report extolling the benefits that Triton and its parent, Fuqua Industries Inc. of Atlanta, would derive from owning Simplicity.

"Last year, pre-tax income and depreciation generated $12 million in cash flow and the pre-tax profit margin in 1983 was 14 percent," the brokerage house said.

"Even though the pattern business has been going nowhere for years because of the declining interest in home sewing, nevertheless pre-tax margins in this proprietary business consistently ranged between 12 percent-14 percent. Pre-tax profits approximated $15 million in 1983."

And then, the real reason that the Simplicity-Fuqua-Triton marriage made so much sense: Triton possessed "a potential tax loss carryforward of about $200 million to shelter future earnings. In order to take advantage of the carryforwards, Triton obviously needs to acquire operating companies with good cash flow and a consistent record of profitability." Translation: The losses run up in earlier years by a long-dead company—the real estate trust from whose corporate shell Triton had been formed—would be used to offset the taxes owed by a profitable firm.

Tax Gimmicks and Givebacks

Triton's losses had originated in a real estate business in Massachusetts called Chase Manhattan Mortgage and Realty Trust, which went into bankruptcy court in 1979. A year later, it emerged with a new name, Triton Group Ltd. It was acquired by Fuqua Industries in 1983.

In a report to Simplicity shareholders after Fuqua assumed control, he offered this glowing assessment: "Simplicity has a dynamic new management team which in only a few months has made innovative moves to more widely use the Simplicity name, which has become synonymous with sewing through many decades of consumer product use … Simplicity is already beginning to pay off a significant amount of the debt incurred to acquire this fine company, and the outlook is indeed bright …"

Did this mean that an innovative new management had made structural changes to turn around a declining company? Hardly. Simplicity's seemingly changed fortunes were attributable to three factors: the tax code, a raid on a company pension fund and concessions by Simplicity's workers.

Triton Group, Simplicity's new parent company, reported profits of $13 million for 1985, $11 million for 1986 and $76 million for 1987. For the three years that it owned Simplicity, profits totaled $100 million. Yet according to records filed with the SEC, Triton paid no federal income taxes on that $100 million.

How could that be? Remember all those losses run up by the defunct realty trust before it went into bankruptcy court and came out as Triton?

Well, Triton merely subtracted the old losses from the taxable income of Simplicity and Triton's other subsidiaries.

Having made use of the tax code, Triton then took aim at the pensions of Simplicity workers. Triton tapped one of the pension funds covering hourly workers in 1986. It removed $7.8 million of the $8.5 million in the fund, according to records filed with the Pension Benefit Guaranty Corp. This was the second raid on a Simplicity pension plan in three years. Before the money was removed this time, the pension of each Simplicity employee enrolled in the plan was backed, on average, by assets of $39,535. Afterward, the average per worker was $3,256.

In the footnotes to a financial report filed with the SEC, Triton explained where part of the $7.8 million in pension-fund money went: "Simplicity's retirement plan for salaried employees was terminated during the year. Refunds received from the termination ... will be held for or applied to redemption of the Simplicity Series B preferred stock until all such shares are redeemed."

And who owned Series B stock? Hurwitz's Maxxam Group Inc., the previous owner of Simplicity, which had received the stock as a part of a $65-million package of cash and notes it received when Triton bought Simplicity. In other words, Triton used the pension fund money of Simplicity workers to help pay for Triton's purchase of Simplicity.

But surely, the change in ownership brought change to the production plant in Niles? Not exactly. Paul M. Borowski, who at the time was Simplicity's general accounting manager in Niles, recalls visits to the plant by the new California owners. "I can remember the guys coming, walking through, making their grand show," he said. "It was one of those things, clean the place up ... get rid of the trash, clean the factory, you know, get it the way it should be every day. I can remember those guys coming in a couple of times. Everybody was scared to death of them."

But what about all those advantages that are supposed to come with corporate reorganization? Surely, the new management introduced ways of making better use of existing equipment and expertise, of expanding into new but related fields of business, of opening up other markets? Not really. Douglas G. Wimberly, a former manager of computer services at Simplicity, said there was a lot of talk about diversifying, but it was all talk. There were discussions about printing national magazines. One salesman even brought in a $1-million printing order, but no decisions were made and the order was lost. "Rumor was that management could never make up its mind," Wimberly said.

Borowski agreed. "We'd bring up at staff review meetings different proposals. The managers would say, 'Yeah, we're going to look into that.' I'd sit there, I'd say, 'I thought we were going to look into that four months ago.'"

Not only did the Triton management not diversify, but Simplicity was losing ground in the business it once dominated. More than 50 percent of all the patterns sold in America had carried the Simplicity label in the 1970s. The figure had dropped to 43 percent by 1983, and to 37 percent in 1986.

The gloomy sales figures aside, Triton did very nicely with its investment in Simplicity, thanks to the tax advantages. But after three years, Triton decided it was time to dump the pattern maker and move on. To manage the sale, it turned to a familiar face—Drexel Burnham Lambert, always ready to collect another round of fees.

That was in November 1987. A month later, Drexel arranged the sale of Simplicity to Wesray Capital Corp., a company that had established a reputation as the most successful get-rich-quick operation in the field of corporate takeovers. Wesray's name was derived from the letters in the names of its two founders, William E. Simon, former Secretary of the Treasury, and Raymond G. Chambers, a tax accountant who became a buyout specialist. By the time of the Simplicity purchase, Simon had moved on to other corporate deals unrelated to Wesray. Although Simon continued as chairman of the board, Chambers ran Wesray.

Why did Triton want to sell? One reason was that control of Triton had shifted from Fuqua to Charles R. Scott of La Jolla, Calif., a stockbroker turned corporate raider. Like Fuqua, he had made millions buying and selling companies. Scott had amended, slightly, Triton's mission. As he described the philosophy in a report to stockholders:

"Triton is in the business of acquiring and adding value to promising American growth companies ... Simply stated, our aim is to build shareholder value by acquiring promising companies, guiding management in restructuring, refinancing and repositioning for accelerated growth and, ultimately, selling our interest in a well-timed transaction."

In the Simplicity sale, timing was everything. Wesray paid $117 million for Simplicity. Triton walked away with a $52 million profit before taxes. In the amazing world of American business, a company that was worth $65 million in 1984 was worth $117 million in 1988—even though its sales and market share had all declined.

How can the value of a deteriorating company grow? It can't. But in the world of corporate and financial paper-shuffling, it happens all the time. With disastrous consequences for workers, taxpayers and the overall economy.

Wesray purchased Simplicity with borrowed money, meaning that Simplicity would have to pay for itself all over again. As it did when Triton bought it. As it did when Hurwitz bought it before that. At this stage, the debt load topped $100 million. And the $100 million that Simplicity had squirreled away in cash and investments when the decade began had long since disappeared. Nonetheless, the people at Wesray thought they had engineered a good deal.

At Simplicity's plant in Niles, the people who ran the day-to-day business knew better. So did the company's suppliers. They were being paid very, very slowly. It was the surefire sign of a business—or an individual—in financial distress: the old check-is-in-the-mail ploy. Paul Borowski, the general accounting manager whose duties included issuing the checks, remembers those days well.

When a supplier would call and ask about payment, Borowski said, "as a good accountant, following directions, I'd say, 'We've got new internal auditors hired and they're reviewing all our payments.' I said, 'I will call him tomorrow morning and have him release your check.' ... You know, give him the line." Borowski said he was disturbed by the practice. But he was even more disturbed when the corporate office in New York ordered him to send the checks to New York for mailing, further delaying payment. After the checks arrived in New York and were approved there, they would eventually be mailed back to the suppliers in Niles.

Borowski said he also was directed to take the discount that suppliers give if payment is made within a certain period, say 10 days, but then delay the payment:

"If I'm dealing with you, I negotiate with you in good faith for a discount. Then I take the discount. Then I don't even mail the check till about two weeks later. We had one vendor, a big paper company they had done business with for 50 years, they refused an order until the check was certified in their New York office."

There was a solution to the cash crunch: more layoffs. About 20 Niles workers were dismissed in June 1988 when Charlotte Mitchell and Edgar Stanley lost their jobs. Douglas Wimberly, the computer services manager, lost his job as well. "The way it was put to me, it came down from New York that X amount of dollars were going to be cut from personnel," said Wimberly.

Borowski survived the June 1988 cuts. But not for long. Late one week in mid-August, on very short notice, he was asked to have checks for suppliers printed by the following Monday.

"I called one of my clerks back from vacation, to come in at noon [that Monday] to work," he said. "We were running two systems to get it all done ... Came in Tuesday morning, had everything balanced ... Checks all signed, you know, through a machine. And the ones that needed two signatures all ready. All checks were stuffed in envelopes. And when I called New York—it must have been about 10 o'clock or so—he says, 'Are they in the mail yet?' I say, 'Waiting for your OK to take them to the mail table.' He says, 'Give them to the mail table right away.'

"I did that myself ...Went down there at 10:15. About 10:30, I get a call: 'Checks out?' "I said, 'Yeah, they're at the mail table.' 'OK, thank you very much.'"

Twenty minutes later, Borowski was summoned to the plant manager's office. He was told his job had been terminated. So had the jobs of another dozen or so employees. But Simplicity by then had so much debt that even reductions in the workforce didn't free up enough cash to make the interest and principal payments.

In an effort to stay afloat, Simplicity reached an agreement in 1988 to merge with one of its main competitors, Butterick Holdings Inc. based in Altoona, Penn. The plan called for closing Simplicity's Niles plant or Butterick's Altoona plant. Each had about 550 employees. But the Federal Trade Commission blocked the merger, contending that a union between Simplicity, the largest pattern maker, and Butterick, the third largest, would create a monopoly.

After the aborted merger, conditions continued to deteriorate. The company stated the obvious in a report filed with the SEC: Simplicity "is highly leveraged as a result of the 1988 acquisition ... This high level of indebtedness results in significant interest expense and principal repayment obligations for the company." Past-due interest and principal on its senior debt then totaled $23.4 million. Past-due interest on notes had reached $8.8 million. In a report to the SEC in 1990, Simplicity painted a picture that was growing more grim with each passing month: "These conditions raise substantial doubt about the company's ability to continue as a going concern."

UPDATE

After years of raids by predatory moneymen, Simplicity Pattern was bought in 1998 by Conso Products Co., a South Carolina-based producer of decorative trimmings for the home. The company was taken private in 1999.

In 2007 Conso closed Simplicity's longtime plant in Niles, Mich., the only manufacturing plant in the U.S. directly operated by the company. By then the plant's workforce, which had been 2,500 strong in the company's heyday, was down to 125. One of the employees' last assignments was to pack up the pattern-making machinery and other equipment to ship to a company in Wisconsin that had been subcontracted to make patterns that had been made in Niles for 75 years. The massive 750,000-square-foot plant was vacated, a monument to the death of manufacturing in the city of 11,000.

In 2019 a marijuana grower, Green Stem, filed applications with Niles officials for permission to grow medical marijuana in a corner of the former plant. If everything is approved, the grower said it would hire 40 people.

Manufacturing Plants Everywhere

If you believe that Simplicity Pattern was an aberration in the sewing industry, consider the fortunes of two other companies. The first is McCall Pattern Co., a Simplicity rival. The second is the Singer Co., the company that makes the sewing machines that turn Simplicity and McCall patterns into clothing.

The raiding of Simplicity Pattern Co.

Before the takeovers: A stable firm

Assets

$100 million in cash reserves, investments

1980 net income: $ 7 million

Founded 1927 in New York City.

By 1981, the world's largest pattern maker.

Factory: Niles, Mich.

1927–1981

First raider

Graham Ferguson Lacey

Chairman/CEO NCC Energy Ltd.

Gains control of Simplicity, becomes chairman/CEO.

Investments with Simplicity cash

- Two New York City buildings.
- A regional airline.
- Oil and gas exploration.
- Gold-mining company bonds.

Jan.–May 1982

Second raider

Charles E. Hurwitz

Chairman/CEO MCO Holdings Inc.

Gains control of Simplicity, becomes chairman/CEO.

Investments with Simplicity cash

- Shopping centers.
- Sugar refineries.
- Golf and tennis resort.

Pension fund raid

- $2.9 million (42%) removed from fund of Niles workers. Originally $10,455 per worker, cut to $6,085.

Labor cuts

- Jobs eliminated, wages reduced, some paid holidays eliminated.

May 1982–Dec. 1984

Third raider

J.B. Fuqua

Chairman, Triton Group Ltd.

Acquires Simplicity.

Erasing taxes

- Corporate income taxes eliminated by deducting losses of a bankrupt real estate trust.

Pension fund raid

- $7.8 million (92%) removed from another fund covering hourly workers. Originally $39,535 per worker, cut to $3,256.

Dec. 1984–Jan. 1988

Fourth raider

Raymond G. Chambers

Chairman/CEO Wesray Capital Corp.

Acquires Simplicity.

Increasing debt

- Borrows $120 million to buy Simplicity.
- By June 1989, Simplicity in default on its loans.
- By April 1990, delinquent on more than $30 million in payments on interest and principal.

Jan. 1988–Fall 1990

Simplicity today: Who owns it?

$100 million reserve gone

"We can't really give out that information."

$100 million in debt, July 1990

McCall, like Simplicity, enjoyed a stable existence for decades. Until 1983, that is, when it became just another card in a deck of corporations that was about to be reshuffled. At the time, McCall was owned by Norton Simon Inc., a New York consumer products and services conglomerate whose many and varied holdings included Avis rental cars, Hunt's catsup and Max Factor cosmetics. The moneymen had targeted Norton Simon for takeover, believing, correctly, that millions of dollars could be made by selling off Norton Simon's assorted operations. The process would result in the closing of plants, the elimination of jobs and the weakening of some companies, but it would create an instant windfall for those orchestrating the deal.

The opening bid was made by Norton Simon's own management. It was so low, though, that it was generally regarded as just a signal that the company was on the auction block. Kohlberg Kravis Roberts & Co., the Wall Street investment firm on its way to becoming the premier buyout specialist, immediately made a counteroffer. But the winning bid came from yet another conglomerate, Esmark Inc., the Chicago-based company once known as Swift & Co., and whose products included STP motor oil, Playtex girdles and Swift ham.

As has been—and continues to be—the case with corporate restructurings, Esmark lacked the money to pay for what it had just purchased. So it began to sell off pieces of Norton Simon. One of the first to go was McCall Pattern. In 1984 a New York investment firm, TLC Group Inc., headed by emerging entrepreneur Reginald F. Lewis, bought McCall. The buyers put up $1 million and borrowed the remainder of the $24.5 million purchase price. Like so many business deals of the 1980s and 1990s, it turned out to be a short-term investment built on long-term debt.

First, Lewis and his associates reaped a quick profit when they extracted $19 million from McCall through a recapitalization plan. Then, three years after the acquisition, they decided it was time to cash in and sold McCall Pattern to the John Crowther Group, a British textile conglomerate. The sale price: $63 million in cash and $32 million in assumed debt.

A news release distributed by TLC Group took note of the extraordinary return: "The sale enabled McCall's stockholders to realize a

90-to-1 profit on their initial investment in the home sewing company ... McCall's stockholders have received aggregate proceeds of more than $90 million on their initial equity investment of $1 million."

Too good to be true, you say? Well, it was very good for Reginald Lewis and his investors. It was not nearly so good for McCall Pattern, the company. Eighteen months after the sale, McCall Pattern—unable to pay its bills—went into bankruptcy court in 1988 to seek protection from its creditors.

Finally, there is the sewing machine used by generations of families to turn their Simplicity and McCall patterns into dresses and suits and coats and other clothes: the Singer. And the company that manufactured it was much older than Simplicity, its origins dating to 1851. For part of the 19th century and most of the 20th century, the Singer Co. dominated the world sewing machine market, its name becoming synonymous with the product it sold.

In the early years, European countries railed against the huge imports of the American-made sewing machine, complaining that Singer, with its emphasis on mass production and its reputation for building low-cost but high-quality machines and providing good service, was dominating the world market. Which it was. At one time, Singer employed as many as 5,000 people at its sprawling production plant in Elizabeth, N.J., where sewing machines were manufactured and shipped to virtually every habitable section of the globe.

No more. The Elizabeth plant closed in 1982 after more than a century of operation. The Singer Co. became a defense and aerospace contractor. The sewing machine business was given a catchy new name, SSMC Inc.

By 1992 SSMC had changed its name back to the Singer Co. and incorporated in the Netherlands Antilles for tax purposes. The company continued to manufacture sewing machines and related products everywhere in the world—Brazil, Taiwan, Mexico, Turkey, Pakistan, Malaysia, Germany, Sri Lanka, the Philippines, Indonesia, Thailand, Bangladesh.

Everywhere, that is, except in the United States.

Chapter Nine

THE DISAPPEARING PENSIONS

INTRODUCTION

In deeply divided America, almost all partisans agree upon one issue:

The country faces a retirement crisis.

In a poll showing rare agreement, the National Institute on Retirement Security found in 2019 that 80 percent of Democrats and 75 percent of Republicans believe that not only is retirement a growing catastrophe, but it's one that Washington has refused to face.

The evidence is overwhelming:

- More than half of working-age Americans have no retirement plan of any kind.

- The median annual value of private pensions is only about $9,600.

- Corporations are abolishing private pension plans at such a rate that they may not exist in coming years except for the very wealthy.

- The median value of 401(k) retirement accounts for workers 60 to 69 years old is only $63,000 —not enough to yield even $3,200 a year at an annual rate of five percent.

- Despite its avowed purpose to keep up with the cost of living, Social Security payments have not kept pace, putting a hardship on nearly half of America's seniors who depend on Social Security for their basic retirement income.

- Poverty among U.S. seniors is nearly twice the rate of those in other developed nations.

The greatest single change to undermine retirement security in the U.S. has been the death of pensions. From 1950 to 1980 more and more Americans were enrolled in pension plans that promised a monthly paycheck of a specific amount for years of service to the company. But in the 1980s, coinciding with other economic decisions by corporations and Washington that would end up harming the middle class, companies began freezing or eliminating pension plans.

With Washington's approval and encouragement, they promoted 401(k) plans as an alternative, a move that saved them money and shifted retirement planning to employees.

No one thought that when 401(k)s were created that they would ever replace pensions. They were touted as an additional way workers could supplement their retirement. But once corporations saw the money they could save by getting rid of pensions, they switched to 401(k)s as retirement plans for their employees.

Every age group within the middle class faces retirement challenges, especially millennials, whose depressed earnings, student loan debt, and high housing costs leave them little money to put aside for retirement. In 2019, The *Wall Street Journal* concluded: "American millennials are approaching middle age in worse shape than every living generation ahead of them."

A Frightening Future

The lesson for today is the American pension system. It is subtitled: What to look forward to when you retire. The text is drawn from the government rule book, with its contradictory and often-overlapping laws relating to pensions.

Here are the highlights:

» The percentage of workers who receive a fixed monthly pension is steadily declining.

» Women who retire from jobs in businesses receive smaller pensions than men.

» The percentage of workers who will receive reduced pension benefits is growing.

» Corporations dip into their employees' pension plans and use the money to enrich the company.

» Conscientious workers who establish their own individual retirement accounts—believing them to be insured by the federal government—one day may discover to their dismay that they are not.

» Workers in the private sector receive far smaller pensions than workers in local, state and federal governments.

» Half of all workers have no pension at all.

» And the people who made all this possible—members of Congress—will continue to receive the best pensions of all.

Barring a massive revision of the rule book by Congress, conditions will continue to deteriorate. In the meantime, watch for the coming war between those who work for government and those who don't. It will come when workers in private industry realize how much power public-employee pension funds wield.

For example, local and state government workers, teachers and community college professors in Oregon benefited handsomely when their pension fund sold its stock in NI Industries Inc. in 1985. NI Industries, formerly Norris Industries Inc., was a manufacturing company based in Long Beach, Calif., that made everything from plumbing fixtures to automobile wheels. The Oregon Public Employees Retirement System had invested $25 million with Kohlberg Kravis Roberts four years earlier to help underwrite the Wall Street investment firm's takeover of NI Industries. When the Oregon pension fund cashed in its chips, it walked away with a return of 268 percent.

In its annual report for that year, the pension fund pointed to the splendid results of its takeover investments, saying that its "leveraged buyout investments ... continue to do well. The sale of the $25 million investment in NI Industries resulted in cash proceeds exceeding $92 million."

That was good for Oregon's public employees. It was not so good for workers at NI Industries. After Kohlberg Kravis took over the company with the backing of Oregon's public-employee pension fund money, it raided the pension plan of workers at NI Industries.

Documents filed with the Pension Benefit Guaranty Corp. show that in 1983 the company's new owners removed $23.3 million from a pension plan—or 61 percent of the plan's total assets of $38.3 million. That left the 2,908 workers covered under the plan with an average of $5,158 each to be invested for their lifetime retirement benefits. By comparison, workers in the Oregon Public Employees Retirement System had, on average, assets of more than $33,000 each to provide for their retirement years. To make matters worse for NI workers, the raid on their pension plan was followed in later years by plant closings and the elimination of their jobs.

Public pension systems across the country are reaping billions of dollars doing the same thing that the Oregon Public Employees Retirement System did. They invest in corporations and then encourage restructuring or other business decisions that lead to curtailed pension benefits for workers in those corporations, the elimination of their jobs, or both.

As a result, workers in private industry who pay taxes that fund the salaries of public employees are losing their pensions and jobs because of investment decisions made by pension funds representing those public employees. To put it more bluntly, the retail employee who lives down the street from a county courthouse worker stands a good chance of losing a portion of his or her pension benefits, job, or both, to provide a better pension for the courthouse worker.

In the past, this would not have been possible. Public-employee pension funds were bit players on the pension scene. The largest pension funds were those of corporations like General Motors and AT&T. While those companies still have big funds, the list of the 25 largest pension funds is dominated by public agencies—entities such as California Public Employees, New York State Teachers, the Wisconsin State Board, Michigan Retirement Systems and Pennsylvania Public Schools. All told 16 of the 25 largest pension funds were public-employee funds in 1992. The assets of public pension funds grew at a much sharper rate in the 1980s than those of private funds. From 1980 to 1989, the assets of private pension plans increased 122 percent—from $496.6 million to $1.1 trillion. During that same period, public pension funds grew by 267 percent—from $198 billion to $727.4 billion.

Public pension funds continue to grow aggressively, and in 2019 comprised 20 of the 25 largest pension funds in the U.S. The largest, California Public Employees Retirement System (CalPERS), had $336.6 billion in assets. The largest private pension fund was AT&T's, which barely made it into the top 10, with $113.5 billion in assets—roughly one-third the size of CalPERS.

With this burgeoning wealth came a newfound power to influence corporate America. Together, the private and public-employee pension funds represent the largest unregulated, untaxed pools of capital in the nation. Managers may invest the money most anywhere they choose, from leveraged buyouts to the purchase of stock in foreign corporations, which may make products that compete with those made by American workers at home. Required by federal rules to maximize the return for the benefit of participants, their loyalty is to the bottom line of their balance sheets, as the NI Industries story illustrates.

In the future, pressure will mount on public-employee pension funds to increase their investment return. That's because most public pension plans are underfunded. Guaranteed, to be sure, but underfunded nonetheless. That means a pension fund does not have enough money to pay the benefits it has promised to the workers enrolled in the plan. As a result, fund managers will be called upon to produce ever greater returns.

The statistics tell the story of the difference between the retirement benefits paid by public and private funds. Take the average annual pensions for 1990: A retired federal worker received $12,966. A retired local or state government worker received $9,068. A retired private-sector worker received $6,512.

Actually, the situation is much worse than the numbers suggest. First, because public-employee pension plans are underfunded, taxpayers eventually may be called upon to provide the additional cash needed to pay the promised benefits. Second, nearly everyone who works for local, state and federal government is covered by a pension plan that guarantees a fixed retirement check every month—long considered the best of all available retirement-plan options. But less than 30 percent of workers in private industry are covered by such defined-benefit plans. Third, many public-employee pension plans provide for mandatory inflation adjustment—that is, the retiree's benefit check is increased as the cost of living goes up. But mandatory inflation adjustments are rare in private pension plans.

UPDATE

The trend of public employees at all levels receiving more generous pensions than private workers has further intensified. Public teachers, sanitation workers, policemen and firefighters receive some of the most generous pensions of all, sometimes as much as 75 percent of their earnings. But it can't last. Estimates vary, but an alarming gap exists between what state and local governments have promised to pay their employees in retirement versus the money they have set aside to make those payments. This unfunded liability of state and local pension funds is at least $5 trillion, and some estimates put it several times higher.

Some state and local governments are already diverting funds to shore up pension funds with tax money that might have been used to pay for broader public services. States and cities with the greatest unfunded liabilities will have to cut benefits or divert money from other services into pension funds, or both.

Finally, the private pension system is deteriorating at the same time that there is a growing recognition—albeit grudging—that the Social Security system will lack the resources to provide for many of these same workers.

Americans can expect little help from their government as they try to wade their way through the morass of laws, rules and regulations that govern pensions in this country. Consider the testimony of a top labor department official before a congressional subcommittee in April 1989. David M. Walker, assistant secretary of labor for pension and welfare benefits, told the members that when a company terminated a pension plan it was required to replace it with an annuity that would provide the retirement benefits that had built up.

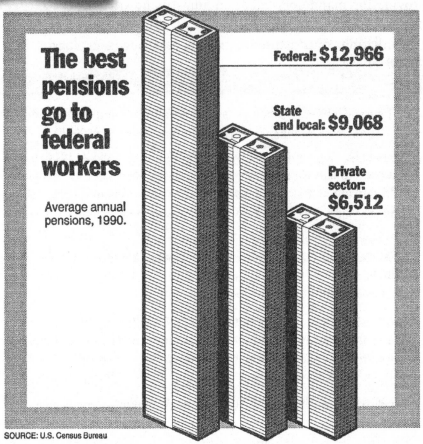

The best pensions go to federal workers

Average annual pensions, 1990.

Federal: **$12,966**

State and local: **$9,068**

Private sector: **$6,512**

SOURCE: U.S. Census Bureau

... WHAT WE'VE FOUND NOW

Workers for federal, state and local government still have the best pensions as the value of private pensions continues to decline. For 2017, the average annual pension of federal workers was $38,000; for state and local employees, $25,818; and for private workers, $15,568.

Source: U.S. Census Bureau

"Annuity contracts must be purchased to secure the value of those accrued benefits," Walker said, adding: "The bottom line is that participants are fully protected with regard to their accrued benefits when there is a termination."

There's one problem with that last statement. It isn't true. Payment of so-called defined-benefit pensions is guaranteed by the Pension Benefit Guaranty Corp., a quasi-federal agency. If a company reneges on its pension commitments, the PBGC issues the monthly pension checks to retired workers. That is not the case with annuity contracts. Annuities are not guaranteed by the PBGC or any other governmental agency.

For this, you can thank Congress, which wrote the rule book in such a way as to permit companies to terminate a pension plan, buy annuities for its workers that will pay the accrued benefits, and keep for themselves whatever accumulated money is not needed to pay for the annuities. It did not require them to guarantee, or insure, the annuities.

At the same time that growing numbers of employees are being asked to make sophisticated judgments on how to set aside their money for retirement, companies that have long provided fixed pension benefits are abandoning such plans in droves. Consider this: Each year, beginning in 1950 and continuing through the 1960s and 1970s, corporations spent a steadily growing amount of money on retirement plans, according to their federal income tax returns. In 1950, corporations claimed $1.7 billion in pension plan contributions. That rose to $4.6 billion in 1960, to $12.2 billion in 1970 and to $51.5 billion in 1980.

That's as it should be. Every year there are more workers. Every year there should be a larger sum set aside for their pensions. And so it went until 1983. That year, corporate pension contributions peaked at $54.4 billion. Then, while the number of workers in the country continued to rise, the money earmarked for their retirement began to go down even though the number of workers enrolled in primary pensions went up.

So what are corporations doing with the money that once went for pensions?

A large chunk of it is going to pay interest on the staggering debt incurred during an uncontrolled borrowing binge. In 1950, for every $1 million that corporations contributed to pension plans, they paid out $1.6 million in interest on loans. As late as 1968, interest payments still amounted to just $1.9 million for every $1 million in pension contributions. But by 1986, corporate interest payments were consuming $5 million for every $1 million that businesses allocated for their employees' retirement.

Looked at another way, in 1986 corporations contributed to pension plans an average of $1,171 for every worker. They paid an average of $5,942 per worker in interest on corporate debt.

America's corporate pension system is especially grim for women. Labor Department statistics show that in 1988 the median private pension income for single women was $2,153. Half of all unmarried women received more than $2,153, half received less. The $2,153, of course, is for a full year. That's $41.40 a week.

More pointedly, the median pension income of single men was $3,820. Thus, single women received 56 percent of the pension income of single men. That was down from 74 percent in 1976. Thus, in 12 years, the amount of single women's pensions fell from about three-fourths that of men's pensions to about half. This despite the fact that women live longer, that more women than ever are working, and that more women than ever are collecting pensions.

Married women in the workforce fared no better. Their median pension in 1988 was $1,848. For married men it was $4,285. That meant the pension of a married woman was 43 percent of the pension of a married man. That figure, too, was down from 12 years earlier. In 1976, married women got $1,310, or 61 percent of the $2,150 pension of married men. Since women outlive men, on average, by seven years, and since most private pensions are not adjusted for inflation, the pension dollars that women eventually receive are worth even less.

All the current evidence suggests that this pattern will continue. Why? Congress's tax-writing committees have heavily skewed the tax law against most women.

FEWER WORKERS HAVE GUARANTEED PENSIONS

Fewer workers with guaranteed pensions, and women retirees are worse off

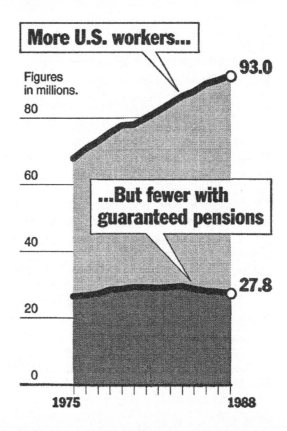

More U.S. workers...

Figures in millions.

...But fewer with guaranteed pensions

93.0

27.8

1975   1988

A smaller and smaller percentage of workers and retirees are covered by any guaranteed pension. In 1988, the figure was 27.8 percent; in 2018 it was 22 percent.

Source: Bureau of Labor Statistics and Pension Benefit Guarantee Corporation

Women who work outside the home are most often employed in the service sector—retail sales, clerical—that generally provides inferior pension plans compared to manufacturing. Even women who work in manufacturing tend to be clustered in businesses with the poorest pension plans, such as the textile industry.

Both male and female workers are victimized by the lack of a coherent pension system. Years ago, the demise of an iconic corporation, Studebaker, brought to light the gaps in pension protection that could have such harmful impact on workers.

The Studebaker Corp. dated from 1852 when brothers Clem and Henry Studebaker built their first covered wagon. They equipped the Union army with wagons during the Civil War and turned out their first horseless carriage in 1904. For the next 60 years, Studebaker manufactured automobiles—sometimes with a styling flair, as with the 1950 Champion—at a sprawling plant in South Bend, Ind.

The same year the Champion debuted, Studebaker Corp. established a pension program. In a booklet distributed to employees, H.S. Vance, the company president, said the plan "carried forward the Studebaker tradition—concern for the employees of the company and their family." The booklet, illustrated with a series of drawings depicting a life of leisure, began: "You may be a long way from retirement age now. Still it's good to know that Studebaker is building up a fund for you so that when you reach retirement age you can settle down on a farm ... visit around the country ... or just take it easy ... and know that you'll still be getting a regular monthly pension paid for entirely by the company."

Reality fell far short of the promise. In 1964, after years of dwindling sales, Studebaker closed the South Bend plant. More than 5,000 workers lost their jobs. Those workers who already had retired, or who were 60 and eligible for retirement, received their promised pensions. Everyone else—more than 4,000 workers—divided up the $2 million or so that remained in the pension plan. That averaged out to lump-sum payments of $197 to $1,757, depending on seniority.

Seven years later, in 1971, when Congress began to seriously study the pension issue, Studebaker workers traveled to Washington to testify before the Senate Labor Committee. Lester Fox, one of those workers, summed up the issue:

"At the time of the plant closing, I was age 40 ... with 20 years of accredited service toward my pension. I received a lump-sum payment of $350 as my share of the residue of the pension trust ... The problem ... is that in this instance, in excess of 4,000 workers who had a promise of a private pension plan witnessed it vanishing before their very eyes ... I commend those who are considering legislation that would provide for a public reinsurance of private pension plans, and I would view that as something similar to the Federal Deposit Insurance Corp., which insures private savings."

More years of congressional wrangling slipped by until 1974, when lawmakers enacted the Employee Retirement Income Security Act (ERISA). The act set standards for the first time that companies would have to follow if they maintained pension plans. A key provision established the Pension Benefit Guaranty Corp., which would guarantee payment of pension benefits if a company failed to pay.

When President Gerald R. Ford signed the law on Labor Day 1974, he declared: "I think this is really an historic Labor Day—historic in the sense that this legislation will probably give more benefits and rights and success in the area of labor-management than almost anything in the history of this country.

"This legislation will alleviate the fears and the anxiety of people who are on the production lines or in the mines or elsewhere, in that they now know that their investment in private pension funds will be better protected ... It certainly will give to those 30-plus million American workers a greater degree of certainty as they face retirement in the future."

So how goes it after the historic passage of ERISA? From 1975 to 1980, the number of workers participating in a pension plan insured by the Pension Benefit Guaranty Corporation rose to 29.7 million, from 26.8 million. But since then the percentage of the workforce covered by such plans has been declining. One reason: Many companies pulled out of the guaranteed-pension program when their PBGC premiums soared. They were getting stuck paying for the insured pensions of the retirees of bankrupt companies.

THE GENDER GAP IN RETIREMENT INCOME

Women lagging behind men in private pensions

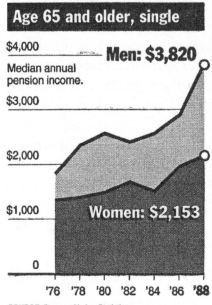

Age 65 and older, single

$4,000

Median annual pension income.

Men: $3,820

$3,000

$2,000

$1,000 **Women: $2,153**

0

'76 '78 '80 '82 '84 '86 '88

Age 65 and older, married

$4,000

$3,000 **Men: $4,285**

$2,000

$1,000 **Women: $1,848**

0

'76 '78 '80 '82 '84 '86 '88

SOURCE: Bureau of Labor Statistics

... WHAT WE'VE FOUND NOW

Women 65 years and older have on average a third less income in retirement than men. Since publication of this book's first edition, the differential has barely changed. In 1988, women had pension income that was 56 percent of that of men. In 2019, women's total retirement income was still only 59 percent of men's. In 2017, the median reirement income for men was $32,654; for women $19,180.

Source: Bureau of Labor Statistics and Pension Rights Center

Only 2 percent of America's private-sector workers were covered by a pension in 2018—down from 28 percent in 1980.

Corporations have killed pensions at a breathtaking pace in the past 40 years, a dramatic reversal from before 1980 when many companies added defined-benefit plans for their employees. From 1950 to 1980 the number of Americans in private industry who were enrolled in pension plans more than tripled, from 10.3 million to 35 million. The number of these plans reached a high of 172,843 in 1983. Since then companies have killed 127,764 pension plans and only 45,079 remain—so far. Fewer private-sector workers have pensions today than at any time since World War II.

While killing pensions, corporations have shifted employees into 401(k) plans. Originally conceived as a supplement to pensions, 401(k)s have become the primary retirement vehicle for 60 million Americans. The median value for all 401(k) accounts—$22,000 in 2019—may not even be enough for many to live on for a year.

The corporate decision to ax pensions and shift workers into 401(k)s has saved companies billions in contributions and administrative expenses but is creating a catastrophe for millions of Americans who will quickly outlive their retirement savings.

The Pension Raiders

While tens of millions of workers have fared poorly under the existing system, corporate managers and takeover artists have profited handsomely from it. They do so by raiding pension funds—a practice made possible by the way the federal government wrote the rule book.

During the 1980s alone, nearly 2,000 businesses dipped into their pension funds and removed $21 billion. That is enough to provide pensions of $800 a month to a quarter-million retired workers. And their spouses. For the rest of their lives. The $21 billion does not count the billions that businesses diverted to other uses after substituting inferior pension plans for the plans that had been in place for decades.

How does a company go about extracting money from its employees' retirement bank? To withdraw money, a company must certify that the pension plan has more assets than are needed to meet its retirement obligations.

As noted earlier, Congress wrote the rule book in such a way as to permit companies to terminate a pension plan, buy for its workers unguaranteed annuities that will pay the accrued benefits, and keep what is left over. The losers in the transaction are the employees, who virtually always end up with smaller retirement checks than under the old plan. What's more, most companies that terminated their defined-benefit plans—plans that promise a specified amount to a retiree—replaced them with defined-contribution plans, meaning, in most cases, even lower retirement benefits in the future.

Under a defined-contribution plan, an employer agrees to set aside a fixed amount of money for an employee's retirement. How much the employee eventually receives depends on how well that money is invested. In most cases, it is substantially less than what a defined-benefit plan would provide. Most significantly, neither the annuities nor the defined-contribution plans carry a government guarantee.

About 23,000 former and current employees at the Cannon Mills Co. textile plants in North Carolina, South Carolina and Georgia learned that lesson the hard way. For years, workers at Cannon Mills, headquartered in Kannapolis, N.C., were covered by a pension plan that was insured by the PBGC. That changed after a corporate raider by the name of David H. Murdock appeared on the scene in 1982.

Murdock was chairman and chief executive officer of Dole Food Co., whose products include Dole pineapples and bananas, and was a member of the Forbes 400, the Who's Who of the nation's rich. Murdock was a major fund-raiser for the Republican Party. In 1988 he hosted a private, $10,000-per-person reception at his 64-room Bel Air, Calif., home once owned by the late hotel baron Conrad Hilton. There, donors mingled and posed for photographs with his friend, President Ronald Reagan.

It was in 1982, during one of his takeover forays, that Murdock picked Cannon Mills. When Murdock launched his takeover of

Cannon Mills, it was the last of the large family-controlled textile businesses. Cannon employed about 24,000 people at 22 plants, producing towels, sheets, other bedding accessories, kitchen products and rugs. The company was profitable, had extensive real estate holdings and no debt. It was run in much the same paternalistic way as it was in 1906 when it was founded. The company still owned 1,600 homes in Kannapolis, which it rented to workers for $20 to $85 a month.

As was the practice in the 1980s, Murdock bought Cannon Mills with mostly borrowed money and then used company revenue to pay the debt. To that end, he eliminated the jobs of 2,000 workers and sold the company houses. Four years after acquiring Cannon Mills, Murdock decided to move on. Before selling the company, he terminated the pension plan covering 23,000 workers.

PBGC records show that the plan's assets at the time were valued at $102.8 million. Murdock removed $36.6 million, contending that the remaining $66.2 million was enough to guarantee pensions. He invested the $36.6 million in stock of two companies that were potential takeover candidates and used the leftover $66.2 million to purchase annuities from an insurance company for Cannon Mills workers. But the annuities, unlike the pensions they replaced, weren't guaranteed by the PBGC.

And they were purchased from Executive Life Insurance Co. in Los Angeles—the same Executive Life that had sunk billions of dollars into junk bonds sold by Michael R. Milken of Drexel Burnham Lambert Inc. The same Executive Life Insurance Co. that was seized by California officials in 1991 in what became the nation's largest insurance company failure at the time. The same Executive Life Insurance Co. that reduced monthly payments to pensioners and other annuity holders, including retirees of Cannon Mills, to only 70 percent of the pension benefits they had been promised before Murdock dipped into their plan.

As for Murdock, he converted the $36.6 million he had withdrawn from the pension plan into a handsome profit. When he sold the stock in the takeover companies, he reaped a $60-million profit on his investment.

While Murdock was raiding the pension fund of a single company, others were launching multiple raids. Among them: Meshulam Riklis of Beverly Hills and Victor Posner of Miami Beach, Fla., the two elder statesmen of American business who were using borrowed money to make their fortunes long before the coining of the phrase junk bonds.

Riklis was possibly best known for spending millions of dollars to promote the singing-acting-entertainment career of his second wife, 36-year-old Pia Zadora, whom he met when she was 17. He underwrote singing and acting lessons, orchestrated commercials and a nude layout in *Penthouse* magazine, arranged stage shows and movies. They included the Harold Robbins production *The Lonely Lady*, which one critic dismissed as a "risible concoction designed to show off the non-talents of a non-star in a film financed by her husband." Through a maze of interlocking companies, Riklis controlled such familiar businesses as McCrory Corp. and J.J. Newberry, the variety stores; Samonsite Corp., the luggage maker, and Culligan Corp., the water-treatment company.

In October 1985, Riklis' Faberge Inc. removed $6.2 million from its employee pension fund of $18.2 million. That same month, Riklis' McCrory Corp. removed $11.1 million from its employee pension fund of $87.5 million. And in March 1986, Riklis' Kenton Corp. removed $12.6 million from its employee pension fund of $18.9 million. Over a six-month period, the three Riklis companies withdrew a total of $29.9 million from employee retirement plans. After the $11.1 million was extracted from the McCrory pension fund, the remaining $76.4 million averaged out to $5,045 to be invested for each worker covered under the plan.

Many of McCrory's 26,100 employees, though, were not eligible to participate in the pension plan. Among them were 9,360 workers who earned less than $4,000 a year. And nearly two-thirds of the 15,140 employees enrolled in the retirement plan earned less than $10,000 a year. As for Riklis, his compensation from the various companies ranged upward of $4 million a year. That was complemented by a retirement package of more than $100,000 a year for life. And then for his wife. For life.

Victor Posner was a Riklis contemporary who maintained a lavish lifestyle using corporate funds at various times to pay for his yachts and horses.

PBGC records show that, like Riklis, he began raiding pension funds in the 1980s. First came the Graniteville Co. of Graniteville, S.C. A textile company with a rich history dating to the mid-1800s, Graniteville was taken over by Posner in 1983. That month, Posner's Graniteville removed $15.4 million from a company pension fund.

In 1984, Posner's Pennsylvania Engineering Corp., a Pittsburgh-based engineering and construction company, removed $2.4 million from a pension fund. The following year, Posner's Royal Crown Companies Inc., a Miami soft drink distributor, removed $1.9 million from a pension fund. In 1986, Posner's National Propane Corp., a New Hyde Park, N.Y., liquefied petroleum gas distributor, removed $1.1 million from a pension fund. Later that year, Posner's Birdsboro Corp., a Birdsboro, Penn., foundry whose corporate ancestors manufactured muskets for the Revolutionary War, removed $4.4 million from a pension fund.

In 1987, Posner's Salem Corp., a Pittsburgh industrial furnace and mining equipment manufacturer, withdrew $3.5 million from a pension fund. In December 1987, Posner's Enro Shirt Co., a Louisville, Ky., shirtmaker, withdrew $1.5 million from a pension fund. Finally, in 1988, Posner's Fischbach Corp., a New York engineering firm, withdrew $35 million from a pension fund.

That brought to $65.2 million the total that Posner companies drained from the pension funds of nearly 4,800 employees.

In the case of one of his companies, Sharon Steel Corp., Posner never put the money into the pension fund in the first place. In a report filed with the Securities and Exchange Commission in 1986, the company said it had postponed $27.8 million in pension contributions that it was required to make for 1984 and 1985. At the time, Sharon Steel's pension plan was $105.6 million in the hole. And the hole was growing.

The Pension Benefit Guaranty Corp. in 1991 listed the steel company's employee-retirement obligations at $264 million and the pension fund's assets at only $86 million, leaving the pension plan short $178 million. That means all the other businesses that contribute to the PBGC would be obliged to pick up the tab for the retirees of Sharon Steel.

In the meantime, Posner was indicted on charges of tax evasion and filing false tax returns. He pleaded no contest in 1987 to charges of filing false income tax returns. U.S. District Court Judge Eugene P. Spellman in Miami ordered Posner to pay a fine of $75,000, back taxes and penalties of $2.1 million, and interest on that sum, which totaled about $2 million. He also ordered Posner to devote 5,000 hours to community service.

There is a historical footnote to this story: In 1977, the SEC had cited Posner for diverting Sharon Steel pension fund assets to his personal use. He signed a consent decree promising not to violate the law in the future.

Government officials and corporate executives are fond of saying that most private pension plans are overfunded.

That is, the plan's paper assets—the value of the stocks, bonds and other investments it holds—exceed the amount of money that will have to be paid to future retirees. Therefore, they argue, the extra money belongs to the company, not the employees—even though in some cases it was set aside for pensions in lieu of raises.

On the other hand, when a plan is underfunded, those same executives often refuse to make the additional contributions needed to make the plan solvent. It is the ultimate coin-toss game: Heads, the company wins; tails, the employees lose.

If a company terminates a pension plan and buys uninsured annuities, it gets to keep the leftover cash. But if the pension fund lacks sufficient cash to pay the promised benefits, it becomes the PBGC's problem. Or if the PBGC insurance fund goes the way of the Federal Savings and Loan Insurance Corp. insurance fund—broke—it will be the taxpayers' problem. In other words, today's overfunded pension plan may be tomorrow's underfunded plan.

Witness the experience of the Boise Cascade Corp. In 1984, assets in the Boise pension fund amounted to $522 million. Employee retirement benefits totaled $373 million. That meant the plan was overfunded. It had $149 million in what pension raiders like to call "excess cash." Just seven years later, the Pension Benefit Guaranty

Corp. released a list of 50 companies with the largest underfunded pension plans. Among those cited: Boise Cascade, which was $32 million short. And the list continues to grow.

UPDATE

Not even all those who have pensions that they thought were guaranteed can bank on them.

Eleven million workers in construction and transportation have pensions guaranteed by the multi-employer program of the Pension Benefit Guaranty Corporation (PBGC). But that program is $65 billion in the red and verging on collapse. Should that happen, workers in those industries would receive only a fraction of what they expected in retirement, some less than $200 a month. No one factor is to blame, but Congressional deregulation of trucking has led to chronic bankruptcies, fewer contributions and more payouts.

The Government Accountability Office (GAO) has estimated that PBGC's multi-employer fund is highly likely to be insolvent by 2025.

PBGC's other major program, which covers employees who work for a single employer, is also facing long-term funding challenges as more employers withdraw. The plan has a surplus, but the GAO has warned that it too might face a deficit if a series of costly corporate failures suddenly occurs, as has happened in the past:

"[The] spate of plan terminations in the airline and steel industries from 2001 to 2006 resulted in more than $20 billion of net claims," the GAO reported in 2019. "The possibility of large, future claims persists ..."

Companies in both the single-employer and multi-employer plans have steadily pulled out of the PBGC program, leading to a shortfall in premiums. Since 1985, the decline in the number of single-employer plans insured by PBGC fell 78 percent—from about 114,000 to about 24,000—and covered 13 million fewer workers by 2020.

Sometimes a company's pension fund serves as an early-warning signal of corporate distress. Our analysis documented scores of instances in which a company's decision to dip into the retirement fund of its employees was followed in a few years by bankruptcy court proceedings, corporate restructurings, the elimination of jobs, or all three.

Take SCOA Industries Inc., a publicly owned, mini-retail conglomerate that in 1985 was headquartered in Columbus, Ohio. In December of that year, a Boston buyout firm, Thomas H. Lee Co., joined forces with Wall Street's money-raising takeover machine, Drexel Burnham Lambert, to take SCOA Industries private. The stock buyout cost more than $600 million—most of it borrowed. Drexel Burnham and the Lee company, headed by Thomas H. Lee, a nephew of SCOA's chairman, picked up millions of dollars in fees as well as nearly 50 percent of the stock in the new company.

At the same time, SCOA Industries dipped into a company pension fund and removed $43.7 million. Soon after, the company began selling off some of its holdings to pare down the debt incurred in the buyout. The $43.7 million extracted from the pension fund amounted to 57 percent of the fund's assets. That left $33.3 million, or an average of $3,299, to provide lifetime retirement benefits for each of the 10,102 employees covered under the plan.

Two years after taking SCOA Industries private, Drexel Burnham and the Lee company announced plans in 1987 to take the successor business, Hills Department Stores, public. They sold more than four million shares of stock and issued $40 million of debt that could be converted into stock.

From those transactions, Drexel Burnham and the Lee company picked up additional millions of dollars in fees as well as millions of dollars in profits from the sale of stock they acquired when taking the company private.

Drexel Burnham issued a report touting the Hills stock to investors, saying that Hills' pricing strategy, "coupled with a strong management team, has produced one of the highest operating margins in the industry." Drexel Burnham forecast a "15 percent annual sales growth over the next five years" and dismissed concerns that the outstanding debt would pose serious obstacles: "While some investors may be concerned about the company's high financial leverage, it appears to be well covered. This risk should be minimized by the company's history of twenty-nine years of consecutive increases in operating profits and sales ... We feel Hills will be able to generate the earnings growth and cash flow necessary to pay down debt and deleverage the balance sheet, while expanding the operation at a faster than historic pace."

Two more years slipped by and Hills was not faring especially well. Nonetheless, Drexel Burnham remained bullish in a report issued to investors in September 1989: "Hills results have been below expectations since going public two years ago, but profits appear to be on the verge of a turning point." Gazing into Wall Street's crystal ball, Drexel Burnham analysts projected that "going out past 1991, we expect earnings per share to grow by nearly 25 percent annually. This growth is a function of leverage created by paydown of debt and improving operating margins." As for all that debt still outstanding, Drexel Burnham continued to exude optimism: "We believe Hills can generate excess cash flow from earnings growth to pay down debt and slowly deleverage the balance sheet."

Once again, the wizards of debt at Drexel Burnham guessed wrong.

In 1991, burdened with a crushing debt arranged by Drexel Burnham and the Lee company, Hills filed for bankruptcy. The 1985 raid on the company pension fund had been a precursor of what was to come, just as similar raids were at scores of other companies. Consider: In September 1982, Branch Motor Express Co., an interstate trucking company headquartered in New York City, removed $4.53 million from a company pension fund. That amounted to 52 percent of the pension fund's total assets, leaving $4.23 million, or an average of $5,221, to provide lifetime retirement benefits for each of the 810 employees covered under the plan. Two years later, Branch Motor Express filed for protection from its creditors in bankruptcy court. The company's 70 terminals across the country were later closed and all employees dismissed. The company no longer exists.

Another: In 1984, the owners of Ames Department Stores Inc., the discount retail chain headquartered in Rocky Hill, Conn., removed $1.7 million from a company pension fund. That was 57 percent of the pension fund's total assets, leaving $1.3 million—or an average of $458—to provide retirement benefits for each of the 2,904 employees covered under the plan. Six years later, Ames filed for bankruptcy protection. The company that once operated nearly 700 stores under the Ames and Zayre names, mostly on the East Coast, closed 220 stores and dismissed 18,000 employees.

Another: In 1985, Ohrbach's Inc., the fashionable women's apparel chain headquartered in New York City, removed $9 million from a company pension fund. That amounted to 66 percent of the pension fund's total assets, leaving $4.7 million, or an average of $6,590, to provide lifetime retirement benefits for each of the 716 employees covered under the plan. One year later, the Dutch company that owned Ohrbach's, which was founded in 1923, discontinued operations. Ohrbach's stores, concentrated in New York and Los Angeles, were closed.

Another: In 1987, the owners of Morse Shoe Inc., operators of the Fayva shoe store chain in Canton, Mass., removed $8.3 million from a pension fund. That was 35 percent of the pension fund's assets, leaving $15.4 million—or an average of $5,477—to provide lifetime retirement benefits for each of the 2,812 employees covered under the plan. Three years later, Morse Shoe filed for bankruptcy protection.

Another: In September 1986, the owners of B. Altman & Co., the 120-year-old New York-based retailer, removed $10.9 million from a company pension fund. That was 45 percent of the pension fund's total assets, leaving $13.1 million, or an average of $4,226, to provide lifetime retirement benefits for each of the 3,100 employees covered under the plan. Three years later, B. Altman's parent company filed for protection in bankruptcy court. A few months later, all B. Altman's stores were closed and 1,700 employees were out of work.

After 10 years and the removal of billions of dollars from retirement plans, Congress got around to rewriting the rules to take some of the profit out of the practice by imposing stiffer excise taxes. But that doesn't mean the pension-raiding era is over. Far from it. Later, Congress quietly slipped a new provision into the government rule book that permits corporations to use their pension fund money for another purpose: to pay for employee health-care expenses.

As was noted earlier, corporations are already cutting back on health-care benefits as insurance premiums soar. Congress gave them a way to attack that problem by using money set aside for employee retirement benefits to pay their health-care costs. For corporations, the best part of the deal is that the retirement payments are guaranteed by the PBGC—and ultimately taxpayers—if the pension fund runs out of cash because money was diverted to health insurance premiums.

Junk Pensions

To better understand what the future holds for the retirement of millions of workers as a result of the way Congress writes the rules, let us visit events that unfolded in two places that are worlds apart—Seneca, Kan., and Washington, D.C.

It was the week of July 13, 1986. On Friday of that week, in sleepy Seneca (population 2,300), employees at the Community National Bank were processing paperwork for two self-directed individual retirement accounts for John G. Kass and his wife, Virginia. The Kasses lived in Topeka, about 75 miles south of Seneca. He was a painter for the Veterans Administration hospital; she worked in the accounting department of the Santa Fe Railroad. Their retirement accounts were among hundreds the bank established for workers living in different sections of the country but were concentrated in the Midwest.

With the bank acting as trustee, John Kass invested $2,400 in senior subordinated debentures—a fancy name for a piece of paper that is a corporate IOU. His wife invested $2,500. The debentures promised a hefty interest rate of 12.5 percent a year. They were issued by American Continental Corp. of Phoenix.

Actually, the Kasses had rolled over their IRAs from another small Kansas bank in yet a smaller Kansas town, the First National Bank of Onaga. Like many others, the Kasses had opened their retirement accounts at the Onaga bank because it catered to the self-directed IRA business. With a self-directed IRA, future retirees tell the trustee—a bank, brokerage firm or insurance company—what stocks, bonds or other investments they want to put in their retirement account.

The Onaga bank encountered financial difficulties as a result of a portfolio of bad loans and was seized by federal regulators. Many of the IRAs, including the Kasses', were shifted to Seneca. The Onaga bank was quickly reorganized and continued to service its IRAs. Now it had competition from Seneca. As more people invested their retirement accounts in American Continental bonds because of the high interest rate they paid, processing the accounts became a sizable part of the work for both banks in a region hard-pressed for jobs.

For the First National Bank of Onaga, the IRA business translated into jobs. "We are a town of 700 people," said Owen E. Duer, the bank's executive vice president, "and we employ 12 people in our IRA department who would not even be here if it weren't for that department. So we are pretty tickled that we have this so we can employ people in our town." In Seneca, the Community National Bank established a separate division, called the Retirement Plans Division, to process and monitor IRA investments.

During 1986, workers from around the country put more than a quarter-million dollars of their retirement money into American Continental bonds at the Seneca and Onaga banks. But soon the money that John and Virginia Kass and many others had set aside for retirement was largely gone. American Continental, a financial services holding company, filed for bankruptcy protection in 1989, virtually wiping out the savings of thousands of retirees like the Kasses.

During that same week in 1986 when the Community National Bank of Seneca was processing the paperwork for what would turn out to be worthless retirement accounts, Charles H. Keating Jr. was in Washington, doing what he did best—lobbying the people who write and revise the government rule book. Keating was a Phoenix homebuilder, fund-raiser for friendly members of Congress and presidential candidates, proprietor of one of California's largest savings-and-loan institutions, crusader for decent literature, and chairman and chief executive officer of American Continental Corp. Back in the 1950s, when he was a Cincinnati lawyer, Keating had founded Citizens for Decent Literature Inc. For years, he traveled the country identifying and denouncing smut.

On July 16, 1986, Keating was making the rounds of Capitol Hill, railing against government regulators and their efforts to impose some controls on financial institutions, such as his Lincoln Savings & Loan Association. Keating's American Continental had acquired Lincoln Savings & Loan, headquartered in Irvine, Calif., in 1984. He promptly abandoned the traditional savings-and-loan business of making home mortgages and opted for pouring hundreds of millions of dollars into junk bonds, luxury resort hotels, assorted real estate deals and foreign investments.

When the Federal Home Loan Bank Board, under chairman Edwin J. Gray, proposed a regulation limiting such investments, Keating mounted a banker's holy war against regulations in general and Gray in particular. He enlisted an army of supporters to lobby both the Federal Home Loan Bank Board and Congress. The army included Donald Regan and Alan J. Greenspan. At the time, Regan was White House chief of staff and Greenspan was a private consultant and member of the President's Economic Policy Advisory Board. That's the same Alan Greenspan who later, as chairman of the Federal Reserve Board, helped make policy decisions that influenced the course of the economy and everyone's standard of living.

In a letter to the Federal Home Loan Bank Board on behalf of Keating's thrift, Greenspan had written on Nov. 1, 1984: "I understand that Lincoln Savings & Loan Association has requested that the board allow me to meet with it or its staff in order to discuss my view that the proposed rule (limiting thrift investments) is unwarranted and could prove harmful if put into effect. I hope that the board will agree to such a meeting ... at the earliest possible time."

The high-powered lobbying notwithstanding, Edwin Gray and the bank board issued the rule. By the summer of 1986, Keating was back in Washington, pushing for Gray's ouster, an end to the regulation on investments and the appointment of more friendly regulators. He had come up with his personal nominee for a seat on the three-member bank board.

His candidate was Lee H. Henkel Jr., an Atlanta lawyer and businessman. During the first administration of President Richard M. Nixon, Henkel had served as general counsel for the Internal Revenue Service and assistant general counsel of the U.S. Treasury Department. Henkel, who was active in Republican politics, had worked with Keating in 1980, when both men were backing John

B. Connally's bid for the GOP presidential nomination. Henkel also had borrowed millions of dollars from Lincoln Savings & Loan to help underwrite some of his investments.

So it was that Keating set off to the Senate to sell Henkel. First, he met with Paula Hawkins, the Florida Republican. Then, he met with Sen. Donald W. Riegle, Jr., the Michigan Democrat. Then he met with Alan Cranston, the Democratic senator from California. Later, Keating's forces would give Hawkins $8,000 in campaign contributions, Riegle $78,250—and Cranston $1.3 million. In the weeks that followed, Keating lobbied other lawmakers on behalf of Henkel. His perseverance paid off when President Ronald Reagan tapped Henkel for a seat on the board.

Henkel was no sooner in office than he proposed new banking rules that would have granted immunity to Lincoln Savings for some of its past lending practices. It seemed that Lincoln had put nearly twice as much money into risky investments as was allowed under the regulation still in effect. For months, federal bank examiners had been poring over Lincoln's books, asking annoying questions about the institution's investments and missing paperwork.

Henkel's attempt to help backfired. When his financial ties to Lincoln were disclosed, and Sen. William Proxmire, the Wisconsin Democrat, demanded a Justice Department investigation, Henkel resigned from the bank board. But Keating's lobbying and incessant attacks on his nemesis, Edwin Gray, had had their effect. Gray left the bank board when his term expired in 1987. He was replaced by another Keating ally, M. Danny Wall, the former staff director of the Senate banking committee. Over the next two years, Wall's actions would protect Keating and his company from the federal auditors who correctly saw that Lincoln's investment practices would bring down the thrift.

But eventually it would all unravel. Lincoln Savings & Loan was seized by federal regulators. Its bailout cost taxpayers an estimated $3 billion. American Continental went into bankruptcy court. The bankruptcy case was the largest in Arizona history and one of the half-dozen largest, in terms of paperwork, in U.S. history. And finally, in December 1991, a Los Angeles County Superior Court jury convicted Charles Keating himself for security fraud in connection with the sale of the worthless bonds. Later, a federal grand jury indicted him of fraud and racketeering charges.

Keating was convicted of fraud, racketeering and conspiracy in both federal and state courts and served 4½ years in prison before the convictions were overturned. In 1999, he pleaded guilty to wire fraud and bankruptcy fraud and was sentenced to the time he had served. Keating died in 2014.

In addition to the hundreds of people who put their retirement money in American Continental bonds, more than 20,000 others, most residents of California, purchased the bonds as an investment. In California, where the debentures were sold at Lincoln Savings & Loan branches, many unsuspecting buyers thought the bonds—like their savings accounts—were insured by the federal government. So, too, did some of the people who bought the bonds for their retirement accounts—including the folks in and around little Seneca, Kansas. They were not.

Owen Duer, the First National Bank of Onaga official, said that a lot of people were confused, assuming that because their IRA was in a federally insured bank that the account, too, was insured. Many IRAs are backed by the government, but only when they are placed in accounts that are federally insured. After the American Continental bankruptcy filing, Duer said, "We had lots of phone calls. I can remember one gentleman who just swore up and down that he was insured by the (Federal Deposit Insurance Corp.), and I assured him that he wasn't, and that I didn't make that investment. He was only insured by FDIC if I made that investment for him. He chose to make that investment. He felt just because we were a bank, anything he did with us became insured ..."

Duer emphasized that the banks acted only as custodians: "We do whatever the customer or his representative says to do with the assets in his IRA. The only thing we do is the paperwork and the government reporting. We make no recommendations on whether to buy or sell ... That's the sum total of our involvement." Duer said it's possible that the people selling the bonds led the buyers to believe that because a bank was acting as custodian, the IRA was insured. Or perhaps the salespeople did nothing to discourage a buyer who jumped to that conclusion.

But how was it, exactly, that people in Iowa and Michigan and Nebraska and Arizona opened IRAs in Onaga and Seneca and invested their future in a piece of Charles Keating's financial empire? Local and regional brokerage firms, among them the Offerman Co. of Minneapolis, sold the bonds. The two Kansas banks acted as custodians.

John Kass, the Topeka painter who put his IRA money in American Continental bonds, remembered the broker's spiel well: "He said, 'John, I think this is pretty good. I think we ought to get into this. It's paying 13 percent' ... or whatever it was. He said his boss had a lot of shares in it. He said it was a real good deal."

The broker's pitch notwithstanding, Kass might have chosen a different investment if he had heard the views a year earlier of the man in charge of the company issuing the bonds. During an appearance before a congressional committee in 1985, Charles Keating, the American Continental chairman, spoke critically of subordinated debentures:

"I do not happen to think (a) subordinated debenture is viable capital. I think it is a sham." Out in the heartland, the story was a bit different.

Another Topeka resident, Duane Hudson, a former telephone company lineman, said he was told that American Continental bonds were "as good as gold. He (the broker) told me this will be there when you retire. You'll have your investment ... The risk was never mentioned. It was just the same as though you had put it in a bank. He said that with institutions of that size, there is never any worry.

"I guess these were junk bonds, but they weren't sold to me as junk bonds. These were sold to me as a security so when I retired I would have some money. I didn't want my IRA in anything that was risky. And that's why I'm bitter. I didn't know what a junk bond was from anything else, but I do now."

Dream Pensions

While all this may seem to suggest an unrelievedly grim picture of America's private pension system, there are a few bright spots.

Suppose you once earned $50,000 in your job. You retire. The years slip by. Now you collect $100,000. Not likely. That's because about 99 percent of the labor force works for businesses that do not adjust pensions yearly to account for inflation. More typical is a pension that amounts to 25 percent, or less, of a worker's salary. Unless you're in Congress.

UPDATE

Average pensions for retired members of Congress range from $41,208 to $75,528, depending on when they served. But many pull in annual six-figure retirement checks. According to a Bloomberg News report, they include former House speaker Newt Gingrich, $100,200; former South Dakota senator Tom Daschle, $105,804; former Mississippi senator Trent Lott, $110,352; former Utah senator Orin Hatch, $139,000. The late Illinois congressman Robert Michel, who died in 2017, took in $211,452 a year—57 percent more than he earned as a congressman in his last year in Congress, 1994.

In addition to their pensions for years in Congress, many lawmakers also have established supplementary pension accounts based on other income. Here again, they have amended the government rule book, time after time, to take care of themselves while assuring workers everywhere they were merely strengthening the private pension system. The result has been ever greater inequities: a system that provides extraordinarily generous pensions for some, meager pensions for others, guaranteed pensions for some, non-guaranteed pensions for others.

Overlying this chaos is another practice that Congress has elevated to an art form: enacting specific legislative packages one year then rescinding or amending them a few years later. This has been especially true in the area of taxes and pensions.

Take tax-deductible Individual Retirement Accounts (IRAs): Congress passed the universal IRA program in 1981. In a report that year, the Joint Committee on Taxation explained the reasoning:

"The Congress was concerned that a large number of the country's workers, including many who are covered by employer-sponsored retirement plans, face the prospect of retiring without the resources needed to provide adequate retirement income levels."

In 1986, Congress took a different position and, depending on income levels, either limited or canceled the deductibility of IRAs. A Congress that five years earlier had said that IRAs should be expanded so everyone could have a retirement plan now said that IRAs should be curbed because people had too many retirement plans.

Bill Bradley, the Democratic senator from New Jersey, spoke for the revisionists: "Just giving a quick scan over the code, you find that it is possible for a family to have six or seven different pension plans. For example, you could have a 401(k) plan ... If you have a spouse that works as a teacher or public employee, you could have a so-called 403 plan ... If you have a little self-employment income, you could have a Keogh plan. If you work for a company, you will have the company pension plan. If your spouse works for another company, you will have two company pension plans.

"If you are like an increasing number of Americans who, in their work life work for two companies, you could end up with two company pension plans. If your wife or husband worked also for two companies, you could end up in a family with four company pension plans. And that is all before we even get to the question of Social Security. So that you could find a family with a 401(k) plan, a 403 plan, a Keogh, two or three or four company pensions, and Social Security."

Such a scenario is indeed possible for about 17 percent of America's workforce. The overwhelming majority are public employees—schoolteachers and college professors and local, state and federal government workers. For the remaining 83 percent of the population, the probability of multiple retirement checks is a fantasy.

Perhaps Bradley was talking about himself. Or about any number of other members of Congress—Robert J. Dole, the retired Republican senator from Kansas, for example. In 1986, Dole condemned IRAs for people who already were enrolled in a pension plan at work, saying "you shouldn't have a double dip." Dole, on the other hand, has multiple dips.

Dole receives a guaranteed pension for his years in Congress estimated to be at least $150,000. He could contribute to a 401(k), and the federal government—make that the taxpayers—will match part of his contribution. He receives a tax-free military pension of $13,728 for injuries sustained in World War II. And he has established a six-figure Keogh account to accommodate his income from honoraria, speeches and writing.

Now contrast that with a worker earning $50,000 a year. If she's lucky enough to have a pension where she works, she also may establish an IRA, to which she may contribute a maximum of $6,000 a year.

This is not just to single out Sen. Dole. Other members of Congress are doing just as well—or better. And some already are collecting pension checks in addition to their congressional paychecks. Even those lawmakers convicted of crimes have done quite nicely under the Capitol Hill pension system. Cornelius E. Gallagher, a Democrat, spent 14 years in Congress as the representative of Hudson and Union counties in northern New Jersey before checking into a federal penitentiary in 1973 after pleading guilty to income tax evasion. Gallagher's congressional salary in 1972, when he was indicted on charges of concealing more than $300,000 of income, was $42,500. His monthly pension checks in 1990 added up to $58,368—or 137 percent of his congressional salary.

Frank M. Clark, a Democrat, represented three Western Pennsylvania counties—Beaver, Butler and Lawrence—for 20 years before voters retired him in January 1975. Three years later, Clark was indicted on charges of income tax evasion, mail fraud and perjury in connection with placing his housekeepers and campaign workers on federal payrolls. He pleaded guilty in 1979 to income tax evasion and mail fraud and was sentenced to two years in prison. Clark's final congressional salary was $42,500. In 1990, he collected a pension of $64,068—or 151 percent of his salary.

While Congress was protecting the pensions of its convicted felons, a few states have enacted legislation terminating the pension benefits of public officials found guilty of criminal acts. West Virginia's three-term Republican governor, Arch Moore, was sentenced to five years in prison in 1990 after pleading guilty to federal charges of tax fraud, mail fraud, extortion and obstruction of justice. He served time at a camp for white-collar criminals at Maxwell Air Force Base in Alabama. As a result of the conviction, Moore lost his annual state pension and any survivor's pension for his wife.

But Moore didn't lose all his retirement benefits. Until his death in 2015, he continued to collect his check from the U.S. Treasury for the years he spent in Congress.

UPDATE

The scandalous practice of allowing convicted congressional lawmakers to collect hefty taxpayer-funded pensions even after they served time in prison was attacked for decades by critics. In 2007 and 2012, Congress bowed to public pressure and enacted legislation aimed at stripping former lawmakers of their pensions if convicted of a felony. But loopholes in the laws have allowed lawmakers to continue to collect their pensions even after conviction.

Chapter Ten
THE POLITICAL CONNECTION

INTRODUCTION

How would you like to earn a million dollars on the job and pay taxes at the same rate as the sanitation worker who picks up your trash?

A sweet deal, yes?

Well, some people have that deal. They're private-equity moguls and hedge funders who make use of a provision in the IRS code called carried interest. This allows them to shift their earnings to a much lower tax bracket.

Thanks to Congress, the tax code has many rich giveaways for those who have access to the halls of Congress. Of all of them, the carried interest provision is one of the most outrageous and may be the best example of Wall Street's enduring power in Washington.

Buried deep in the tax code, the carried interest provision allows hedge fund and private-equity managers to earmark part of their earnings from managing investment funds as capital gains rather than salary, which would be taxed at a higher rate. For those who have very high incomes, salary income is taxed at almost double that of capital gains income. Critics point out that Americans who manage other kinds of companies do not receive any special tax break simply because they are managers. Why should money managers be different?

For years some Democrats and Republicans have lambasted this tax break, which enriches only a few Americans. Donald Trump campaigned in 2016 to repeal it. Even some in the industry acknowledge it's not right.

"It is just not fair for teachers and firefighters to subsidize a special interest tax break that costs billions of dollars a year," one venture capitalist told Congress in 2007.

Yet every time the carried interest giveaway is attacked, Wall Street marshals an army of lobbyists to protect it. When a determined effort at repeal gained steam in 2007, Wall Street counterattacked: In the best Washington tradition, private-equity firms formed the Private Equity Council, the first Washington-based lobby in the industry's history, and dispatched some of the industry's most high-profile figures, including Henry Kravis of Kohlberg Kravis Roberts, to personally lobby lawmakers.

It worked. Repeal failed and it's never been close to repeal since. And Wall Street, according to Congress's Joint Committee on Taxation, is $15.6 billion richer.

Investing in Capitol Hill

In Washington, where 11,000 organizations are lobbying Congress, there is an old adage: Successful lobbies are measured by the legislation they stop, not by the laws they get passed.

By that yardstick, the Alliance for Capital Access was phenomenally successful. Let's watch the Alliance in action in 1985, the year it stopped a big one. At the time, pressure was building on Congress to do something about the wave of hostile takeovers, leveraged buyouts and corporate mergers that were sweeping America.

Rep. Timothy E. Wirth, the Colorado Democrat who was then chairman of a House subcommittee, was concerned that "shareholders, companies, employees and entire communities have been harmed in these battles for corporate control." He wanted hearings to "assess the fairness" of the takeovers.

To schedule witnesses and set the agenda for the hearings, which were expected to lead to new legislation, Wirth turned to a close aide, David K. Aylward, the subcommittee's staff director and chief counsel. Aylward indicated that the hearings would go beyond a probe of the tactics used by raiders and explore the role that high-yield (junk) bonds were playing in financing corporate takeovers. "We really don't know where this money is coming from, and whether it could be better used for something else in the long term," Aylward told The *New York Times*.

Shortly after the hearings convened, Aylward resigned from

Wirth's staff and took a new job. He joined a lobbying company whose first clients would include the newly formed Alliance for Capital Access. Its sole aim: To block any legislation that would restrict junk bonds. Describing itself as an organization of high-yield bond users, the Alliance was in reality a Washington lobby for Michael R. Milken, Drexel Burnham Lambert Inc.'s junk bond chief, who helped create the group just as junk bonds came under mounting criticism.

Over the next few years, the Alliance became one of the capital's most successful lobbies—wining and dining lawmakers, passing out checks to House members and senators to make speeches, testifying before congressional committees and extolling the benefits of junk bonds.

In the end, its success could be measured by a simple standard: Congress never enacted legislation to scale back the virtually unlimited deduction for interest on corporate debt—the engine that had driven the junk-bond movement. In 1991, the Alliance disbanded, its job done.

"I charge people money when there is something I can do for them," Aylward said. "There's no legislative activity on the horizon that would justify people contributing to that kind of organization any more." That's good news for supporters of the Alliance.

But it's bad news for you if you're a middle-class man or woman, single parent, child or senior citizen, factory worker, middle-level manager, or shopkeeper. For successful lobbies like the Alliance for Capital Access have helped frame the content of the government rule book, the agglomeration of laws and regulations that direct the course of the American economy.

That rule book is responsible for the decline of America's middle class, for the triumph of special interests. It determines whether you have a job that pays $15 an hour or one that pays $6; whether you have a pension and health-care insurance; whether you can afford to own a home. It governs everything from the tax system to imports of foreign goods, from the bankruptcy system to regulatory oversight.

But just as important as the laws and regulations that make up the rule book are the potential changes that are never enacted by Congress, never implemented by regulatory agencies—owing to the influence exercised by lobbies.

Health care is Washington's largest lobby, dwarfing all others in the amount of money it spends to lobby Congress and federal agencies—$594 million in 2019, according to the nonpartisan Center for Responsive Politics. The largest component of the lobby is Big Pharma, which spent $295 million in part to keep drug prices in the U.S. higher than anywhere else in the world. As a result, any significant change in America's health insurance system faces formidable barriers.

Yet in poll after poll, Americans put health care at or near the top of their list of greatest concerns. Rising deductibles, more out-of-pocket charges and the mind-numbing health-care red tape discourages treatment for millions of Americans. Even so, the U.S. spends more per capita on health care than any other country —18 percent of Gross Domestic Product (GDP). Germany spends 11 percent, Canada 10.7 percent, and Japan 10 percent. Unlike the U.S., those countries cover the health care of all citizens. Even though the U.S. spends more, Americans don't live as long. Life expectancy in the U.S. is 79.7 years; in Germany it's 80.5, Canada 83 and Japan 84.7. On the global roster of nations whose citizens live longest, the U.S. ranks 46, just ahead of Panama.

The second-most robust lobbying presence in Washington is the finance industry—Wall Street, insurance and banking, which spent $499 million. Together, the health-care and finance industries invest more than a billion dollars a year—nearly one-third of all the money that flows into Washington each year for lobbying. By contrast, the U.S. oil industry and the defense industry, which have outsized reputations as powerful influence peddlers in Washington, spent $125 million and $111 million respectively in 2019.

Because of powerful lobbies, Congress has failed to rewrite the laws that permit foreign-owned companies in the United States to pay taxes at a lower rate than American-owned companies.

It is because of lobbies that Congress has failed to rewrite the laws that permit companies to escape their financial obligations to

THE SWAMP THRIVES

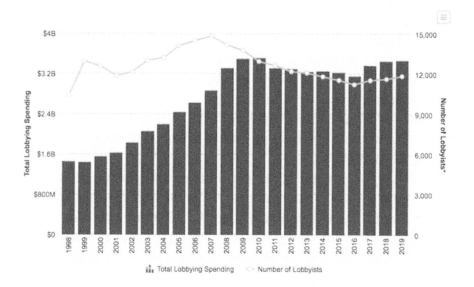

Corporations and other interests are spending twice as much to lobby Congress as a generation ago. In 1998, lobbying expenditures totaled $1.45 billion; in 2019 they were $3.47 billion. The amount increased during the first years of the Trump presidency, averaging $3.4 billion a year compared to the Obama presidency, when the yearly average was $3.3 billion.

Source: Center for Responsive Politics

employees and retirees, suppliers and customers, by seeking sanctuary in bankruptcy court.

It is because of lobbies that Congress has failed to rewrite the laws that permit wealthy citizens to pay combined income tax and Social Security taxes at a rate well below that paid by individuals and families earning less than $20,000 a year.

It is because of lobbies that Congress has failed to do anything to help millions of Americans who are going without health-care insurance and millions more who have insurance that provides only limited protection.

It is because of lobbies that Congress has failed to rewrite the laws that permit wealthy foreign investors to pay taxes on their U.S. income at a rate well below that paid by individuals and families earning less than $30,000 a year.

It is because of such lobbies that Congress has failed to rewrite the laws that permit banks to deduct most of their bad loans, thereby shifting the cost of flawed business decisions from themselves to the American taxpayer.

And it is because of such lobbies that Congress has failed to even consider rewriting the laws to impose taxes on dealings that have long gone untaxed.

Like, say, a 1 percent excise tax on the trading of stocks, bonds, futures and options. That's the kind of tax that middle-class families pay every day. Look at your telephone bill. See that 3 percent excise tax added onto your charges? Look at the gas pump the next time you fill up the car. See the 18-cent-a-gallon federal tax? That's an excise tax.

But the idea of an excise tax on securities transactions has been blocked each time it has come up in Congress. Lobbyists asserted that such a tax would fall on pension funds—the largest pools of money that are presently untaxed.

While Wall Street pours billions of dollars into leveraged buy-outs, hostile takeovers and mergers, it invests just as enthusiastically in Washington. Investment bankers, banks, trade groups, stock exchanges, and brokerage houses gave millions in campaign contributions to senators and House members on crucial committees that write the rules by which the economic game is played.

Members of Congress can no longer accept speaking fees, which were once a rich source of revenue for them and a powerful lever for special interests, but there is a replacement: the personal congressional foundation or related tax-exempt organization. Contributions may be made directly to any number of foundations established by members of Congress. However worthy the cause of these tax-exempt organizations, contributions to them bring to special interests something beyond the reach of middle-class Americans—access to the people who write the rule book.

So, too, do campaign contributions. Many lobbying groups also contribute to the campaigns of members of the tax-writing committees.

Consider this sampling of contributions to those committees during the period Congress considered, then rejected, taking any action to roll back the unrestricted deduction for corporate debt in the 1989-90 period. While the names of lawmakers have changed, the practice remains the same to this day: Morgan Stanley & Co.'s political action committee, the Better Government Fund, made contributions in 1989-90 to Sen. Max Baucus, Montana Democrat; Sen. Bill Bradley, New Jersey Democrat; Rep. Beryl F. Anthony Jr., Arkansas Democrat; Rep. Thomas J. Downey, New York Democrat; Rep. Barbara B. Kennelly, Connecticut Democrat; Rep. Robert T. Matsui, California Democrat; Rep. Guy A. Vander Jagt, Michigan Republican, and Rep. Charles Rangel, New York Democrat.

The Public Securities Association's political action committee contributed to the campaigns of Sen. Lloyd Bentsen, the Texas Democrat; Sen. Thomas A. Daschle, a South Dakota Democrat; Sen. Robert Dole, the Kansas Republican; Sen. Steve Symms, Idaho Republican, and Rep. Byron L. Dorgan, North Dakota Democrat.

The Chicago Mercantile Exchange's political action committee gave to Sen. Dave Durenberger, Minnesota Republican; Sen. Charles E. Grassley, Iowa Republican; Rep. Fred L. Grandy, another Iowa Republican; Rep. Sander M. Levin, Michigan Democrat; Rep. Donald J. Pease, Ohio Democrat; Rep. Martin A. Russo, Illinois Democrat, and Rep. Donald K. Sundquist, Tennessee Republican.

When members of Congress aren't busy taking care of such contributors, they're busy taking care of themselves. In 1950, members of Congress received annual salaries of $12,500. That was six times the $2,065 salary earned by a department store clerk. By 1992, members of Congress, who by then had enthusiastically endorsed America's shift from a manufacturing to a service economy, did much better. Their annual salary of $125,100 was 12 times the $10,480 earned by a department store clerk.

But that higher salary is important because, without it, ordinary workers who would like a seat in the Senate would be unable to afford a life of public service. That, at least, is the way the late Sen. Robert C. Byrd, the West Virginia Democrat, saw it. He said so in July 1991 when he introduced legislation providing for a 23 percent pay increase to bring the salaries of senators in line with that of representatives.

Said Byrd: "We must not perpetuate an arrangement which effectively shuts people out of serving in the Senate. To continue down this road means there will not be any welders that come out of the shipyards in Baltimore and stand in this place.

"There will not be any more meatcutters that come out of the coalfields of southern West Virginia or Indiana or Illinois or Kentucky or Alabama to stand in this place.

"There will not be any garbage boys that come out of the hills of West Virginia, or produce salesmen or even small, very small, small business operators that will come here to give of their talents ... Let us open the doors to a few poor folks who may aspire to run for U.S. Senate ..."

 UPDATE

Money and politics are an old story in America, but a new chapter was written when the U.S. Supreme Court sided with corporate interests in the *Citizens United* case in 2010. The 5 to 4 ruling opened the floodgates to a gusher of corporate money into U.S. elections.

Before *Citizens United*, it was illegal for companies to make contributions to committees that supported or opposed specific political candidates. The ruling gave corporations the green light to spend unlimited amounts of money through ads and other measures supporting those seeking political office. Corporations are still banned from contributing directly to candidates. But after *Citizens United* they could for the first time contribute unlimited amounts of money to political committees that were backing specific candidates.

The ruling also lifted the prohibition on corporations contributing to nonprofit organizations involved in political campaigns, triggering a surge in "dark money," contributions to tax-exempt nonprofits that are not required to disclose their donors. This means that powerful interests such as the American Petroleum Institute as well as wealthy donors, including gambling mogul Sheldon Adelson, can secretly make big contributions to organizations that support the candidates of their choice.

News accounts are careful to say that the *Citizens United* decision applies to both corporations and labor unions, that it allows each to spend unlimited amounts of money on elections. While that is technically true, it is terribly misleading. There is a huge disparity in money between the two as data compiled by the nonpartisan Center for Responsive Politics regularly shows. Corporations, not unions, have the access to the most cash. When it comes to money for elections, "business interests dominate, with an overall advantage over organized labor of about 16 to 1," the Center reported in 2019.

Citizens United turned the country over to corporations and the wealthy to a degree unprecedented in modern America and against the wishes of the vast majority of Americans. Anyone worried about the state of democracy need look no further than *Citizens United* as a case study in how the will of the people is being thwarted. Public opinion polls regularly show that a substantial majority of Americans—both Republican and Democrat—want to repeal *Citizens United*. Yet efforts to do that go nowhere in Congress.

Grassroots movements across the U.S. have mounted petition drives calling for a constitutional amendment to overturn *Citizens United*. By 2020, legislatures in 20 states and 800 cities and towns had adopted resolutions calling for a Constitutional Convention to adopt such an amendment. Eighteen more states would have to act. That's a high bar.

Caring for the Privileged

Longtime inequities in the tax code assure that the wealthy escape payment of taxes. For all the talk in the 1980s about repealing tax breaks benefitting the rich, Congress preserved some long-standing tax benefits that have been the special province of the wealthy for decades. Like tax-exempt interest.

Tax-free income is everyone's dream, but only the very wealthy can make this fantasy come true. When former IRS Commissioner Sheldon Cohen, a leading Washington tax lawyer, told an audience that the 1986 tax reform bill did not even "come close" to wiping out loopholes, he had tax-exempt bonds uppermost in mind: "We have a client who owned investment real estate, retired, and sold out for about $8 million. He invested every penny in tax-exempt bonds. He is a millionaire many times over. He did not pay any taxes before tax reform, and he still won't pay taxes after tax reform."

It was only fitting that tax reformers preserved this privilege of the very rich. Congress has kept it intact for a century. The oldest loophole in the code, the exemption goes all the way back to the income tax law in 1913.

The 16th Amendment gave Congress all-encompassing power to tax income "from whatever source derived." But the first income tax law excluded interest from state and local bonds, ostensibly because of uncertainty over Congress's right to tax them. Under the Constitution, federal and state governments cannot tax each other, and so opponents argued successfully that it would be unconstitutional to levy a tax on state obligations.

Support for the idea came from the U.S. Supreme Court decision that overturned an earlier income tax law in 1894. The court held that the tax was invalid because it would tax municipal securities, which it regarded as "a tax on the power of the States and their instrumentalities to borrow money and consequently repugnant to the Constitution." The 16th Amendment ratifying the income tax overrode the decision, but Congress refused to press the issue, and the exemption for state and local bonds continues.

Opposition arose at once and some of the bitterest battles in the income tax's early years were fought over this loophole. From the start, Republicans and Democrats, liberals and conservatives, presidents, secretaries of the treasury, other political figures, and the press singled out exempt securities as among the tax code's worst loopholes. On few tax questions has opinion been so consistent, so evenly dispersed through both parties, and so unified in its philosophical opposition. A sampling of comment through the years shows the range and consistency of the opposition.

Sen. Philander C. Knox, a Republican from Pennsylvania, in 1918: "Exemption of the income from state bonds from taxation in the hands of their holders is against a sound public policy. It frees vast fortunes from taxation by the federal government without regard to the obligations or necessities of that government."

President Warren Harding in 1923: "I think our tax problems, the tendency of wealth to seek non-taxable investment, and the menacing increase of public debt, federal, state, and municipal, all justify a proposal to change the Constitution so as to end the issue of non-taxable bonds."

Rep. Ogden L. Mills, a Republican from New York, in 1923: "Tax-exempt securities constitute, in my judgment, the greatest evil in the whole field of taxation—an evil so far-reaching in its consequences, both social and economic, as to be deserving of the most serious and immediate attention on the part of the people of the country. Of one thing I am perfectly sure: A progressive income tax at high rates and tax-exempt securities cannot exist side by side. Tax-exempt securities must inevitably destroy the progressive income tax, and I am by no means sure that the evil has not already reached such proportions as to make any possible action too late to save our present federal income tax."

President Calvin Coolidge in 1923: "Another reform which is urgent in our fiscal system is the abolition of the right to issue tax-exempt securities. The existing system not only permits a large amount of the wealth of the nation to escape its just burden but acts as a continual stimulant to municipal extravagance. This should be prohibited by constitutional amendment. All the wealth of the Nation ought to contribute its fair share to the expenses of the nation."

Andrew Mellon, Secretary of the Treasury, in 1924: "It is incredible that a system of taxation which permits a man with an income of $1,000,000 a year to pay not one cent to the support of his government should remain unaltered."

President Franklin D. Roosevelt in 1939: "It is difficult for almost all citizens to understand why a constitutional provision permitting taxes on 'income from whatever source derived' does not mean 'from whatever source derived.' ... A fair and effective progressive income tax and a huge perpetual reserve of tax-exempt bonds could not exist side by side."

John W. Snyder, Secretary of the Treasury, in 1951: "The exemption of state and municipal securities is a long-standing barrier to the achievement of equity in the distribution of the individual income tax burden."

John Tunney, a Democratic senator from California, in 1969: "The tax-exempt bonds that are owned by individuals are concentrated in the hands of the wealthiest 2 percent of the population ... It will be possible for a select few to receive vast amounts of tax-free income, while persons with incomes of one-hundredth the size will be taxed at effective rates of 20 to 30 percent."

Stanley S. Surrey of Harvard Law School in 1976: "The tax-exempt subsidy is as inequitable as it is inefficient ... Such a tax escape is distinctly unfair, and morally wrong. It is unfair to the millions of individuals who pay their federal income taxes and are often hard-pressed to do so."

Every attempt to revoke this tax break for the wealthy has failed. The first real effort came in World War I when the House Ways and Means Committee—supported by the Treasury Department—wrote a provision into the pending Revenue Act of 1918 to tax future state and local issues. With the nation fighting its first European war, the committee contended that "justice requires that at least in time of war the holders of these securities should share the burdens equally with the holders of Liberty bonds."

After the House gave overwhelming approval, the measure came under sharp attack in the Senate where Frank B. Kellogg, a Republican senator from Minnesota, called the House provision a "doubtful and dangerous experiment" that could "destroy or render ineffectual state governments." That was all the encouragement the Senate Finance Committee needed to strike out the House attempt to tax the bonds. It also marked the beginning of what would become a long tradition in the tax-law process.

From then on, the Senate Finance Committee would play the role of spoiler both on tax-exempt bond reform and other steps toward making the income tax more progressive. Through Republican and Democratic administrations, peace and war, prosperity and recession, the committee would seek to preserve tax privileges of the wealthy.

After the war, as the volume and the tax loss grew, a strong movement developed once again to end the exemption. Treasury Secretary Mellon charged that exempt bonds were diverting capital from private financing and channeling money into unproductive municipal make-work programs. In 1922, the House Ways and Means Committee adopted a resolution to amend the Constitution to authorize reciprocal taxation of state and federal securities. The House approved the resolution by a two-thirds vote in 1923, but the Senate rejected it.

Another attempt came the following year. It, too, failed, mainly because of opposition from states and local governments which contended that repeal would greatly increase their borrowing costs, a refrain that has been repeated over and over ever since.

The cause was revived in the 1930s, when no less than 80 resolutions were introduced calling for a constitutional amendment to end the exemption. After hearings in 1938 before a special Senate committee, the Public Bond Tax Act of 1940 was introduced in the Senate. While the bill would have taxed only future issues of federal, state, and local securities—leaving outstanding bonds untouched—states and local governments campaigned successfully to kill the measure. In 1951, Treasury again sought to eliminate the loophole, but states and local governments teamed up once more to kill the proposal before it even came to a vote.

The closest Congress has come in recent times to scaling back the break was in 1969, when the House version of the Tax Reform Act of 1969 proposed a surtax on some exempt bonds. Most state and local securities were to remain tax-free, but even that half-hearted swipe at the exemption proved enormously controversial.

States and local governments attacked the "unwarranted incursion on state and local sovereignty." Municipal bond dealers painted a bleak picture of the bond market if the House bill carried the day. As before, the Senate Finance Committee opposed the measure, and when the bill emerged from conference, the section was gone.

There is no longer, if there ever was, any legal basis to support the tax exemption. Supreme Court decisions and subsequent legislation have stripped away the concept on which the exemption was originally based. Nevertheless, there is, if anything, even less interest in Congress to repeal this tax break than in the past.

When the tax reform bandwagon rolled around again in 1986, tax-exempt bonds were not even on it. Reformers pointed to outrageous tax shelters and other avoidance schemes and attempted to show how such widely used middle-income deductions as Individual Retirement Accounts (IRAs), sales taxes, and consumer interest were really loopholes of the rich that should be repealed. Yet the most enduring income tax subsidy to the rich—tax-exempt bonds, which annually deprived the Treasury of more tax dollars than IRAs—was preserved.

With Congress's decision to protect their special status in the tax code, tax-exempt securities looked even better after tax reform than before. What with all the publicity about the death of tax shelters, reductions in tax preferences and changes in other tax programs, tax-exempt bonds were one of the undeniable tax shelters left. Wall Street, appropriately, responded in breathless fashion. "Whew! What a relief," proclaimed one of the largest of the tax-exempt bond firms, the Nuveen Bond Trust, calling the new tax law "a breath of fresh air."

UPDATE

For the very wealthy, tax-free bonds remain one of the most lucrative tax breaks. A total of 627,415 individuals and families earning more than $500,000—fewer than 1 percent of all tax filers—reported receiving interest of $24.9 billion on tax-free bonds in 2017 on which they paid no taxes. That same year 15.1 million middle-class taxpayers who put what savings they could into interest-bearing bank accounts rather than tax-exempt bonds received $12.3 billion in interest—all of which was taxable.

In other words, wealthy taxpayers collected twice the amount of interest as middle-income taxpayers and paid no taxes on that income, while those in the middle were taxed on their modest gains.

Destructive Debt

If Congress was unable to bring itself to even suggest the repeal of tax-exempt bonds, it should come as little surprise that lawmakers were unable to deal with a wave of buyouts, takeovers and corporate restructurings. This even though the tax code helped to underwrite, in part, the corporate restructuring that so often led to the collapse of companies, the shutting of plants and the wholesale dismissal of workers.

For middle-class Americans, the process has been wrenching. Ask Robert Trent.

Trent was born and raised in Clarksburg, W.Va., served a stint in the military, then followed the path of his father and uncles. In 1962, he went to work at the Anchor Hocking Corp. glass-manufacturing plant, the largest employer in Clarksburg.

Over the years, Trent progressed through a series of jobs, eventually becoming a personnel supervisor at the factory, which turned out such familiar objects as the *Star Wars* and Camp Snoopy glasses distributed by McDonald's during promotional campaigns.

In the fall of 1987, Trent, along with 900 other men and women, found himself out of work for the first time in his life when the Clarksburg plant was closed after an unfriendly takeover.

Trent liked to say that "just about every meal that I've ever had has come out of this plant." He worked there 25 years. His father worked there 44 years. His brother worked there 37 years. Even his mother worked there briefly. There were uncles and cousins and altogether, he said, "the Trent family's logged about 200 years in this plant. There were many families like that."

For Trent and his coworkers, it all came to an end when Anchor

Hocking was acquired by a smaller company, Newell Co. of Free-port, Ill. A manufacturer and marketer of a variety of household products, Newell had been growing through acquisitions. In the process, Newell was fashioning a reputation as a takeover company that moved swiftly to eliminate jobs, reorganize the operations it intended to keep and sell off or shut down the rest.

An unsuspecting Clarksburg discovered how swiftly Newell could move. Just 40 days after it acquired Anchor Hocking, Newell announced it was closing the West Virginia factory, eliminating the jobs of 900 workers. It cited excess production.

Robert Trent remembers it well: "We were really excited about some Newell people coming down and looking at our facility, because we thought we were doing very well. They came in about 10 in the morning. We saw them come in. They went to the plant manager's office ... and told him they were closing this facility ... And that was it. They were out of here by 10:30."

For the employees, it was painful. "One of our supervisors right now is working in a local store at minimum wage," Trent said. "It's a shame. He was one of our best supervisors. A very knowledgeable person. Again, in his mid- to late 50s, working for minimum wage now. That's a shock."

Victor M. Cunningham, the manager of the West Virginia Department of Employment Security office in Clarksburg, said many of the workers moved into service and retail jobs, which are low-paid, with fewer hours and little or no benefits.

"It's so hard to convert someone who packed glass for 20 years to manage a convenience store," he said. "You don't know what kind of a struggle it is for them to think and apply themselves to something new. I don't know what the answer is."

More than 3,000 miles to the west, in another small town, in another industry, excessive debt produced a similar result. Ira G. March watched it happen. A husky, full-bearded outdoorsman, March spent most of his working life at a sawmill in Martell, Calif., in the foothills of the Sierra Nevadas. He rose from laborer to sawyer, the highest classification among the hourly workers.

During that time, the mill had four owners. The first was a lumberman, Walter Johnson, who founded the mill's parent company,

American Forest Products, in 1925. "Johnson didn't care whether you were the cleanup guy or who you were," said March. "He would come into the mill and stop and talk to you. He knew all the old guys. That was the kind of guy he was."

Johnson's personal attention earned him the long-term loyalty of employees, many of whom went to work for American Forest Products out of high school and stayed until they retired. "We once had four generations of one family working at the mill," said Jerry Kirchgatter, the Lumber and Sawmill Workers union representative at the mill. "People thought it was a good life, both for them and their kids."

The company, with more than a dozen sawmills, box factories and plants scattered throughout the Sierras, remained under Johnson's control for 45 years, until Bendix Corp., the defense and aerospace contractor, bought American Forest Products in 1970 as part of a diversification plan. That was a time when Wall Street was profiting by putting together conglomerates.

In 1980, when Wall Street began profiting by taking apart conglomerates, Bendix sold the Martell mill and other American Forest properties to an investment partnership headed by New York buyout specialists Kohlberg Kravis Roberts & Co.

March recalled an immediate change at Martell. There was great pressure to work harder as the new owners who had bought the mill largely with borrowed money struggled to cut costs to pay the interest on the debt. "The debt was the problem," said March. "It seemed to be known throughout the plant. That's why they were pushing the plant so hard. So we had to struggle, and we did struggle here for years trying to pay off that debt and make a profit."

But in vain. Even though American Forest Products posted a larger operating profit in 1987 than in the late 1960s when it was an independent company, it recorded a loss for the year. The reason: Most of the company's operating profits went to pay interest on its debt. Kohlberg, Kravis began selling off pieces of the company. In 1988, it sold the mill to Georgia-Pacific Corp., a manufacturer of forest and building products.

Georgia-Pacific itself faced a corporate debt spiraling toward $2.5 billion, with interest due in 1989 alone of $272 million. To help raise cash, Georgia-Pacific, with annual sales of $8.6 billion in 1987, cut expenditures and dipped into the paychecks of workers at the Martell mill. It could do so because in the 1980s, the National Labor Relations Board ruled that new owners could scuttle existing contracts, making it easier to reduce the pay of employees of companies being acquired. In the past when one company bought another, it usually inherited the obligations of the selling company, including labor agreements.

But before the Martell mill changed hands, Kohlberg, Kravis fired all the workers and sold the assets to Georgia-Pacific. This effectively terminated the labor contracts that had been in place, allowing Georgia-Pacific to reopen the mill and rehire some of the fired workers—at wage cuts of 10 percent to 15 percent.

For longtime mill workers at Martell, the wage cut was another setback in working conditions at a plant that had once been a good place to work. Ira March took early retirement. Pablo Iturri, a native of the Basque region of Spain who had worked at the mill for nearly three decades, stayed on briefly, but was disillusioned. "They cut everybody's wages," he said. "That was a big mistake. A lot of people had worked here their whole lives. This was no good."

While debt was undermining companies like American Forest Products, Anchor Hocking and hundreds of others, Congress stood by, watching and listening. It listened more often than not to financial experts who said that everything was all right—that the dizzying round of mergers, buyouts, takeovers and corporate restructurings was a healthy, natural process for the economy.

To turn back any challenge in Congress, the money industry relied on spokesmen to articulate the new values. One such value was the theory that debt is a positive force in corporate management. Advocates contended that debt forced executives to manage more efficiently and pay closer attention to the bottom line.

Among those who held this view was John A. Pound, an assistant professor of government at the Kennedy School of Government at Harvard University and a principal in a Cambridge-based consulting firm called the Analysis Group. It did work for a number of takeover artists, such as the Belzberg family of Canada. Among Pound's studies was a 1989 report he compiled for the Massachusetts Pension

Reserves Investment Management Board, the state agency that oversees the pension funds of Massachusetts state employees.

Pound's Analysis Group extolled the benefits of leveraged buyouts in the report, calling them "part of the ongoing restructuring of corporations that is necessary for the economy to remain competitive." High debt-load levels were, in fact, a positive force, the report argued, because they made companies "more efficient." As proof, the report cited the Campeau Corp., headed by Robert Campeau.

Campeau had run up more than $7 billion in debt in 1986 and 1988, acquiring a *Who's Who* of American retail establishments, including Bloomingdale's, Brooks Brothers, Jordan Marsh, Abraham & Straus, Ann Taylor, Garfinckel's, Bonwit Teller and Filene's. By September 1989, Campeau Corp. was unable to make a payment on its debt. With default looming, Campeau's financiers intervened and arranged what Pound described as a "fix for the credit crisis."

To Pound, the swift action of Campeau's financiers was proof of how high debt loads compel those holding the purse strings to step in before bankruptcy becomes inevitable. The result was a "more efficient and informal way to monitor corporate performance" than having to declare bankruptcy.

Pound wrote: "Default no longer necessarily means bankruptcy or even signals severe or prolonged financial distress. The Campeau liquidity crisis was resolved with a dispatch unimaginable a few short years ago. Most important, the resolution led to a significant shift of corporate control and corporate strategy.

"In the past, prior to LBOs (leveraged buyouts), such a shift in strategy and management would have been virtually impossible to accomplish until performance had slid to a terrible degree. This case demonstrates that high debt loads, and the default that they sometimes cause, cannot be measured by traditional yardsticks."

Pound's report on the Campeau rescue was dated November 28, 1989. Forty-eight days later, Campeau's Federated Department Stores Inc. and Allied Stores filed for bankruptcy protection. It was the largest retail bankruptcy ever and the sixth largest corporate bankruptcy in U.S. history.

Sometimes, the lobbyists extolling debt are the moneymen themselves. Men like Bruce Wasserstein, who with his partner Joseph

Perella made a fortune buying, selling and restructuring businesses through their investment banking firm, Wasserstein Perella & Co.

In September 1987, during an appearance before a House Energy and Commerce subcommittee, Wasserstein discussed corporate debt and the unique abilities of sophisticated financial advisers to determine which companies are capable of carrying large amounts of debt. He cited as an example Harcourt Brace Jovanovich Inc., the book publishing company that had expanded into other areas, including Sea World theme parks and insurance. In May 1987, Robert Maxwell, the late British publisher, sought to buy Harcourt for about $2 billion. To fend off the bid, Harcourt had taken on $2 billion in debt and distributed cash to stockholders.

Wasserstein approved: "The shareholders have every reason to be ecstatic over what happened at Harcourt ... We are confident that Harcourt will do very well, and that is reflected in the marketplace today."

Notwithstanding the sophisticated financial advice Harcourt received, the company was unable to meet the interest payments on a staggering $2.5-billion debt without selling off properties, closing certain operations and laying off employees. For the year it took on the new debt, Harcourt reported net income of $83.4 million. The year after, the company lost $53.5 million. In 1989, Harcourt reported net income of $12.4 million. But that was due to the sale of its theme parks for $1.1 billion. Without the sale of assets, Harcourt would have lost $242.2 million on its operations.

As for the company's stock, in 1986—the year before the money industry moved in—it traded at a high of $104 a share. By late 1991, it was selling for as low as 63 cents. After the restructuring Wasserstein oversaw, Harcourt lost money, sold assets and scrambled to make ends meet.

Unable to manage its debt, the company became a division of General Cinema Corp., a Newton, Mass., retailer and movie theater operator, in a $1.5-billion merger in 1991 and disappeared as an independent company.

Harcourt's casualty list is long: companies sold, jobs lost. There were financial casualties among holders of Harcourt's stocks and bonds. There was a corporate casualty, the story of a once-strong company brought down by debt. And then there are the human casualties.

One of them, Robert L. Edgell, is worthy of special note. A charismatic man, Edgell headed HBJ Publications, the business magazine and school supplies division of Harcourt. Under Edgell, HBJ Publications grew from 16 magazines in the early 1970s to more than 100 in 1987, making it one of the nation's largest business publication companies. But to pay off some of the debt it took on to defeat Maxwell, Harcourt in 1987 had to sell assets fast. One was HBJ Publications.

Long a steady source of income, HBJ was one of Harcourt's prized possessions. Fearful that an outsider might buy the company and split it up, Edgell and other top executives bought HBJ Publications themselves in a $334-million leveraged buyout in 1987. The division was renamed Edgell Communications Inc., with Edgell as chairman and top executive.

Despite the large debt, Edgell said no layoffs or other cost-cutting measures would be implemented. He predicted that the company's revenues and profit would continue to grow at a rate of 12 percent a year. That would enable the company to make more acquisitions and start new publications, he said. "It will be business as usual, only better," Edgell told a reporter at the time.

Wall Street liked the deal, too. Ivan Obolensky, a publishing analyst with the New York brokerage house of Josephthal & Co., saw only sunny days ahead. "The future is a beautiful thing for Edgell. This is a fire sale," Obolensky was quoted as saying about the $334-million acquisition cost.

Despite the optimism, the company had problems from the start. The projections to pay off the debt were based on a robust growth in advertising lineage among the business publications. They did not factor in a downturn that began in 1988. The company lost $65 million that year. The biggest problem was making debt payments. Interest costs were staggering—$42.1 million in 1988 and $38.5 million in 1989.

By contrast, interest charges had been less than $1 million in 1987, when the division was part of Harcourt Brace. To make those steep payments, Edgell Communications, for the first time, began eliminating jobs. The company also sold publications to raise cash, a move that Robert Edgell found especially distressing.

By early 1990, the company was in grave financial condition. Edgell had recorded another large loss in 1989. In March, Standard & Poor's Corp. lowered the rating on Edgell's corporate bonds and said the company faced "potential violations of senior debt financial covenants."

All of this took a heavy toll on Robert Edgell. Not only was the company he had built coming apart, but the investment of many who worked for him and had joined him in the buyout was rapidly evaporating. On May 6, 1990, Edgell resigned and left the company. Richard B. Swank, a former executive with Dun & Bradstreet Corp., was brought in as the new chairman.

Edgell tried to put the firm's troubles behind him. In August, he and his wife, Yvonne, bought a luxury condominium on Florida's Gulf Coast, near Sarasota, seemingly far away from the troubled Edgell empire. The Edgells chose a corner apartment on the seventh floor of a new building on Longboat Key, overlooking the Gulf of Mexico. From the balcony, they could take in dazzling sunsets. The Longboat Key Club called the new development "Sanctuary."

But for Robert Edgell this idyllic setting was not a haven. The Edgell Communications debacle would not go away. When the company failed to make a $7-million interest payment, the default set off a frenzied effort to restructure the debt. Seven business magazines were put up for sale. Rumors were rife that the company might soon have to seek bankruptcy court protection. The company missed a deadline for second $7-million interest payment on its debt.

On New Year's Day 1991, the Edgells had lunch in their condominium with old friends from out of town. After the two couples had finished the meal, Edgell excused himself from the table. At 2 p.m., while his wife and friends were in another part of the apartment, Edgell quietly stepped out to the balcony, climbed up on the railing and, in full view of several people, jumped seven floors to his death.

Edgell left tape recordings to his family and a suicide note. Although the contents of the note were not disclosed, the Longboat Key police chief said the note indicated Edgell was distraught over the reversal of the company's fortunes.

Private equity and its henchman debt have played a powerful but shadowy role in the decline of another crucial American industry—newspapers. Granted, the Internet and other factors have deeply eroded the financial base of this once robust industry. But as newspapers faltered, private-equity funds, hedge funds and other large investment groups have steadily moved into the field to scoop up hundreds of mostly small and medium-sized newspapers.

Many of these acquiring companies did not exist 20 years ago. But by 2016, seven investment firms were among the 25 companies with the largest holdings of American newspapers, according to a 2016 University of North Carolina study. These new chains "surpass in size the large chains of the 20th century," the report observed, and "are still growing as they continue to snap up more and more ink-on-paper newspapers at bargain prices while disposing of unprofitable ones."

The report, "The Rise of the New Media Barons and the Emerging Threat of News Deserts," found that the new owners are focused "almost exclusively on driving the performance of their holdings."

Newsroom staffs and budgets have paid the price. All told since 1990, the newspaper jobs of about 275,000 reporters, editors, photographers and business employees have been abolished.

The control of so many newspapers by hedge funds, which have no stake in their local communities, raises worrisome questions about "the vitality of community journalism and the future of democracy at the grassroots level," concluded the report.

How a Tax Break Was Saved

Whatever the cause of Robert Edgell's suicide, there is no mistaking the cause of Harcourt's demise: excessive debt made possible by a tax code that provides for a nearly unlimited interest deduction. It was this deduction that the Alliance for Capital Access lobbied so intensely to preserve.

The Alliance incorporated in Washington in 1985 as a trade association representing companies dedicated to blocking any changes in the rules on junk bonds. Its articles of incorporation spelled out the group's goal: "To prevent a negative impact on the free flow of capital due to unreasonable corporate or governmental restriction, interference, or regulation."

Dozens of the companies that paid membership dues to the Alliance owed, if not their existence, at least their temporary prosperity to Michael Milken, who had peddled junk bonds on their behalf. Two of the three directors—Carl Lindner, president of American Financial Corp. in Cincinnati, and Richard Grassgreen, president of Kinder-Care Learning Centers in Montgomery, Ala.,—headed companies that had been part of Milken's junk-bond network.

Over the next five years, more than half of the 120 companies that contributed to the Alliance had ties to Milken. Like all successful Washington lobbies, the Alliance lined up a politically well-connected lawyer to do the actual lobbying: David K. Aylward, fresh from a stint as a top aide to Timothy Wirth when he was chairman of the House telecommunications, consumer protection and finance subcommittee.

As executive director of the Alliance, Aylward began to sing the praises of junk bonds. "High-yield bonds ... have become a critical financing source for some of the fastest-growing, most dynamic ... companies," Aylward said when releasing a survey of high-yield bond financing. His main job for the Alliance was "combating misunderstandings" about high-yield bonds and educating the "media and government officials" about the type of companies that used such bonds, Aylward said.

To get this point across, Aylward said Alliance members often went to Washington to pay personal calls on members of Congress. "The messenger is as important as the message," he said. "The best thing was for these people to come to Washington and tell congressmen why they should be left alone. Very simple basic lobbying."

While the Alliance lobbied on a number of legislative issues, most centered on efforts to scale back or limit the deduction for interest paid on corporate debt. "If you wanted to fool with junk bonds," said Aylward, "the way you did it was interest deduction."

At the start, the Alliance estimated "monthly expenses at nearly $11,000 per month to paid lobbyists." In fact, the organization raised and spent much more—$4.9 million from 1985 through 1990. With this war chest, the Alliance became a familiar organization on Capitol Hill. Lobby reports from 1985 to 1989 tell the story:

"Mayflower Hotel ... Breakfast Meeting with members of Congress."

"Joe and Mo's ... Lunch with Congressional Staff."

"Cafe Berlin ... Lunch with Senate Staff."

"The Washington Palm ... Lunch with Senate Staff."

"La Colline ... Lunch with Congressional Staff."

"Hunan of Capitol Hill. Lunch with Senate Staff."

"Banquet Services. Congressmen and staff. Botanic Gardens."

"Joe and Mo's ... meeting with Congressional staff to discuss corporate finance issues."

"U. S. Senate Restaurant ... for Congressional staff luncheon."

"Refreshments for reception with Members of Congress and Congressional Staff."

"Gifts to Congressional and Senate Staff."

"Limousine services for members of Congress and staff."

"Bird's Florist ... Floral arrangements for Congressional Dinner."

On May 20 and 21 of 1986, the Alliance catered two receptions in the House of Representatives restaurant in the Rayburn House Office Building. On the night of May 20, the Alliance sponsored a dinner at the Hyatt Regency Washington for members of Congress. The events came at a time of rejoicing for the organization and its members.

The tax-writing committees in both houses had just completed preliminary work on the massive Tax Reform Act of 1986. In that historic legislation, the tax writers repealed numerous tax breaks— from IRA accounts to the deduction for most consumer interest. But they left intact the deduction for corporate interest on debt.

The Alliance had been in the forefront of the drive to oppose limitations on the deductibility of interest and any other measure that might restrict mergers, acquisitions or takeovers.

When a House subcommittee weighed legislation, Alliance representatives urged lawmakers to leave the system intact. Nelson Peltz, chairman of Triangle Industries in New York, praised junk bonds before a House subcommittee on telecommunications and finance on June 11, 1987, and urged lawmakers to refrain from enacting any measures "limiting high-yield bond financing." He testified: "We can't have legislation that limits access to capital for certain companies that lack investment-grade ratings, that limits the use of debt in acquisitions, that restricts investment in high-yield securities or that imposes arbitrary limits on corporate debt levels."

Peltz went on to say that high-yield bonds were crucial to America's industrial future—that they would help finance companies to "rebuild our manufacturing base."

"They are a vital source of financing for those firms that are creating and saving jobs and helping to push America back to prominence in all the world markets," Peltz said.

Two years later, in 1989, Erwin Schulze, appearing on behalf of the Alliance at a House Ways and Means Committee hearing probing the tax aspects of mergers and acquisitions, urged lawmakers to preserve the unlimited deduction for interest paid on corporate debt. "I believe that an interest cutback will have a far reaching and damaging effect on the ability of entrepreneurs and growth companies to build their businesses," testified Schulze, then chairman of CECO Corp., a Chicago-based supplier of materials to the construction industry. "The Alliance believes that the big losers from a drop in the interest deduction would be these very companies."

Just what were these entrepreneurial companies that were "creating and saving jobs"? They were, it turns out, not exactly the kinds of enterprises likely to rebuild America's industrial base or to make products that could compete with goods from abroad.

They were companies such as SuperCuts Inc. of San Rafael, Calif., the nation's first discount hair-cutting chain. And Fair Lanes Inc. of Baltimore, the nation's largest independent operator of bowling alleys. And LivingWell Inc. of Houston, the nation's largest owner and operator of fitness salons. And they were companies like Public Storage Inc. of Glendale, Calif.

Public Storage is one of the nation's largest owner of mini-warehouses. The company's orange Public Storage logo is a familiar sight along interstate highways. Of all the Alliance members who contributed to the lobbying effort that blocked rules changes, Public Storage best illustrates the fallacy that junk bonds created jobs. Founded in 1972, the company grew spectacularly in the 1980s with the help of Drexel Burnham Lambert, its investment adviser.

Drexel helped the privately held company raise millions of dollars through limited partnerships that acquired land and built mini-warehouses, then leased the facilities back to Public Storage. By 1992, the company and its partnerships had 233 installations in 35 states.

And virtually no employees. Once a mini-warehouse is built, staffing requirements are minimal, a Drexel Burnham report pointed out. Users get in with an ID code that opens a computer-locked door. Some of the facilities have caretakers, but as an investment report of Frederick Research Corp. stressed, those jobs are low-paying: "Usually the properties have a man and wife employee living free in the facility but at minimum-type wages to keep an eye on things."

Mr. and Mrs. Wallace Christina of Lincoln City, Ore., were one such couple. In 1988, they took over as resident managers of a 546-unit Public Storage facility in Gresham, Ore., near Portland, earning, ostensibly, $4.80 an hour.

Mrs. Christina was the manager and worked 40 hours; her husband worked 20 hours. Together they grossed about $1,250 a month in hourly wages. From that was deducted $300 a month rent on a two-bedroom 1,100-square-foot apartment adjoining the storage lockers. By the time they went to work for Public Storage, the company was charging managers rent for their on-site living quarters.

That left them with about $950 in gross monthly earnings, meaning their hourly wage rate was about $3.60 an hour—just slightly above the U. S. minimum wage in 1988.

"You can't live on the money those jobs pay," Christina explained.

He and his wife were able to do so because they were retired and had outside income. But "anybody with small children or a family," Christina added, "just couldn't do it."

Consequently, there was a high turnover in managers, he said. Finally, the Christinas, weary of the low pay and working conditions, quit caretaking in 1991, when the U.S. minimum wage of $4.25 an hour exceeded their takehome pay.

In addition to mini-warehouses, fitness salons, bowling alleys and hair-cutting salons, Alliance members sold tax shelters (Integrated Resources), bought junk bonds (Centrust, Columbia, Imperial and Lincoln Savings), sold annuities (Executive Life Insurance), provided day care (Kinder-Care), owned a professional hockey team (Delaware North Cos.), leased computers (Comdisco), built retirement villages (Forum Group Inc.), arranged retail displays (Action), operated ice cream shops (Brigham's Inc.), managed investments (Shamrock Holdings Corp.), sold insurance (Zenith National Insurance) and leased medical equipment (American Shared Hospital Services).

Whatever their business, companies that had used junk bonds were regularly portrayed before Congress as successful ventures that were creating jobs and building for the future. They were, as Andrew G. Galef, chairman of MagneTek, described them in testimony before the House Ways and Means Committee on May 17, 1989, "the very companies leading America to economic renaissance."

So how goes the renaissance? Four savings and loan associations that contributed thousands of dollars to the Alliance lobbying blitz became insolvent and were seized by federal regulators. The four—Centrust Savings Bank, Columbia Savings & Loan, Imperial Savings & Loan and Lincoln Savings & Loan—collapsed when the junk bonds that propelled their rise sank in value. The parent companies of Imperial and Lincoln in turn were forced into bankruptcy court. The bailout of the four thrifts cost American taxpayers billions.

Another group of Alliance members—Doskocil Cos., First Executive Corp., the Forum Group Inc., Integrated Resources, LivingWell Inc., Southmark Corp. and U.S. Home Corp.—also sought bankruptcy court protection. The reason: inability to generate sufficient profits to cover the high debt service of their junk bonds.

Ingersoll Publications Co., which acquired a string of daily and weekly newspapers in this country and Europe with cash raised from junk bond sales, was forced to sell all of its U.S. publications to stave off default on its bonds. Kinder-Care Inc., the nation's largest day-care center operator, used millions of dollars in junk bonds to diversify into fields other than day care. The company bought savings and loans and a hunting magazine as part of a strategy that left it saddled with so much debt that it had to be restructured.

So it is that many of the companies that bankrolled the lobbying of the Alliance for Capital Access have fallen victims of the very philosophy they embraced.

When David Aylward was asked how it had come to pass that Congress chose to preserve the interest deduction for junk bonds—a deduction that had resulted in the destruction of so many businesses, so much decline for America's middle class—he replied:

"There was not an organized constituency in favor of restrictions on these bonds."

Epilogue
HOW TO MAKE IT RIGHT

It doesn't have to be, this relentless assault on the middle class by government action.

How do we know this?

Because at other times in our history, our government—urged on by the people—has stepped forward to balance the rights of all Americans and to safeguard their health and economic security so that everyone could share in the promise of the American dream.

Yet for the past four decades, the prevailing philosophy of those who run the country has been to help the few, though they never express it that way. What they say—when questions of jobs, the economy, or health care come up—is "let the market decide what's best for America. Keep government out."

The word *government* has taken on an unsavory meaning over the past few decades thanks in part to Ronald Reagan, who in 1986 uttered the memorable phrase: "The nine most terrifying words in the English language are: I'm from the government and I'm here to help."

In truth, the federal government has been a huge help to all Americans in the past by creating jobs and strengthening social stability—sparking railroad development in the 19th century, enacting Social Security in the 1930s, adopting the G.I. bill in the 1940s, starting Medicare in the 1960s, and funding research that led to the Internet. Americans have greatly benefitted from the foresight of previous leaders who created government programs with the specific goal of helping people. Imagine how much more severe the Great Recession of 2008 would have been without the safety nets of Social Security and Medicare.

To reverse government policies that have been in force for decades and to shape new programs that will benefit all Americans will be very difficult. Those at the top who have had their way with policy for so many years will not easily relinquish power. As we noted in Chapter 10, the *Citizens United* decision has further marginalized individual voters whose power pales against those of wealthy vested interests.

But we must not let this stop us from trying to change those policies. The continuing decline of the middle class has disastrous consequences, not only for millions of Americans, but for our democracy itself. For without a middle class, there isn't really an America.

Our history tells us that we can change the system; it's been done before.

And it can be done again.

Once, Congress and the White House responded to the nation's needs by enacting sweeping legislative and regulatory reforms. More often than not, they acted only after events had pushed the country to the edge of crisis—or beyond. Even then, opposition was intense.

But at least they responded.

So it was in 1906. That was a time when Americans were routinely swindled—and often died—when they bought and consumed adulterated foods and drugs. Machine oil was canned and sold as "genuine olive oil." Glucose was colored with coal-tar dye and sold as plum preserves. Cocoa was diluted with starch.

Patent medicines were laced with opium, cocaine and other addictive or poisonous substances. A dose of any number of widely available cure-alls often proved fatal. A Fall River, Mass., couple administered something called "Nurses' and Mothers' Treasure" to their child. The medical examiner concluded that the child's death was caused by opium poisoning. A 28-year-old man in Chillicothe, Ohio, suffering from a cold, took a dose of Hardman's Magic Cure. He died 20 minutes later.

Stories abounded about the sale of rotten meat, foods packaged in poisoned preservatives and patent medicines spiked with narcotics that killed unsuspecting consumers. Nonetheless, many lawmakers vigorously opposed taking action—just as their predecessors had done on other issues, just as their successors would do for the rest of the century. In fact, just about every effort to enact legislation to correct social and economic injustices has first had to overcome powerful opposition within Congress.

When legislation was proposed to regulate food and drugs, opponents argued that it would represent the first step toward a police state, that it was unconstitutional for the federal government to intrude in matters that were the province of the states. The states, they said, were better equipped to enforce such laws.

Rep. Charles H. Grosvenor, an Ohio Republican, dismissed the notion that the federal government should protect the health of residents of one state from adulterated food or drugs produced in another. He said that it was no more logical to do so than it would be for the federal government to close brothels in New York City because "that business is spreading disease into the states of New Jersey and Connecticut."

Nonetheless, Congress finally responded by passing the Pure Food and Drug Act of 1906. It did so only after substantial pressure by reform-minded citizens and lawmakers. As Rep. William H. Ryan, a Democrat from New York, put it during debate, "There is a demand for this legislation ... The people are demanding pure food. They are demanding that articles of food shall be correctly labeled and that Congress prevent, by the enactment of this bill, the adulteration or misbranding of foods or drugs."

The most far-reaching food and drug legislation ever enacted, it made adulteration and misbranding criminal offenses. President Theodore Roosevelt, who signed it into law on June 30, 1906, later described its importance:

"The enactment of a pure food law was a recognition of the fact that the public welfare outweighs the right to private gain, and that no man may poison the people for his private profit."

Congress responded again in 1913.

That was a time when working-class Americans were paying a disproportionate share of the cost of running the federal government, when their living standards were declining. In those years, federal revenue was derived largely from the tariff—a tax added to imported goods—which, as the House Ways and Means Committee concluded, "is the principal cause of the unequal distribution of wealth. It is a system of taxation which makes the rich richer and the poor poorer." The committee explained:

"The amount each citizen contributes is governed, not by his ability to pay tax, but by his consumption of the articles taxed. It requires as many yards of cloth to clothe, and as many ounces of food to sustain, the day laborer, as the largest holder of invested wealth; yet each pays into the Federal Treasury a like amount of taxes upon the food he eats, while the former at present pays a larger rate of tax upon his cheap suit of woolen clothing than the latter upon his costly suit."

To correct the growing imbalance in American society, Congress took up legislation calling for an income tax. Again there was intense opposition in Washington. Sen. Henry Cabot Lodge, the patrician Massachusetts Republican, complained that it was an attempt "to punish a man simply because he has succeeded and has accumulated property by thrift and intelligence and character..." Others charged that the income tax was a communist plot.

But once more, as a result of pressure by reform-minded citizens and politicians, Congress responded, this time by passing the Revenue Act of 1913. The most dramatic overhaul of the tax system in the nation's history, it provided the framework for the progressive income tax. President Woodrow Wilson signed the measure into law on Oct. 3, 1913. Clyde H. Tavenner, a Democratic congressman from Illinois, summed up its intent:

"Under this bill a man will be taxed according to his ability to pay. If he has a small income he will pay a small tax, and if he has a large income he will pay a large tax. John D. Rockefeller, for instance ... would pay an annual tax of more than $2 million. Heretofore Mr. Rockefeller has paid little if any more toward defraying the expenses of the national government than the poor man with a large family."

Congress responded again in 1933.

That was a time when many Americans, who had lost their life savings when banks folded and who had lost their jobs when companies collapsed, were struggling to survive the Great Depression. Public anger was rising over tales of wealthy and powerful citizens who peddled unsound stocks, engaged in rigged securities dealings, encouraged speculation with borrowed money and cut special stock deals for their friends.

That's what J.P. Morgan & Co., the Wall Street investment house, did when it offered to sell Alleghany Corp. common stock for $20 a share to one of the firm's clients. A partner at J.P. Morgan had explained the deal in a letter to the client: "I believe that the stock is selling in the market around $35 to $37 a share ... We are reserving for you 1,000 shares at $20 a share, if you would like to have it." The Morgan client later became Secretary of the U.S. Treasury.

Again, after years of such stories and pressure by reform-minded citizens and lawmakers, Congress finally responded by passing the Securities Act of 1933, the most sweeping overhaul of the securities system ever. When President Franklin D. Roosevelt signed it into law, he described its importance:

"This measure at last translates some elementary standards of right and wrong into law. Events have made it abundantly clear that the merchandising of securities is really traffic in the economic and social welfare of our people ... The Act is thus intended to correct some of the evils which have been so glaringly revealed in the private exploitation of the public's money. This law and its effective administration are steps in a program to restore some old-fashioned standards of rectitude. Without such an ethical foundation, economic well-being cannot be achieved."

Throughout American history, whenever excesses within the economy resulted in private gain for the few and hardships for the many, Congress and the White House responded. Often reluctantly. Usually after interminable delays. But in the end they responded.

Until the 1980s. For the past 40 years the two branches of government have been in legislative gridlock. Except for two relatively modest steps—enactment of a tax on upper-income taxpayers under President Bill Clinton in 1994 and adoption of Obamacare in 2010 to aid the uninsured—no significant legislation has been adopted aimed specifically at bolstering the middle class.

The government rule book has become a catalog of special-interest provisions, like the 2017 giveaway to multinational corporations that allowed them to bring into the U.S. billions of dollars in offshore earnings at a bargain-basement tax rate. That's one of many reasons why America's middle class finds itself in a death spiral. And this is why that spiral won't be reversed by weak measures such as the measly tax cut given to some middle-class Americans in the 2017 tax bill.

It will be reversed only by citizen action to bring about broad legislative programs that are designed to correct structural imbalances that the powerful have built into the economy over many years. And these need to be accompanied by programs that address the problems of a global economy. Even then, to be fully effective, legislative action will have to be supplemented by other social and educational reforms.

Changes like these are a starting point:

TAXES. Tax rates should be raised on both the wealthiest Americans and large corporations. For individuals, the top rate should be increased from the current 37 percent to at least 40 percent for the upper 5 percent of taxpayers, and higher for the wealthiest Americans, those earning $1 million or more a year.

Capital gains income—the money derived from the sale of stocks, bonds and other assets—should be taxed at the same rate as earned income. This is one of the most lucrative tax breaks of the very wealthy, but there is no justification for taxing a working person's wages at a higher rate than a billionaire's earnings from selling stocks and bonds.

If you are wealthy and make a profit by selling some of your stocks, you pay a tax of just 23.8 percent on the capital gain—the difference between the purchase price and sale price of the stock. If you had earned that same amount of money as a high-salaried executive, you would have paid 39 percent in 2017.

The 16,900 taxpayers with income of more than $10 million that year reported total capital gains income of $301.7 billion. If they had been taxed at the top rate for salary earners, they together would have owed taxes of $117.6 billion. But because the tax rate for long-term capital gains income is nearly half that for salaries and wages, their tax bill would have been $57 billion—a savings of $60 billion. The main beneficiaries of the lower capital gains tax rate are taxpayers earning $1 million or more a year. They took home 62 percent of all capital gains income.

For corporations, whose tax rate was lowered to 21 percent in the 2017 Trump tax bill, Congress should increase the rate to 30 percent and eliminate or drastically reduce the value of certain highly prized corporate deductions such as the ability to write off interest on borrowed money. Eliminating that deduction would yield hundreds of billions of dollars in tax revenue. Equally important, it would reduce the tax advantage that private-equity firms use to take over other companies, often to the detriment of workers.

Corporations deducted $10 trillion in interest payments for the 10-year period leading up to 2015. The IRS does not list the total amount of taxes saved as a result of the deduction. But if the corporations that took the deduction paid taxes at the top rate, the deduction would have saved them more than $300 billion. That's the amount that seven million individuals and families earning $40,000 to $50,000 pay in taxes a year.

HEALTH CARE. Some day the U.S. will have a single-payer health-care system in which one agency will insure basic health care coverage for every American, a plan similar to Medicare, which covers everyone 65 years and older. Virtually every study of health-care costs shows that a single-payer system would be the most efficient and least costly, and in 2004 we called for such a plan in our book, *Critical Condition: How Health Care in America Became Big Business— and Bad Medicine*. Yet despite its advantages, a single-payer system isn't likely to happen any time soon without forceful citizen pressure to overcome the power of the health-care lobby and its misinformation campaign about how the system would work.

What should be done? In the immediate future, a so-called public option plan seems to us the most politically feasible course until we ultimately adopt a single-payer system. With a public option, the federal government would provide a form of health insurance that citizens could purchase. In this way, every American could be covered, unlike in 2020, when more than 28 million Americans still don't have health insurance because they can't afford to purchase it from private insurers. Another possibility would be to lower the Medicare eligibility age to 55.

Congress should tackle a long list of other health-care issues from "surprise" medical bills to soaring drug prices. Congress should at least authorize Medicare to negotiate with the pharmaceutical industry to obtain lower prices for prescription drugs. Due to aggressive lobbying by the drug industry in 2003, Congress specifically barred Medicare from negotiating with Big Pharma to lower drug costs.

JOBS. Much was made in 2019 before the coronavirus crisis about low unemployment in America and the nation's near full-employment economy. But what do many of those jobs pay? Labor department data shows that wage growth remains sluggish even with low unemployment. Many workers compensate by holding more than one job.

The private market alone isn't doing the job. We need to invest in infrastructure, new industries and research. That would stimulate good-paying jobs.

We need to raise the federal minimum wage. In late 2019, conservative pundits pointed to an uptick in wages among the lower-paid workers as an indication that the Trump administration's deregulation and tax policies were raising wages at the bottom. But a study by the Economic Policy Institute concluded that the increase was almost solely in states that had increased the minimum wage above the federal minimum of $7.25 an hour. The federal minimum hasn't been increased since 2009 and was 35 percent lower in 2019 than it was in 1968, adjusted for inflation.

Along with a wage increase, lower-paid workers as well as the entire middle class would benefit greatly from one other national benefit: universal child care.

On trade policy, the source of massive losses in manufacturing jobs by American workers, President Trump has initiated a tougher stance than any of his predecessors, but his approach has been counterproductive. Rather than targeting one country—China—and bringing on board other industrialized nations that have also suffered because of China's trade policies, he's gone it alone, with the result that many other sectors of the U.S. economy have suffered, and the gains he's eked out of China in the trade war so far are minimal.

RETIREMENT. This is one of middle-class America's gravest challenges. The death of pensions has set the stage for a bleak old age for millions of hard-working men and women. Only 7 percent of retired Americans have income from all three potential sources of retirement income—pensions, savings and Social Security. Most working Americans can't save enough for their retirement because they need every penny they earn to meet their basic needs. The lack of good-paying jobs for wage earners has intensified the problem.

The most immediate way to help middle-class Americans would be to increase monthly Social Security payments for those who most need it. Contrary to fears that the Social Security trust fund is endangered, there is money to pay benefits for many years to come. To increase payments, though, would require additional revenue. That could come from additional taxes on the wealthy or on large corporations or some combination of the two. As of 2019, Social Security is the only retirement income for 40 percent of older Americans. Unless their monthly payment is increased, they will live their final years in poverty.

STUDENT DEBT. As with Medicare for All, any move to forgive student debt, however needed, isn't likely to happen any time soon. So we must find other ways to help the 40 million-plus Americans who are burdened by life-altering indebtedness.

First of all, we need to restore strong public oversight to the operation of this multi-billion-dollar-a-year venture. For years this program has been operated largely by private contractors who are rewarded by how much money they can squeeze out of debtors. Many approaches could be used to ease the burden short of forgiving the entire debt. One would be to make former students responsible for only the money they actually borrowed, minus interest payments and in some cases fines. Such a step would drastically reduce total indebtedness. Another might be total forgiveness for those most in need.

There is no doubt in our minds that a majority of Americans would support many of these actions. Just as they would support efforts to enact legislation that would repeal or restrict the net operating loss deduction that Wall Street financiers often use to lower their taxes.

Or to end tax subsidies for companies that eliminate jobs in the United States and create jobs offshore. Or to impose a capital gains tax on wealthy estates. Or to impose an excise tax on the sales of stocks and bonds.

Most people would probably endorse legislation that would put an end to a practice that allows members of Congress and other public employees to draw pensions larger than their final salaries. Or legislation that would end, once and for all, a variety of practices that allow profit-making companies and wealthy individuals to pay taxes at a lower rate than middle-class families. Or legislation that would halt the federal government's use of Social Security tax revenue to fund its other programs.

Other potential legislative changes would require study and debate. For example, legislation might be enacted to make Social Security taxes more progressive. Or to limit or end Social Security benefits to the wealthy. Or to more closely regulate the sale of stocks, bonds, commodities, and other securities in a global marketplace. Or to require corporations to secure a federal charter in order to stop companies from playing one state against another. Or to require all corporations, public and private, to disclose the amount and type of taxes they pay in the United States and in other countries —country by country.

With the global economy ever more dominant in American economic life, criminal statutes relating to securities and other economic-related offenses must be overhauled. Illegal practices need to be spelled out more clearly. New penalties could be tested. One possibility might be to apply penalties based on drug-forfeiture laws to economic crimes. Under the existing system, financial felons such as Michael Milken, whose activities led to the collapse of companies and major job losses, serve time in prison and pay a fine but retain hundreds of millions of dollars they made. Under a forfeiture system, their assets—their cars, their houses, their investments—would be seized by the federal government.

These are just some of the revisions to the government rule book that would help restore balance to the system. You probably can think of others.

What is clear is that at this point we need a new way of thinking and a fresh approach to rescue America's middle class. The solution isn't a $500 tax cut, no matter how welcome any additional money might be to financially strapped Americans.

At the heart of this fresh approach is a structural change in the way America forms public policy. We must face the fact that the private market alone cannot solve the problems undermining the middle class—that, in fact, it is that unregulated market itself that has caused so much of the distress. The crisis of the middle class cries out for bold action by government to bolster opportunity and restore a sense of optimism and bold citizen pressure to make that happen.

Nothing has driven home the need for a radical change in our approach to government more than the coronavirus crisis. Lacking any governmental oversight, the nation was totally unprepared for the logistical challenge that mitigating the pandemic would require. Even if the U.S. had a universal health care system, the nation would have been stressed, but the lack of federal oversight made things much worse as shortages of masks, protective clothing and test kits reached epidemic proportions along with the virus itself.

The breakdown in health care was a direct result of the philosophy the U. S. has pursued for the last 40 years of taking a hands-off position on matters of the economy, and the economic wellbeing of citizens, under the mistaken notion that the market will deliver prosperity to everyone. It hasn't and it won't.

To deal with this, the solutions need to be long-term: We must first conceive and then enact new policies, and then stick with them for years to come. Only then will most Americans have the economic security in place to fulfill the promise of the American dream.

It is, of course, easy to come up with a list of potential legislative initiatives that would create a level economic playing field for everyone and thereby reverse the decline of the middle class. It is even easy to put forth legislative goals that would attract broad support. It's the hard part that follows.

Powerful lobbies fiercely oppose any change that would erode their privileges, deploying armies of paid agents and political-action committees to protect their interests. The average citizen has no such advocates.

This has always been so. When lobbyists mounted an intense campaign to block enactment of the progressive income tax in 1913, President Wilson observed that "it is of serious interest to the country that the people at large should have no lobby and be voiceless in these matters, while great bodies of astute men seek to create an artificial opinion and to overcome the interests of the public for their private profit ... Only public opinion can check and destroy it."

Yet the power that average citizens do possess can be decisive if wielded wisely. Over the years many Americans have written to us to offer solutions to the crisis affecting the middle class. Many displayed a clearer grasp of the problems confronting the country than the rulemakers in Washington. And many saw reason for hope, rather than despair. As one reader concluded:

"To the extent that federal policy, rather than impersonal economic factors, is responsible for the hardships our citizens are suffering, there is reason to hope for the better ... *We* make those policies through our elected representatives. What we make, we can unmake."

ACKNOWLEDGMENTS

It is impossible to thank everyone who helped us with this book, but we would like to start by thanking those we interviewed, many of whom are quoted, as well as many others whose observations and insights were invaluable to us in telling the story of the crisis of the middle class. In addition to those we interviewed when we first began the research for this work, many middle-class Americans have written to us over the years to urge us to continue to write about these issues in hopes that this will ultimately bring about changes in government policy.

We would like to express our appreciation to the employees of state, local and federal agencies and of state and federal courts throughout the country who patiently assisted in the difficult task of locating records and documents. As always, we are indebted to librarians at public, private and university libraries, including those at the Lippincott Library of the University of Pennsylvania, the government publications room of the Free Library of Philadelphia, and Michigan's Niles Community Library.

To those who are most directly responsible for helping bring this book to publication we must begin with Maxwell King. Max is a reporter's dream—an exceptionally talented editor and an incredibly supportive leader. As editor of The *Philadelphia Inquirer* when "America: What Went Wrong?" began as a newspaper series, his commitment to that bold project was central to its success. In the foreword to this book, Max sums up in remarkably few words the continuing crisis affecting our nation and what we must do to solve it.

We are grateful to Tom Stites, a contributing editor for the International Consortium of Investigative Journalists and one of the finest editors anyone will ever work with, who line-edited the manuscript for this book and clarified its most crucial points. We also want to thank Donna Martin, who brought her encouragement, her wise counsel, and her deep experience as a book editor to this new edition; Barrie Maguire, who created the handsome cover design; and

Allison Steele, who applied her excellent reportorial skills to ferret out obscure statistics and deeply buried data.

Special thanks are due to Nancy Steele, an editor whose exceptional expertise and sound judgment have been important to this book at every stage of its development.

We are also grateful to Doug Weaver and the talented team of professionals at Mission Point Press. Doug's generous advice, support, and creative suggestions have been invaluable. We thank Heather Lee Shaw for creating the lively, engaging design, Ruth Campbell for copy editing, Jodee Taylor for marketing and promotion, and Collleen Zanotti for updating the book's charts.

We remain doubly indebted to all those who had a role in creating the first edition of this book. Our research for this work began many years ago as an investigation for The *Inquirer*. What we learned about the struggles of middle-class Americans shocked us, and we reported the results in a nine-part series published by The *Inquirer* in 1991 titled "America: What Went Wrong?" The series generated the largest response from readers in the newspaper's history and encouraged us to expand the series into a book of that title.

Of all the debts we have incurred in researching and writing about middle-class America, the largest is to The *Inquirer*. Our series for the newspaper filled 25 pages and was typical of the commitment to investigative journalism that readers had come to expect from the newspaper. It is a tradition that began for us when the late Executive Editor John McMullan brought us together in our first reporting collaboration in 1971 and that continued under his successor, Eugene L. Roberts, who expanded the horizons of investigative reporting and made the newspaper's name synonymous with the best of the investigative genre. That tradition flourished under Roberts's successor, Maxwell King. Their belief in us and their commitment to long-form journalism made our work possible.

We would like to recognize all those who edited the original *Inquirer* series, an exceptional group who did so much to make this subject come alive for readers: the late Managing Editor Steve Lovelady, Assistant Managing Editor Lois Wark, and Deputy Features Editor Marietta Dunn. We also had the benefit of the expert copyediting skills of Julie Stoiber and Hope Keller. We also want to thank graphic artist Bill Marsh for his splendid charts, the newspaper's talented graphic arts director, David Milne, for his guidance, and the staff of The *Inquirer's* library, who spent many hours assisting us by retrieving information from electronic databases. Thanks also is due Bing Mark, an *Inquirer* editorial assistant who performed critical research, and to the late Bill Robbins, whose editing skills were crucial to the first edition of this book.

To each one we offer our heartfelt thanks.

SOURCES

In our research for this book, we relied primarily on public records and data drawn from a wide variety of sources in the U.S. and Mexico, including federal, state and local sources in 50 cities and 16 states, and interviews with dozens of Americans, from assembly-line workers to mid-level managers.

For the heart of our findings, we analyzed data compiled in Statistics of Income (SOI), published each year by the Internal Revenue Service. There are multiple ways to measure income and income inequality in the United States, but we believe that IRS data, which is based on tax returns filed by 150 million Americans, is the most accurate.

In the Introductions and Updates to each chapter, we have relied upon the latest available in 2020. And charts that show trends in previous decades are supplemented with recent data. For individual income taxes, the most recent statistics available are from tax return filings for 2017. For statistics of corporate income, census data, labor market statistics on wages and salaries, and other financial and economic data, the year of the most recent data varies.

Other essential findings are based on data and reports from these U.S. departments and agencies: Administrative Office of the U.S. Courts; Bureau of Economic Analysis; Bureau of Labor Statistics; Census Bureau; Congressional Budget Office; Department of Commerce; Department of Education; Department of Labor; Department of Treasury; Federal Election Commission; Federal Reserve Banks of New York and St. Louis; Federal Reserve Board; Government Accountability Office; Interstate Commerce Commission; National Center for Education Statistics; Office of Public Records, U.S. Senate; Office of the Clerk, U.S. House of Representatives; Patent and Trademark Office; Pension Benefit Guaranty Corp.; Resolution Trust Corp.; Social Security Administration; Office of the U.S. Trade Representative, and the Securities and Exchange Commission.

Agencies outside the U.S. whose staff members provided valuable assistance included the Japan Economic Institute, Embassy of Japan, and the Business Development Office of the State of Tamaulipas, Mexico.

Detailed information on corporations in this book is derived from filings of individual companies with the SEC and numerous filings with state or federal courts across the country. The records of bankruptcy courts were invaluable in documenting what happened to longtime companies and their workers after the companies were plundered by corporate raiders. For these we drew on filings in many jurisdictions, including New York; Boston; Los Angeles; Miami; Cincinnati; Pittsburgh; San Diego; Washington, D.C.; Charleston, W.Va.; Topeka, Kan.; Rockville, Md.; Dallas, Tex.; Jacksonville, Fla.; Phoenix, Ariz.; Akron, Ohio; and St. Louis, Mo.

We also benefited from the work of many nonprofit groups that have been tracking the fate of America's workers and the loss of their benefits. These include the Center for Responsive Politics, the Commonwealth Fund, the Economic Policy Institute, the Institute for College Access and Success (TICAS), the Kaiser Family Foundation, the National Institute on Retirement Security and the Pension Rights Center.

To develop the profiles of the middle-class Americans you see in this book, we crisscrossed the country to interview men and women who worked in glass plants and department stores, shoe factories and packing houses, trucking terminals and brokerage houses, lumber mills and airlines, as well as corporate managers and government officials. We are indebted to each of them for taking time to explain what has happened to their jobs, their paychecks, their health care and their retirement.

Any errors are ours alone.

INDEX

Charts are listed in bold.

deduction for carried interest, 255-56
on dividends and interest, lower rate for, 131
estate, 29, 60, 95-96
exempt bonds, 14, 15, 264-69
foreign investors, breaks for, 131
inequality, as driver of, 60
payroll, 10
progressive, 265-67, 287, 295
television industry (U. S.), 52-53
Temple-Inland Inc., 62, 63, 64,93, 94
Tesla, 30
Texaco Inc., 41
Thatcher Glass Co., 20
Thompson, Betty Jean, 194
Thornburg Mortgage, 120
Thune, John, 96
Tilray, 30
Time Warner Inc., 85-86
TLC Group Inc., 220
Toppers Meat Co., 108, 109
Toshiba Corp., 140
Toys R Us, xi, 123
trade, 46, 51, 52, 55-57, 291
  deficit in, 124-25. *See also* global economy
Tradevest Inc., 196
Trans World Airlines Inc. (TWA), 41, 156
Transcon Lines Inc., 162-163, 168, 169, 170, 171
Treasury, U.S. Department of, xi, 23, 46, 95, 139, 147, 215, 265, 266, 267, 268, 287
Trent, Robert, 269, 270
Triangle Industries, 280
Trico, 50
Triton Group Ltd., 201-202, 203, 211-16
Trotter, Smith & Jacobs, 113
Trump, Donald, viii, ix, xviii
  administration, and lobbying, 259
  and the deficit, 83-84
  and the economy, xi, 134
  and Michael Milken, 35
  and regulation, 149, 182, 291
  and taxes, 2, 9, 61, 67, 68-69, 70, 75, 89, 135, 255
  and trade, 46, 51, 55, 125, 291
Tunney, John, 266
Turnaround Management Association, 104
Twin Fair Holdings Inc., 210

U

U. S. Home Corp., 91
Ullman, Al, 81
Uniroyal Inc., 41
United Airlines, 156
United Arab Emirates, 130, 131

United Auto Workers (UAW), 55
United States-Mexico-Canada Agreement (USMCA) 51, 55
United Steelworkers Union, 144, 146
Universal Manufacturing Co., 5, 47-48
University of Chicago, 118, 199
University of North Carolina, 277
University of Virginia Health System, 198
Upjohn Co., 139
USA Truck, 164
USMCA. *See* United-States-Mexico-Canada Agreement

V

Van Tatenhove, James M., 104
Vance, H. S., 232
Vander Jagt, Guy A., 261
Varity Corp., 177, 180-82
Vasquez, Alberto, 56
Vasquez, Rosa, 47, 56-58
Verizon Wireless, xi
Vitro S. A., 25
Vornado Realty Trust, 123

W

wages, 17, 50, 55, 281, 291
  downward pressure on, 5, 8, 14, 17, 22, 26-27, 30, 33, 138, 157, 158, 159-60, 162-64, 166, 171, 194, 206, 211, 272
  in Mexico, 5, 50, 53, 54-55
  minimum, xix, 17, 138, 186, 198, 270, 281, 282, 291. *See also* deregulation; income, median family; manufacturing
Wagner, Leslie, 151, 159
Walker, David M., 227, 229
Wall, M. Danny, 248
Wall Street Journal, 10, 33, 40, 45, 79, 157, 223
Wallop, Malcolm, 119
Walmart, 95, 187
Walton, Sam Moore, 187
Walton family, 95
Waltons Bond Ltd., 207-209
Warnaco Group Inc., 48
Warren, Elizabeth, 149
Washington Mutual, 100, 120
Wasserstein, Bruce, 45, 273
Wasserstein Perella & Co., 42, 273, 274
Ways and Means Committee, U.S. House of Representatives, 10, 72, 86, 129, 266, 267, 280, 282, 286
Webb, Rosalind, 98-99
Weikel, Larry, 18, 19, 21, 22, 23, 25, 42
Wesray Capital Corp., 203, 215
Wesray Corp., 23-24, 25

NICK KEISH

ABOUT THE AUTHORS

DONALD L. BARLETT and JAMES B. STEELE are the nation's most honored investigative reporting team. Their work has received two Pulitzer Prizes, two National Magazine Awards and upward of 50 national journalism awards. Two of their eight books have been *New York Times* bestsellers. They first began working together at The *Philadelphia Inquirer*, and since then their writing has appeared in *Time*, *Vanity Fair*, The *New York Times* and The *Washington Post*. They live in Philadelphia.

They can be reached at *info@barlettandsteele.com*.

Made in the USA
Coppell, TX
11 October 2020